A KILLER'S CONFESSION

A KILLER'S CONFESSION

and a Mother's Fight for the Truth

KAREN EDWARDS
with
DEBORAH LUCY

HEADLINE

First published in 2019 by
HEADLINE PUBLISHING GROUP

1

Cataloguing in Publication Data is available from the British Library

Hardback ISBN 978 1 4722 6665 1

Typeset in Monotype Sabon by CC Book Production
Printed and bound in Great Britain by Clays Ltd, Elcograf S.p.A.

Headline's policy is to use papers that are natural, renewable and recyclable
products and made from wood grown in well-managed forests and other
controlled sources. The logging and manufacturing processes are expected
to conform to the environmental regulations of the country of origin.

HEADLINE PUBLISHING GROUP
An Hachette UK Company
Carmelite House
50 Victoria Embankment
London EC4Y 0DZ

www.headline.co.uk
www.hachette.co.uk

To Becky, my beautiful, spirited, complex daughter
All my love, Mummy

CONTENTS

PART THREE

INTRODUCTION

I have lived every parent's worst nightmare. In April 2011, on what would have been her twenty-ninth birthday, a police officer knocked on the door and told me my beautiful daughter, Becky, was dead. Not only was she dead; she had been found buried in a shallow grave in a remote field in the Gloucestershire countryside. Becky had been brutally murdered. She had been lying in her makeshift grave since 2003.

The only reason police knew she was there was because of the disappearance of another girl, Sian O'Callaghan. When police closed in on a taxi driver, Christopher Halliwell, they were unaware that he had been hiding a dark secret for many years, but he finally met his match in Detective Superintendent Stephen Fulcher, the man leading the enquiry. Halliwell made a shocking confession to Steve Fulcher, leading him to the exact spot where he had buried Becky.

My world shattered the day I was told Becky was dead. To me, she would always be my baby, my little girl. Like most parents, when she was born, I imagined how her life would be when she grew up. As a young girl, she was so sweet-natured, always giggling, always loving. We all loved her. I had such hopes and dreams for her; she would be happy, successful. She would marry well, have children and generally live a worry-free life filled with love, laughter and good times. We would be able to sit and see her children play, watch as they grew up. I would be there for her, for them. In the wonderful life I imagined for her the sun shone in blue cloudless skies and there were only ever smiling faces. There was no trouble in the future I imagined and wanted for Becky. The day I was told she had been robbed of her life, I was robbed of my dreams for her.

But after the knock on the door, our family was plunged into a complex world where we had to navigate the intricacies of a major police investigation and the criminal justice system. The legal terminology, technicalities and endless processes that we were expected somehow to absorb and understand became almost overwhelming. This was foreign territory for me and my family, but we trusted the British legal system; we had faith in it. We had to. Because when your loved one is murdered, there's not a lot else to have faith in.

We could never have imagined what happened next. We never dreamt that we would have to fight to see Halliwell convicted of Becky's murder.

Steve Fulcher's actions in talking to Halliwell and allowing him to take them to where he had hidden his victims were treated by the judiciary, police and some commentators as if they were worse than the barbarous acts committed by Halliwell. For having the audacity to confront a serial killer, DSupt Fulcher was severely punished.

Too often, the events of that day are referred to as a 'police blunder'. Nothing could be further from that. Because of the actions of one police officer, Becky was returned to us. For that I will be eternally grateful. In the midst of our grief, Steve Fulcher enabled our family to feel the peace of being reunited with Becky.

Ask any family who are missing a loved one and they will tell you they would give anything to have them back. Ask any family in a 'no-body murder' what they want most; it is the chance to find their loved one, to give them a decent burial. To stop the endless torture of wondering where they are.

For years I kept pushing for the truth to be heard. When I should have been grieving for Becky, I had to do all I could to fight to keep her story in the public consciousness. I had to let people know that I wasn't going to go away until I had justice for Becky.

I still don't know if the full extent of Halliwell's evil actions is known or whether there may be more victims out there. These are questions that I continue to wrestle with. Perhaps I will never be able to make sense of the evil that befell our family.

Even now, after everything we've been through as a family, when I look back over the events that have occurred, I am left in disbelief. Disbelief that I can't see my beautiful Becky. Disbelief that she was murdered, that I now have to tend her grave. And disbelief at what happened after. We were just a normal family, going about our business like millions of others, until that knock on the door. But I am finally in a position where I can try to reflect on our battle for the truth and start to grieve for the daughter I have lost.

PART ONE

I

THE BEGINNING
OF THE END

'Mum, I think you should come to the door. *Mum*, I think you need to come here.'

My son, Steven, had answered the knock on the front door. Now he was calling me from the kitchen. I knew then, even before I looked down the hallway. Maybe I caught the tone of Steven's voice, a nuance that would have been lost on anyone else. A mother's instinct perhaps. I'd been listening to my instincts for days and I was sensitive to any sign, any indication that might confirm my fears. I'd voiced my concerns to my husband, Charlie, and to Steven. They'd tried to reassure me, but it hadn't worked. So, now, I didn't want to go to the front door. Because I knew.

Cold fear gripped me. As soon as I saw the police officer I knew why he was standing there. *Becky.* I recognised the officer straight away because I'd seen him on the television. Everyone knew his name.

Only three months earlier, we had seen blanket news coverage of police investigating the disappearance and murder of

3

Joanna Yeates, a young woman from Bristol. Now there was another crime investigation even closer to home. For the last two weeks a police investigation had played out through the media as police looked into the disappearance and murder of Sian O'Callaghan, a pretty local girl who had gone missing on her way home from a nightclub in Swindon, in the early hours of Saturday, 19 March 2011. The officer in charge of the case, Detective Superintendent Stephen Fulcher, had delivered all the news updates on the enquiry. He was now on my doorstep.

Like thousands of others in Swindon and around the country, I had been glued to the news. It was a dreadful story that so many people could relate to. There was a huge public response, as it had hit the national headlines. The investigation into Sian's disappearance dominated every news bulletin, radio station and newspaper. It was all anyone could talk about, me and Charlie included, as Sian had gone missing on our wedding anniversary.

I had felt an enormous sympathy for Sian's parents, as I imagined what they must be going through. I had seen them and Sian's boyfriend, Kevin Reape, on the news, appealing for help to find her. I saw the pain and worry etched on their faces. The man now at my door had been sitting next to them.

He had hero status in Swindon. There had been such an outpouring of gratitude in the media and on Facebook. Not only had he captured Sian's abductor and murderer, but he had discovered Sian's body so she could be returned to her family. But there had also been an extraordinary twist. When DSupt Fulcher had first ordered the arrest of a local taxi driver, Christopher

Halliwell, for Sian's abduction, no one could have predicted what would happen next.

Halliwell repeatedly replied 'no comment' to other officers when they used emergency interview provisions to ask him where Sian was. They hoped she might still be alive somewhere so they had to find her fast. The quickest way to do this was to ask the only man who knew – Halliwell – but he refused to co-operate. So before he was taken to the police station, DSupt Fulcher himself asked to speak to Halliwell. He wanted to look the man he had spent days hunting in the eye to persuade him to reveal where he had taken Sian.

It worked. Halliwell told DSupt Fulcher he would lead him to Sian. He then took officers on a long car journey, directing them out of Wiltshire, where all the searches had been focused for days, and into the Oxfordshire countryside. During the journey, Halliwell indicated he had killed Sian and had left her body somewhere down a steep verge along a stretch of road. He hadn't been able to locate the spot exactly, because he'd left her there in the black of the night. In the daylight, he was not so sure where she was, but knew the road he had driven along.

While a helicopter was searching the area for Sian's body, and before he was taken into custody, Halliwell requested to talk further to DSupt Fulcher. He had Halliwell driven to a quiet spot and asked him what he had to say.

'Do you want another one?' Halliwell asked.

He told the officer he had murdered a woman some years earlier, in either 2003, 2004 or 2005; he couldn't be more precise than that. But he could take him to the spot – the exact spot – where he'd buried her. He directed officers through the countryside, driving down winding, single-track lanes until they reached a remote field in Eastleach, Gloucestershire. By the time they'd arrived, the helicopter at the original location had found Sian O'Callaghan's body.

Halliwell got out of the police car and climbed over a dry-stone wall. Once in the field, and taking a reference point from a dip in the wall, he paced steps to a spot in the ground and indicated that was where he had buried the woman. A day later, the skeletal remains of a body were discovered a little way from where Halliwell indicated in the field. But he had given no name for his victim, so who was she?

When I heard on the news about another body being found in a field, the O'Callaghan family's story suddenly became very personal to me. Until then, of course, as a mother, I felt enormous empathy for them – a sort of 'there but for the grace of God, go I' kind of empathy – along with any other parent who heard the story and who had a young, pretty, vibrant daughter.

But another body . . . something inside me, something instinctive, told me it was Becky. She had been a vulnerable, troubled teenager, disappearing for weeks and months at a time. But she always came back eventually. However, I hadn't actually seen her for many years by now. The last time I'd seen her, she'd promised me that she would come home when she was ready. So I'd waited. In the years that had passed since, as recently as just a few months ago, other people had told me that they'd seen Becky. People had spoken to her, told me of their conversations with her. One told me she was having a baby. Even her grand-

6

father had spoken to her. Although I was hurt that she wasn't ready to return home to me yet, I convinced myself that I had to be patient. I remembered her promise and waited. It would be like she'd never been away.

But despite all the sightings of her, something deep inside nagged at me. As I watched the news unfold, I couldn't shake the feeling that the newly discovered body was Becky. I felt it so strongly I spoke of it to my family. An inexplicable feeling of dread had settled on me. 'What if it is Becky?' I asked them. 'It can't be,' they said, as, like me, they'd relied on what people had told us over the years. But, still, what if it *was*? For some reason I knew it was her. I just knew it. All through the week that followed I drove myself mad with fear and worry that it was Becky. It was all I could talk about.

My husband and son were so concerned for me, they went out to look for Becky again, remembering the sightings and the conversations people had told us they'd had with her. In the intervening years, I'd lost count of the times Charlie had driven me around trying to find her. I'd even get up in the middle of the night and drive round myself, convinced I might see her, only to return disappointed. They said they would go out and find her, bring her to me, put my mind at rest, stop me from going on about it. But despite their efforts and people saying she was living locally, Charlie and Steven couldn't find her. As they looked for her, I realised I had been taking what people had said to me at face value. It had been eight years now since I had seen or heard from her myself. All the years I hadn't seen her, I thought she was avoiding me, that we were estranged because

7

she had chosen a life I didn't agree with. I'd wanted to find her, see her for myself, check that she was alright, as people had told me she was. But I'd never been able to find her. Thinking about it now, I couldn't believe that if she was in the neighbourhood she wouldn't have come to see me. After all, there was no bad blood between us.

In all the years I hadn't seen Becky, it never once occurred to me that she might be dead. As a mother, I'd never felt that. I never expected 'the knock on the door'. And yet, as soon as I heard about the body in the field, it triggered something powerful inside me, an awful certainty that I'd never felt before. Suddenly, none of it made sense and my fear worsened.

When I knew I was alone in the house, I sat in my bedroom, pen in hand at my dressing table. I finally picked up the phone and dialled the police. Dread was burning inside me. I was so frightened. But I had to do it.

'Hello, Wiltshire Police, how can I help you?' the call operator sounded quick and efficient.

'My name is Karen Edwards. My daughter, Becky, has been missing for a while and I'm concerned it could be my daughter found in the field at Eastleach.' I was choking back the tears, trying to stay calm, not really believing what I was saying. But the words came tumbling out.

I heard the quick tap of fingers on a keyboard as I relayed Becky's details. As the operator spoke, she tried to reassure me by saying that 464 other people had also rung in to report their loved one missing since the body had been found. I seized on what she said, writing the figure 464 on my note pad. She told me not to worry too much. At last I put the phone down. Relief at having made the call flooded through me but I felt sick at the same time. I couldn't stop crying. I wanted to take comfort from what the call taker had said; there were 464 other people with fears like mine. But there was only one body. As much as I tried to stop myself thinking it, I just knew it was Becky.

Now, here was Stephen Fulcher at the front door. My heart was racing. I could hear the rapid pulse in my ears. It was deafening. I knew why DSupt Fulcher was there and yet I so wanted it not to be true. My mouth went dry in reaction to the fear that racked me. As I walked towards the door I created a delay. I didn't want to hear what he had to say, so I bought myself a few precious seconds while I tucked some tea towels on to a radiator. I knew what I was doing. I was desperately trying to hang on to normality, the familiar world I knew. The world in which Becky still existed for me. I didn't want to hear what he had to say. I felt sick.

As I walked down the hallway towards him, my stomach churned. My palms were sweating. I knew. I just knew. I seemed to float towards him in slow motion. There was no more delaying. This was it. We stood facing each other.

'Mrs Edwards?' His voice was low and steady.

'Yes? My god, is it my Becky? Is it my Becky? *It is*, isn't it?'

There was the merest hesitation before he answered. His eyes stayed fixed on mine.

'Yes,' he said clearly and calmly. 'May we come in?' Stood beside him was another policeman, with two women officers behind them.

'Please, no, *no*, not my Becky!' I cried. The tears were instant, as was a huge wave of fear, sadness and utter hopelessness. I'd known for days in my heart, in my gut, but here was the awful confirmation.

Nothing can ever prepare you for the shock. That Monday will be for ever etched in my memory. It had started out so well, so ordinary. My son, Steven, had come round in the morning. He was excited. On Saturday, two days earlier, on the same day I had rung the police and reported Becky missing, he had come round with his wife, Kelly, and their three young children to tell us that they had a surprise for us.

'Get your coats and shoes on and follow us.'

We went out of the house and walked down the lane, going on for about ten minutes, past the village pub. All the time we walked, the conversation I'd had earlier with the police call operator spun round and round in my head: 464 people had made the same call as I had. All those people with fears like mine – why should it be Becky? There were 464 others it could be. So why was my gut leaden with certainty that it was her? What did I seem to know that others didn't? Steven and Kelly stopped suddenly and turned. We were standing in front of an old cottage, a place I'd driven past so often I'd stopped noticing it.

'It's ours!' they both said and told us that for the last few months they had secretly been buying the cottage so we could be nearer one another. In any other circumstances, it would have been a lovely surprise, but my mind was elsewhere. Thinking of a body found in a field.

'What did you say, love?' I heard myself ask as if from a distance.

'I said it's only a small garden, but you can work your magic on it, Mum.' Steven was grinning from ear to ear. I smiled back at him. I did my best to sound interested; I didn't dampen the mood by telling them that I'd phoned the police about Becky. Maybe I was being over-sensitive. In two days' time, we would be celebrating Becky's birthday, along with my eldest grandson Nathan, who shared a birthday with her; she would be 29 on Monday, 4 April 2011. Perhaps this was why I was so anxious. I desperately wanted to see her. Maybe this year she would come home for her birthday? If she did, I would be able to laugh at my fears.

So today, on the day of Becky's birthday, Steven had turned up on the doorstep and asked me what my plans for the day were. Charlie had gone to work and I had nothing to look forward to except cleaning and ironing. When Steven said he was going to go round to the cottage and start stripping it, I volunteered to help. The place needed an awful lot of work, but that could be sorted; it was close to us, which meant we'd get to see lots of our three other grandchildren, Chelsie aged four, Chanel, three and six-month-old Charlie Thomas. Another reason I wanted to go and help Steven was to distract myself from dwelling on thoughts about the body found at Eastleach. I was still hanging on to the remote hope that Becky might come home today, to celebrate her birthday.

When we arrived at the cottage, I immediately started work. Steven was laughing at me as I was wearing a black velvet tracksuit with pink wellington boots. He wanted to lift the old wooden flooring so we set to it. I channelled my nervous energy into the task, grateful for the physical nature of the job. It was backbreaking work. As we pulled up the planks, the air in the cottage became stale and dusty. It had got to lunchtime and I suggested that we pop back home for a drink and a sandwich, so we did. I was just about to put the kettle on when we heard the knock on the front door.

Now the police officers were closing the door behind them. I ran to Steven who was in the living room, standing by the fireplace. My worst fears had been confirmed. The body was Becky's. My lovely baby was dead. It was as if my instincts had been trying to prepare me for the shock. I had had a feeling it was Becky for days, ever since I'd heard about the body in the field. And yet despite my feelings, despite my certainty, the news still came as a terrible shock and something I couldn't seem to absorb. My world shattered. To hear this today of all days was devastating. On the day she'd been born, I was told she was dead.

I clung to Steven and just broke down. I wasn't in control any more. I felt an actual physical change, as if something died inside me. I couldn't function, I couldn't hear or speak. The only thing I could do was cry hysterically. Steven went straight on the phone to Charlie, who came back from work immediately. The world didn't feel real any longer. We'd descended into a kind of hell.

A policewoman helped me to sit down. All I could see was my lovely daughter, Becky. I continued to sob uncontrollably. They were talking to me, but all I could take in was it was Becky they had found in the grave.

'But it's her birthday, it's Becky's birthday.' It was all I could manage to weep.

'Could we please see Becky's room?' DSupt Fulcher asked gently, after a while. I looked at him through a haze of tears; I could see that he was tired, but there was a determination about him that I'd seen in him on the television.

'Of course,' I answered, tearfully.

I led the way upstairs and opened the door. I'd always kept the room ready for her, waiting for her to come back, as she had many times over the years. It still had all her things there; it was just as she'd left it, despite the fact she hadn't been here for so long. It was Becky's room. Typical of many teenage girls, it was full of her personality; the double bed where she would lounge on her pink cushions with her teddy bears, while listening to R&B music. Her artwork hanging on the walls, her fluffy slippers by a bedside cabinet. Now, I was standing in her room with a police officer. He was out of place in there. It was wholly surreal.

As he looked around, taking it in, I opened the wardrobe. 'These are some of her presents from the birthdays and Christmases we've missed since she left. There's more in the loft . . .' It was all I could manage to say before the words choked in my throat. Again, the tears brimmed and blurred my sight. He looked at me. Piled in neat columns were parcels wrapped in Christmas paper. This was where I kept some of Becky's presents since we'd last seen her, in 2002. They were ready for her to unwrap as soon as she came back. Just because she wasn't here, I hadn't forgotten her; she loved Christmas and birthdays. There were two more presents for her today. As I looked at them now, I knew she would never open them. I started sobbing again.

The officers asked for photographs of Becky and gently started to probe about her history. However, as the news started to sink in I became too distraught to carry on. I couldn't speak, only cry. I was useless. My head was thumping and all I could think of was Becky. I'd been expecting *her* to knock on the door today, instead it was the police to tell me she was dead. This couldn't be happening. Not to Becky.

The police stayed for about an hour or so, saying they would return tomorrow. The house started to fill with family and friends as the news spread. There were so many people around me, so many tears being shed and questions being asked. I couldn't take anything in. I was completely overwhelmed. I didn't want all the people around me. I couldn't deal with their grief too. I couldn't cope with my own.

My nightmares had come true, but now I was in a state of disbelief. It was as if my body was refusing to accept the news. I was shutting down. None of this was real. Becky dead? *Not my Becky*. I kept seeing her face, seeing her as a baby, on the day she'd been born. This day, 29 years ago. And now she was dead. It was too much.

I was in such a bad way that the local doctor was called. I was put to bed. Whatever tranquilliser she gave me worked well because I didn't wake until the following morning. As soon as I opened my eyes the reality of the day before hit me like a hammer blow. The nightmare that had begun yesterday was there again today, and would be every day now. There was an indescribable pain in my chest. My heart felt as if it had literally broken in two. I started to retch, I was going to be sick. I got out of bed and fell to the floor. Crawling on my hands and knees, I made it to the bathroom and threw up.

Out of my drug-induced sleep, my mind went to a new, dark place, somewhere I'd never been before, a kind of torture chamber, where all manner of horrors greeted me. Becky was dead, so what had happened to her? How had she come to be buried in a field? How had she been murdered? What had that vile animal done to her? His name went round and round in my head, a name I'd heard on the news. Who was he? What had happened? My mind spun with these thoughts. I would have to know. In the meantime, my mind filled in the blanks.

This was a new form of torment that replaced the fear which had sunk deep into the pit of my stomach when I'd first heard of the body discovered in the field. When I thought of Halliwell, I felt a strong new emotion: pure hatred. I hadn't woken up with this feeling yesterday, but within the space of 24 hours, things were very different. I knew if I ever found myself near him, I would kill him.

With these dark thoughts in my mind, I knew somehow I had to face the day. The policewoman returned to see me. She wanted to ask me lots of questions about Becky and in the fog of grief and a relentless stream of tears, I did my best to answer them. I had trouble stringing a coherent sentence together. The sheer pain of knowing she had died in terrible circumstances was overwhelming.

In my grief I told those around me that I couldn't live without

Becky. I wanted to die too; to me, it was logical. It was the only way I could be with her, to comfort her. My need to be with her felt greater than the need to be here, with everyone else. I scared Charlie; he knew that I meant it. I didn't want to be in this world any more. Not without Becky. He was on suicide watch from that day on.

The days followed in a frenzy, as the discovery of Sian and Becky dominated the news. The media went mad, with journalists climbing over the gate and camping en masse outside the house. The local press were running a public appeal for information – 'Did you know Becky?' – and were already highlighting other women who had gone missing from Swindon. There was such a hunger for information, we eventually had to put a note on the gate requesting privacy.

The television was permanently off now; the case had reached saturation coverage and we didn't want to hear it. We didn't need to, we were living it. The phones wouldn't stop ringing, and in the end Charlie walked around carrying our mobiles and the house phones in his pockets. The police had advised us to screen all calls. Ordinarily, when the phone rang, we picked it up without thinking; now we were told to look at the incoming number and if we didn't recognise it, to cut it off. Apparently, there were some very strange people out there, who could be threatening and abusive in these circumstances. The same went for our cards and letters of condolence. This was a world that was alien to us and I couldn't believe what was happening.

There was a constant flow of visitors, phone calls, cards and flowers. Steven and Kelly moved in with our grandchildren. We all wanted to be together at this time, to stay close and safe. Kelly was absolutely amazing at fielding all our visitors, keeping the house tidy, making a constant flow of tea and coffee, all the time with six-month-old Charlie Thomas attached to her hip. Our normal, routine lives dissolved into a disconsolate turmoil of loss, sadness and numb disbelief.

I continued to help police to build up a picture of Becky and we went back to her room. They needed to go through her things, read her diaries, letters, and try to understand her. They asked me for her story so they could determine what had taken her into the path of her killer, Christopher Halliwell. They wanted to know anything that could contribute to the investigation. There was nothing too small or insignificant I could tell them.

This gave me a reason to function while I dealt with the pain of knowing I would never see Becky again; the pain of knowing she had been murdered. I was helping them with their enquiries, helping them with their investigation. I could do that. I needed to do that. Anything that would help bring her killer to justice. And so, still unable to believe what was happening to us, I started from the beginning.

2

THE EARLY YEARS

Over the coming days, I told officers all about Becky and us as a family. They wanted to know everything. It was exhausting answering all their questions, but I was grateful for it because it meant I could think of Becky in happier times. Remembering Becky as a baby and a child now helped to keep the dark thoughts at bay. At least, it did for a few hours.

Becky was born at precisely 9.20 a.m. on 4 April 1982 at Princess Margaret Hospital, Swindon. My husband John was with me as we watched Becky being delivered into the world. She was a beautiful little baby and so perfect, weighing 7lb 14oz. We wanted a girl so we were over the moon with our lovely new baby. I couldn't stop cuddling her, she melted my heart.

My mother chose her name; we drew names from a hat, my mother pulled out Rebecca Louise, which she liked, and so that's what we called her, Rebecca Louise Godden. Her brother, Steven, was three years older and he clearly loved his little sister. I remember crying with joy as I looked round at my little family; Becky had completed us. I had two beautiful blonde-haired, blue-eyed children.

Unlike Becky, Steven had been quite a demanding baby; he would keep me awake all night long, refusing to sleep. He would cry constantly, particularly any time he was laid down. Becky was different altogether. She was perfect. She would sleep right through and was very easy to handle. She was a very contented baby, who looked utterly angelic. Everyone who saw her fell in love with her. It was a happy time for us as a family; importantly, I felt we had proved the naysayers wrong.

I'd married John Godden in 1978. We had known each other for two years before we were married when I was only seventeen and a half years old. Because I was under eighteen, I'd had to get signed permission from my parents in order to marry. Both my parents naturally had reservations about me marrying so young, and they weren't enamoured of my choice of husband.

My mum was a very quiet woman. I didn't take after her, being anything but quiet; it was my sister, Tracey, three years younger than me, who seemed to have Mum's personality. However, quiet as she was, Mum left me in no doubt that she wasn't keen on John. Like most mums with their daughters, she thought he wasn't good enough.

My father also made it plain how strongly he felt. He asked me to name my price and said he would happily sign me a cheque for any amount if it stopped me marrying John. I hadn't quite realised the strength of their feeling towards him until then, but I was a rebel. Like many teenagers, all I saw was a life that was independent from my parents and John was my way to it. Perhaps their dislike of him made him all the more attractive to me.

He was good-looking and I certainly thought I was in love.

Perhaps subconsciously, in the two years I'd known him, I had already decided that I could influence him enough to change him into the person I thought he could be. The person I wanted him to be. And, for all I knew, he was thinking the same about me. I thought I knew what I was doing, but I was so naive. Little did I know at the time that my thoughts of independence would be very short-lived, as I fell pregnant within three months of our marrying. What was it my parents saw that I clearly had not? I was strong-willed, defiant, determined – I knew what I was doing. If they didn't give their blessing I threatened to run away to Gretna Green. Reluctantly, they signed the consent form and we were married.

At the time of Becky's birth three years later, both Steven and I were living with my mum and my sister in Swindon. By then, Mum and Dad had split up. John was working away in Newport, South Wales and staying with his parents there. We had been living apart like this for nearly ten months, as John had to move to where the work was and that happened to be in Wales. He'd recently found a better job and I was waiting to move there too, where we were hoping to buy our first house instead of going into a rental property.

Not that I wanted to leave my family in Swindon. With a toddler and a new baby, I had my hands full while John worked away. I was so grateful for the amazing support Mum and Tracey gave me. They spoilt Steven and baby Becky with love and attention. Nothing was too much trouble, even though it seemed we turned the house upside down. Steven had an enquiring little mind and would get up to all manner of things. We had to have eyes in the back of our heads. Once, we found him behind the television merrily sticking a screw driver in the back of it, which he thought he was fixing. With his antics, I needed all the help I could get.

However, with John in Wales, we had no choice but to leave. Somehow I would have to manage without them. Within a few months of Becky's birth, I made the move down to Newport and, for the first time, all four of us were together. While I missed my family back in Wiltshire, I was determined to make a go of things.

With our new home, John's new job and our two adorable children, I felt as though I had it all. I loved our children so much as they gave me so much joy. I used to dress them in co-ordinating outfits when we went out, with Steven always managing to stay clean and Becky always managing to get something down her. Steven continued to be a typically lively little boy, while Becky was completely different, quieter with a lovely gentle nature. Despite the differences in their personalities, they got on very well together, which was so special to watch.

The little community we lived in just outside Newport was perfect. The location of the house was so pretty, with a small river nearby. I quickly made friends with our elderly neighbours, who would look after us with veg from their garden, and I would fetch them bits of shopping and look in on them. They loved to see the children. I used to take Steven and Becky down to the river, where we'd sit with a little picnic and watch the birds. The countryside around there was so tranquil and beautiful. We made friends with other couples and easily integrated into life in Wales.

This idyllic time was unfortunately short-lived. Things were not quite how I had imagined they would be. The time that John had spent without me had seen him carve out a single life for himself, which he seemed reluctant to give up now we were back together. I could understand him wanting to find his own company after work, particularly as he had been living with his parents for the best part of a year. He now had a good social life, largely governed by going to pubs and nightclubs with his colleagues. But now I was there with the children, he still wanted to carry on doing this as if nothing had changed for him. The fact that he now had a wife and children to go home to didn't seem to register. I knew he needed downtime after working all week, but I started to resent the number of hours he spent away from us at the pub.

I quickly started to see that the time we had spent apart had totally changed us as a couple. Unfortunately, we seemed to want very different things. John came from a large family and soon made it clear that he wanted more children, as many as four, he said, whereas I was happy with two. He also wanted me to be a stay-at-home mum, but within a short space of time, with a mortgage on our new home, the burden of finances soon became an issue. We argued about money, with him spending what little we had left going down the pub, fishing and buying bootleg records. This behaviour wasn't what I was expecting; we were no longer teenagers, we were parents, with responsibilities. With two young children, there were more pressing things to spend our money on than records. For some reason, John couldn't see that.

Contrary to John's wishes, I decided I needed a job and found one as a supervisor at Tesco's in Newport. This was a job I could do in the evening, just for a few hours, to help us financially. I wanted more for us, and didn't know how to make that happen by any other way than hard work. A few hours soon grew into more; I found myself able to earn good money if I included a night shift, so one night a week I worked from 6 p.m. to 6 a.m.

After two years, I realised I wanted to move back to Swindon to be nearer my family. I liked it in Wales, because of my friends and my job, but I missed the support system of my mum and sister. I was struggling to juggle work around the children, and with John working all day it started to feel we were being pulled in different directions. With large cracks appearing in our relationship, John and I put our house near Newport up for sale and looked to find another back in Swindon.

While the house was on the market, I made the move back with the children to live with my sister and her husband-to-be, Tony. This left John to carry on working and oversee the sale of the house. With the help of Mum and Tracey to look after the children, I quickly managed to find a job. Luckily, Steven and Becky enjoyed each other's company and played well together, which made looking after them easy. Becky was a little giggler and would play with her teddy bears and dolls for hours. In fact, she was like a little doll herself: she was very petite, taking after my grandmother Iris, who was also very tiny.

Eventually, the house in Wales sold and we managed to buy a house in the Rodbourne area of Swindon. Houses here were more expensive than in Newport, so it was difficult to find something that compared with what we had. We settled on the only house we could afford for the location we wanted to live in. The property was built in the 1960s and nothing had been done to it; it didn't even have any central heating. Because we'd had to pay more, we didn't have any spare money to fix it up. But we were together, in our own home, and at the time that was the only thing which mattered. I had every hope that things would improve between John and me now we were back in Swindon. I was determined to make things work between us.

My grandfather found John a job working in Yorkshire Imperial Plastics as a forklift driver. Unfortunately, despite all these positive aspects, we continued to have different ideas for our relationship. John continued to envisage us having more children. I was adamant I didn't want that. For a start, we could barely manage financially with two children as it was. Because we were both working, the only day we had together as a family was Sunday. Not unnaturally, John would also like to go to the pub on Sunday, the only day he could.

Again, I started to resent this. As I saw it, instead of playing with his children, or spending time with them, he preferred to go to the pub. I couldn't ignore it any longer; as I looked ahead all I could see was this becoming our routine, the norm. He was carving a groove for our life that I had no intention of following.

The trouble was, I seemed to have lost the ability to influence him. Financially, we had taken a step backwards returning to Swindon and I was keen for us to turn the situation around. Things needed doing in the house, the children were getting older and the only way we were going to get on was by working hard. I enjoyed working, which I felt John resented me for.

Despite the problems between us, the children were happy. I made sure they weren't witness to our rows and deepening discontent, as they continued to spend time with Mum, Tracey and our grandparents. When Tracey married her husband, Tony, in 1988, I was matron of honour, with Steven a pageboy, dressed in his smart little bowtie and cummerbund, and Becky, in a pretty cerise pink dress, also a bridesmaid. They behaved wonderfully. Tracey looked beautiful and she and Tony made a lovely couple. They were obviously so right for each other. A week before, John and I'd had a massive row and on the day of the wedding we weren't speaking. Despite that, it was a really special day and I was determined that John wouldn't spoil it for us.

On the following Monday, I took the children to school and went on to work. That night, John didn't return home. I thought he had gone out on a drinking session and that he would be back, but he never returned. He had left us. Steven was nine and Becky was six.

I tried to keep it from Steven and Becky at first by making excuses for his absence, but, of course, they were quick to notice after only a few days, that he was gone. Naturally, they wanted to know where he was, but I couldn't tell them as I didn't know myself. It was a shock to them. As they cried, I was left to comfort them. I still thought John would return.

I tried to hide the fact that John had gone from his parents, but that became impossible when John's mother was hospitalised and I had no way of making contact to tell him. I had to admit to his father, Pete, that I didn't know where he was. John had gone off the radar. Pete and I had always got on; he used to say I was John's backbone and that he would crumble without me. He sympathised with my predicament, but now we needed to find him.

Pete managed to track John down; he'd been sleeping at one of his friends' houses. Pete tried to help sort things out between us, but it was now beyond that, such were our differences. I wanted a better life for us and wanted to work hard to get it, but John only saw me as a housewife with more children. He accused me of being a workaholic, saying that was all that interested me. I was frustrated with John as he seemed to show no ambition or drive to want us to get on in life. It was as if it didn't occur to him. He just wanted to do his own thing, which now predictably involved the pub and fishing. He wanted a stay-at-home wife, surrounded by children. I felt that if that was how it was to be, we were better off without him. I think Pete appreciated this too. Things had finally come to a head. The tension between us over these issues was insurmountable. We wanted different things from life.

With John gone, I tried to keep Steven and Becky occupied so that life remained as normal as possible for them. With me having a full-time job to hold down, they spent a lot of time after school and at weekends with Mum and Tracey, with John's sister, Lynn, also keeping in touch. I'd known Lynn since she was a little girl and had always got on with her. I had a very good friend as well, Shirley Bunn, who also helped out with childcare after school, as did my good neighbour Sharon. It was a struggle to keep it all together and I was lucky having such good friends and family at so difficult a time.

Due to the sudden turmoil of John leaving, Steven and Becky

remained my priority. Things were different for them and I was determined to do all I could to lessen the impact. I had to be both parents now, as well as the main wage earner. Despite everything, they both continued to be well behaved and well mannered, something I always strived to instil in them. Even Steven, my little rebel, was well behaved at home, although he struggled to be the same at school. The notion that he would need to sit still and learn things from books was lost on him. To Steven, school was a penance, something to be endured until he could escape and do his own thing. He never enjoyed his school experience.

By contrast, Becky was clearly happy at primary and junior school, despite what was happening at home. She liked to be top of her class and would work hard at attracting praise from teachers. She was a favourite with them. She may have been the smallest in the class, but was one of the brightest. She loved learning, soaking up information she gained from school projects she undertook such as on history, anatomy and the universe. She particularly loved reading and poetry and always had her head in a book. In fact, she would rather stay inside and read than go out in the playground. She was the same at home, wanting to continue reading when it was time for bed.

'Come on, Becky, turn your light off now,' I'd have to say to her.

'I just need to finish one more page,' she would answer.

'No, come on, read it tomorrow.'

'OK.'

And as she turned off her light, I would pretend to go. Instead,

I'd watch at the door as she pulled up her duvet over her head and, using a torch, she would carry on reading under the cover. It made me smile as I'd done exactly the same at her age. Despite being a shy little girl, she was very popular, with lots of friends. She loved gymnastics and the activities at the Brownies. But, despite her outward behaviour, deep down Becky missed her dad terribly. The shock of John suddenly leaving certainly had an enormous effect on Becky, and to a lesser degree Steven too. There were times when they would both cry to see their dad, so John started visiting them.

I suggested that he could come to the house on a Saturday and have the kids while I was at work. That way, they would be in their home with their toys and would be more relaxed. I would bake and cook the night before so they all had a meal they could eat together. Steven and Becky certainly seemed to enjoy him coming to see them. He was so laid-back with them; not for the first time I would return home to hear John saying: 'Just you wait till your mum comes home, I'm going to tell her you've been naughty and then you'll see.'

The arrangement worked well for a few weeks, but then John started to turn up late, then not at all; he had been out drinking, or had overslept. The novelty quickly wore off. I couldn't rely on him to look after the children on Saturdays while I worked and had to make alternative arrangements, many times at short notice, when he failed to show up. It was disruptive, both to me at work and for the children to not know where they were, or who would be looking after them.

With this turn of events, I started divorced proceedings. There seemed little point in delaying things. I wanted a clean break. The children also deserved more stability and certainty. It was proving to be a constant struggle to keep things going financially as, by now, John hadn't been contributing to our finances for some time, and although I'd kept up with my half of the mortgage payments, the house became subject of a repossession order. It was an extremely stressful time.

I explained to the children about the divorce and what it meant in terms they could understand. There were books for children on the subject which helped me to describe what would happen. However, I didn't feel it was appropriate to mention the issue of custody. A hearing was set to resolve this but John failed to turn up.

In court, in his absence, I was awarded £1.25 per child per week. It didn't even cover their school dinners. I was outraged. I felt it was the ultimate insult from him. I didn't care about not receiving any maintenance for myself, but I was incensed on behalf of Steven and Becky. Neither could I believe such a sum was acceptable to the judge.

'Is that what you think my children are worth?' I asked the judge. 'Well, you can tell him to stick his £1.25 a week. Tell him to put it towards another pint. I will bring my children up myself.'

I was so disgusted. I wanted the judge to be in no doubt how I felt, so I immediately left the courtroom with my solicitor running after me.

'You can't do this,' he said as he struggled to keep up with me as I strode out of the court, 'You can't walk out and leave the court like this.'

'I just have,' I told him. I was so angry.

I was granted sole custody of the children, but was stung by such a paltry offer of £1.25 a week for each of them. How on earth were they meant to survive on £2.50 a week? Well, I was determined to make up for it; I would make sure they didn't go without.

I had been awarded the house, so I immediately remortgaged and saved it from repossession. We at least had a roof over our heads. But I was living on my nerves as I was well aware everything rested on my income. I felt as if I was living on a tightrope, trying to keep my balance with the mortgage like a millstone round my neck.

At the time of the divorce, I was working in Debenhams on the YSL cosmetics section. I knew I needed to earn more money, and when I saw a new bridal concession was joining the store, I applied for and was offered the manager's position. In the circumstances, it probably wasn't the ideal job at that stage. I found myself wanting to tell everyone I saw trying on wedding dresses not to do it. My experience of married life had left me cynical. Men were fickle and unreliable and I was better off without them. But this was my job and I needed the money, so I put on an encouraging smile for prospective brides and helped them to choose a dress for their big day. Hopefully, they'd be luckier than I had been.

The hours were nine to five thirty with a late night on a Thursday, and days off on Friday and Sunday. I was a single mum now with a mountain of bills and financial responsibilities. I certainly felt the weight of the situation. My wages were stretched to breaking point. But I was ridiculously proud and would not ask for any financial help. Luckily, I had good people around me who could see our little family unit depended entirely on me.

My friends were so kind to me; they knew my position and would give me clothes their children had grown out of. I was so grateful for this. They would even buy me sandwiches for my lunch, knowing that I couldn't afford to feed myself during the day. Everyone rallied round us. My Nan would buy me a joint of beef at the weekend, enough for us to have a decent Sunday roast, with vegetables from granddad's garden. Mum and Tracey would buy Steven and Becky items of new clothing; they loved their gifts. It was hard, but with help from friends and family, we were just about managing to scrape by. Then I discovered I was to be made redundant.

I knew I couldn't wait for it to happen, so I immediately applied for a different job within Debenhams, this time for Equator Luggage. I got it, along with £5,000 more a year – I was elated. It turned out to be a good move. It was hard work, but I threw myself into it. Then, within six months, I was promoted to area manager with a region to look after.

But it wasn't all work; I made sure that me, Steven and Becky did things together. We all had push bikes and, especially in the summer months, we would all go out riding together. On one occasion we went out bike riding and I fell off. Steven and Becky's co-ordination on a bike was much better than mine and I soon found myself flat on the pavement. We were near to Tracey and Tony's so in we went for a cup of tea and for me to clean up my bloodied hands and knees. We were all in the garden and as we were about to head back Tracey asked Tony to get some apples for us from a large apple tree. Not needing to be asked twice, Tony climbed to the top where the apples were largest.

As he was doing this, we suddenly heard a large crack and the branch Tony was holding on to started to fall, unable to hold his weight. As he held on tight, the branch gradually came away from the rest of the tree. Tracey and I sat laughing, it was such a funny sight, but as we laughed, Becky was crying, fearful for him falling to the ground. Tony and the branch came to earth with a small bump with no harm done. The children rushed to make sure he was alright while Tracey and I were in hysterics.

Although the branch had broken off the tree, Tracey managed to successfully replant a part of it in the garden, something that the children were particularly pleased about. It was an incident that we still laughed about in the years to come and which we remembered at a most poignant time in the future.

Not long after, thanks to a tax rebate, the three of us went abroad for the first time. My friend Jenny, who I had met through work, offered the three of us her apartment in Spain. It was an extra treat for Becky, who had fallen off her bike a few weeks before and chipped her kneecap, resulting in surgery and a plaster cast. It came off a week before we were due to go, and then just a few days later she hurt her leg again! I called an ambulance and as she was put in the back she announced to the paramedics, 'My mum is a spare parent.' They laughed as they knew she meant 'single' parent. Fortunately, nothing was going to stop us going. We got some crutches and the three of us had our two-week holiday in Spain. We had an absolute ball, thanks to Jenny. It was just what we all needed.

We all became even closer over the next few years as we made a good team. Becky was coming up for leaving junior school. She was 11 years old by now and after the summer holiday would be starting senior school. Till now, she remained the same sweet-natured girl who helped me around the house. On Sundays my grandparents would visit for tea and we'd bake, with Becky helping to make the cakes and decorate them.

She was a very loving little girl, who liked sitting in my lap for cuddles and was constantly giggling – in fact she was known as 'the giggler'. She used to put her hand across her mouth as she giggled, as if she was shy. She loved nature and animals and gravitated towards any cats and dogs. She especially liked learning about all the different creatures there were in the garden. She would often stay with me in the garden for this reason and help plant seeds with me in the greenhouse. Her love of Disney grew out of her love of animals, as she loved to watch the films depicting the animation of her favourite characters. Things were settled and seemed to be going well for us.

As the kids grew older the demands on my income increased; I was also struggling to pay the mortgage and didn't want to keep relying on my family. My sister, Tracey, had a boy and girl of her own now – Sam and Laura – and would still support me by looking after Steven and Becky when I was working. She was marvellous; however, trying to keep things all together financially was a huge struggle. But I knew I couldn't give up.

I was still working full time with my area supervisor job. My workload had become greater as I travelled around the region to London and Bristol. But, as time went on, we needed more money. I couldn't rely on John for anything. I felt he had long nailed his colours to the mast. Moreover, he'd also found a new partner.

Becky felt this keenly, feeling pushed out. She continued to miss him, but I felt John had washed his hands of us. Well, I was determined to make up for him, we didn't need him.

During this time, I started studying aromatherapy at college once a week. I realised that I needed another string to my bow, something that I could fall back on in an emergency. The threat of redundancy a few years ago had shown me how financially precarious my situation was. With everything resting on me, I knew I needed a skill I could perhaps develop into a further income stream. This had to be something I could fit around my day job and the children. Aromatherapy was something that interested me. After discussing this with my mum and grand-parents, they generously offered to pay for the course and my books. I rose to the challenge. I loved it; it was so different from my nine-to-five job and I really enjoyed learning. After studying for two years and juggling home and work, I passed the exams with flying colours.

Once I qualified, I quickly found an evening job practising aro-matherapy at the local Health Hydro. I found it really rewarding helping other people and I gradually built up a client list. Then, very slowly all the hard work started to pay off. I soon found that I was able to put money aside, and saved enough for a small car. It was an enormous boost as it gave me my independence.

It meant that I could now travel and practise aromatherapy at clients' homes, as well as going to the Health Hydro. My aromatherapy work also paid for extras and holidays for us, which gave me a huge sense of satisfaction, as I didn't want the children to feel too disadvantaged coming from a single-parent family. I treasured my little car, making sure I cleaned it inside and out every Sunday, polishing it until it shone. Steven and Becky thought it was great too.

Things were looking up; these were happy times for us. I felt we'd turned our backs on the hard times and we were moving forward. Looking back, I had no chance of foreseeing what was to come.

3

THE START
OF BECKY'S TROUBLES

The police presence at home quickly became the new norm, as they continued with their questioning. They were eager for any information we could give them so that they could piece together every aspect of Becky's life. We were suddenly completely subsumed in a murder investigation which only days ago, like everyone else in Swindon and the country, we had been horrified spectators to. We were an ordinary family like any other and I was an ordinary mum. All I could think of was, why Becky? Why my baby? It seemed all we had to cling to was the fact that her murderer had been caught.

Becky had had her problems. We'd managed to keep the depth and scale of them largely within a tight circle of friends and family. The police already knew some of the details but DSupt Fulcher's puzzlement was obvious. How could a young girl who came from a loving family and a good home end up as a drug addict and sex worker, much less in a shallow grave in a lonely field? It was a question I had wrestled with myself over the years, pinpointing the moments where things had gone wrong, revisiting the ways we had tried and failed to help her, and the many lost years. But I didn't want Becky to be seen in this way now. That Becky was a sex worker was true. I knew that. She had worked in the red-light districts in Swindon and Bristol. I had seen her as a 'working girl' for myself, on one of my many attempts to bring her back home from that life. It had broken my heart to see her like that. But notwithstanding her life-style, Becky's life was no less important than Sian O'Callaghan's. Becky's murder was as tragic. DSupt Fulcher said he would do all he could to prevent Becky being dismissed in the media as a prostitute. I understood what he meant and I was grateful.

Looking back, it was clear to me where Becky's problems started. Our little family had had to negotiate John walking out, the divorce and the change that had brought. Mum, Tracey and I explained things to Steven and Becky so they would understand; we took time to sit with them, talk it through, ask how they felt about things. Steven seemed to cope well enough, but Becky in particular continued to badly miss her dad. I don't think I quite appreciated how much at the time, despite offering all the reassurances I could to both of them. John leaving turned her little world upside down.

I certainly didn't stop John from seeing his children; on the contrary, that was something I was keen to encourage. I'm not sure what more I could have done to try and get him to engage with them. The only barrier was John himself, and what little interest he did show waned in a short space of time. He knew where we were and seemed happy for me to get on with things.

I tried to make up for his shortcomings, but I guess, all things considered, there was still one parent missing. Becky loved her dad and I know now that she felt his absence intensely; it made her feel unsure and vulnerable. Before she transitioned to senior school, she had had the familiarity of her school and little friends around her, which probably helped her as she tried to make sense of it all. The continuity of junior school provided her with security during this time. As soon as she went to senior school, the new environment, different teachers, different pupils, her world turned upside down again. The safe and secure setting that she knew at junior school, in which she was able to learn and thrive, disappeared. She was still trying to cope with one fundamental change in her life, when along came another.

She showed no outward anxiety about starting her new school. We had had a lovely summer school-holiday break as we normally did; if anything Becky was excited to get back to school. She had been due to go to a school whose reputation was not good for bullying. Steven was already there and had dealt with some minor issues, but Becky was different. She was shy and quieter than Steven; I didn't want her coming up against that sort of behaviour. I wanted things to continue for her as they had. So I chose to find her an alternative school.

But she had not been at senior school for many weeks when I received a phone call at work. Becky had run away, hiding from some girls. When I spoke to her, she told me they had made her take off her cardigan and had put it in dog mess and made her put it back on. They were bullying Becky and she was breaking her heart over it. I went straight to the school and took her home.

This was new territory for both of us as up until that point, we hadn't had to deal with anything like this. Until now, school was somewhere I knew Becky was safe and was somewhere she loved to be. She loved to learn and furthermore, she was a clever girl. Needless to say, what she was now experiencing made her reluctant to return, so I contacted the school and explained what was happening. I wanted this to stop. I wanted them to intervene. As a parent, I expected them to put an end to it.

Bravely, Becky returned the next day, but the bullying continued. I couldn't understand it; perhaps it was because she was smaller than her classmates, perhaps it was because they knew her father wasn't at home. This did mark Becky out as different and all kids want at that age is to fit in. Despite me telling the teachers what was going on, they continued to do nothing. Why wouldn't they listen? I couldn't understand why they wouldn't do something. I wasn't prepared to put up with it; if they wouldn't do anything, I would. I was so incensed, I went into the school one morning and took Becky out of the classroom. She never returned.

I approached another school for a place for Becky and they took her. I wanted to see her settled and able to concentrate on her lessons again. She couldn't learn all the time this was going on, so I looked forward to a better time for her. But it wasn't long before the same happened there too. Becky made some new friends at school, as they came to the house regularly for tea, but like her, they weren't able to stand up to this amount of harsh bullying. She started to become withdrawn.

I didn't know what to do for the best. She had to go to

school, there was no alternative. Up until now, she had enjoyed school, enjoyed learning. I just wanted things resolved so that she could be happy again. I was at a loss as to why bullying was seemingly tolerated in schools. One Saturday evening, when Becky was nearly 12 years old, I returned home from work and seeing Steven asked him where Becky was. He told me she was in her room, so I called up to her but there was no answer. After a few minutes, I went up to see her. She was in her room, in bed with the curtains drawn; the room was in darkness. As I walked towards the bed, my foot kicked something in the gloom. I turned on the light.

To my horror, the floor was covered in empty bottles and packets, a mixture of Paracetamol, Ibuprofen, Imodium, anti-histamine tablets and some sleeping pills. I recognised them all from our bathroom cabinet. Becky had not stirred despite the light being on. I pulled back the covers; she was lying curled up in a ball, not moving. I panicked and began to shout. I shook her. There was no response from her; she remained still, lifeless.

I was sick with fear but picking her up I lifted her out of the bed. Walking over the packets on the floor, I rushed her straight into the bathroom. The only thing I could think of was to plunge her head under cold water to revive her. She started to respond to this, so I wrapped her in a towel and rang the hospital. Taking the boxes and bottles with me, I drove as fast as I could to A&E. When we arrived, doctors were waiting for us and they took Becky straight into a side room. I was so worried as I watched them going about their work to revive her. It was a shock to see her in this state. Whilst I knew she was being bullied, I never for a moment thought it would lead to her taking an overdose. I hadn't realised it was affecting her to such a degree she would consider taking her own life.

They took her blood for analysis and then started to get her to drink a black liquid that I later found out was activated charcoal which stops poisons being absorbed into the body. She looked so ill lying there. At last I could go to her and hug her. As I held her in my arms she was sick all over me. It was such a relief. She had survived, she was going to be alright. But my lovely little girl was in such a mess. We needed to get to the bottom of whatever was going on. The doctor said she would need to stay in overnight, so that she could be monitored. Becky was very tearful. She was sorry she had done it, causing so much trouble, and upset. I comforted her, it wasn't her fault. As I hugged Becky tightly, I told her that we loved her and would help her. I rang Tracey, who was really concerned and immediately came to us. We all remained so close, but we decided to hide this from Mum, as I didn't want to cause her to worry.

Becky's blood continued to be analysed, and the next day a child psychologist visited to assess her. It was clear that Becky had problems that required expert help. Why had I not seen this coming? She obviously hated school, hated the kids taking the mickey out of her parents being divorced, added to which she continued to be upset that her dad had gone. Becky was hurting and this had been a cry for help.

She came out of hospital. During this time, we gave her all the love and support we could. We all ensured she was told she was special to us and gave her hugs and kisses, along with advice about what to do with the bullies. She eventually returned to school. I had visited the head teacher and told him what had happened, hoping the bullying would now stop.

Not long after this, one Sunday evening, Becky came home early from playing out, which was unusual. My good friend Shirley Bunn had come round for a coffee, and after she left Becky came downstairs, into the kitchen.

'What do you want for your tea, Becks?' I called out, over my shoulder. Turning round, suddenly I took a look at her and could see cut marks up her arms. They were dripping with blood.

'What the hell have you done, Becky?' I shouted. I was frightened. This was something I hadn't encountered before.

She looked back at me and burst into tears, crying uncontrollably. I wrapped her arms in clean towels and called Shirley, who had only just left. Shirley came straight back and came with us to A&E. As we watched the nurses dress Becky's arms, I was stunned. I didn't know what to do. I was out of my depth. I was unsure how to deal with this, but Becky obviously had very deep-seated problems and her way of letting us know this was first the overdose and now by self-harming. My little girl was a deeply troubled soul. Once again, she was referred to a child psychologist.

I put my faith in the system. At least we had help. Through a psychologist, we would now get to the bottom of Becky's problems and sort her out. Or so I thought. The trouble was, after only a couple of sessions, like before, Becky no longer wanted to engage with them. I was at my wits' end. She had to go to school but she was clearly finding the move to senior level very difficult. If only the bullying would stop, she would have a chance to settle into her new surroundings and gain in confidence. In the meantime, all I could do was continue to watch her and, along with the rest of the family, support her and provide her with love and reassurance.

Becky went back to school; she had good days and bad days. I continued to work all day and one evening a week at the Health Hydro. Steven and Becky were looked after by Mum and Tracey after school. The Health Hydro continued to provide me with the chance to earn extra money and improve my aromatherapy skills. It gave me as much pleasure as it did my clients. It also felt liberating to do something different from my day job which could earn us extra money at the same time.

While I was there, one of the clients was a very smart-looking man who had been referred to me by his doctor. He had been suffering from severe migraines and aromatherapy had been recommended to him. He had a weekly appointment, and over the months I treated him we slowly became friends.

During the treatments, he confided in me about his work and family and I provided a listening ear. He had gone through a messy divorce. The treatment went on for several months. Then one evening, out of the blue, he asked me to go for a drink sometime, no strings attached. I never said yes, but neither did I refuse. I had to think carefully. I had worked so hard at my diploma and at finding a nice little niche at the Hydro that I didn't want to do anything that might spoil things. I ignored the question. He asked again a few weeks later, I said maybe. He asked again, I said perhaps. Then one evening, I'd had a particularly bad weekend and when he came in, I said, 'Do you fancy going for that drink tonight, Charlie? I could do with a chat.' By now, we had come to know one another quite well, and I was pleased when he agreed.

Following this, Charlie Edwards and I decided we would see each other again, but I was insistent his visits to me at the Health Hydro had to stop. He would need to seek aromatherapy treatment elsewhere. We continued to see each other and within a short space of time, Charlie and I became serious. He was such good company, although I proceeded with caution.

I hadn't been looking for a relationship; I had the children, a good network of friends and family, so I wasn't lonely. I was happy as I was. Also, Charlie was fifteen years older than me. But he was lovely and easy to be with. He was a hard worker with his own business. Meeting him had come as a complete surprise; I had been so focused on work, the children and keeping our heads above water that I hadn't given a thought to any long-term, serious relationships for myself. I simply didn't need to.

I remember broaching the subject with my mum, wondering what she would say.

'Mum, I've met a man. I can't wait for you to meet him. There's just one thing though, he's a lot older than me.'

Her opinion was important to me. She had provided me with so much support. If she had misgivings about what I was doing, I needed to know.

'Don't you worry about that,' she said. 'You deserve some happiness. When are we all going to meet him? I want to see the man who's put a smile on your face.'

I was so relieved. I wasn't quite sure what I'd have done if she hadn't liked the idea of my seeing Charlie, but after not listening to her about John, her blessing meant a lot to me. Tracey and Tony's views were also essential and I introduced Charlie to them too. I needn't have worried. Reassuringly, they liked Charlie a lot. But, most importantly, when they met him, Steven and Becky took to Charlie straight away. Over the weeks that followed, I met Charlie's three daughters, and they met Steven and Becky. We all got on and seemed to come together without any problems. I was warmly welcomed by other members of his extended family and his friends.

Within three months of us first going out together, Charlie asked me to marry him. We had been out for Sunday lunch at The Bull Inn in Charlbury, and on the way home he stopped the car. As he said the words I panicked so much that I chose to totally ignore the fact he'd asked the question! It was sudden and such a big decision. I had been on my own for years now with the children and we were just fine like that. The divorce from John had hit hard – once bitten, twice shy was never more true as far as I was concerned. I enjoyed my independence; it was tough, but I'd got used to there being just the three of us. The children were my world and I was happy with this. Besides, I felt we had come through the worst and had good times ahead.

Finding someone like Charlie was so unexpected and things had moved pretty fast. But we seemed to have so much in common and we made each other laugh. He was very easy to love. We seemed to be really in sync with one another; family and hard work were important to both of us. Three weeks later, he bravely asked me again. I consulted Steven and Becky. Charlie had made a huge impression on them; they loved what they saw in him, the fact that he wanted to look after us all as a family. They told me he made them feel safe.

What was I waiting for? This time, I said yes. We were to be married. Steven and Becky were over the moon and very happy for us. Although I vowed over the years I wouldn't do *that* again, I hadn't bargained on meeting Charlie. We were so well suited and everyone seemed to wish us well. This time, it was very different.

With the decision made, we then had to look around for a house big enough to accommodate our two families. It didn't take long before we fell in love with an old farmhouse in west Swindon. It sat in large grounds and came with outbuildings in the shape of a couple of old small barns. I knew I could make it into a lovely family home for us all. It was perfect, or at least it would be in time.

We rented it for a few months while the mortgage was sorted out and then bought it. Charlie was old-fashioned; he wouldn't have us living together before we were married. So Steven, Becky and I moved in on our own until the wedding. I hadn't sold our family home yet, as we were considering renting this once the wedding was over. There was so much to think about in the meantime.

Steven had turned 17, so Charlie saw to it that he passed his driving test and bought him a small car. Steven was over the moon. Charlie had made such a difference to us. It felt as if our lives had turned a corner, there was a lot of fun and laughter, and as I looked around me I saw a lot of smiling faces. I only had a few months to arrange everything, but the wedding plans were going well. We were to be married on 19 March 1997.

We were completely swept up in the romance of it all, with Becky as thrilled as I was. Becky was now 15; she was going to be my bridesmaid and was helping me to organise everything. It seemed she was very good at wedding planning and relished the task. I was also stumped as to what to wear. What style, colour, long or short? Becky was in her element and persuaded me to have an ivory wedding dress: at my age – I was 37! I thought back to when I'd worked in the bridal shop – I would never have dreamt then I'd wear another wedding dress.

Our wedding day arrived and it was a wonderful occasion. In the morning the house was filled with beauticians, hairdressers, and family and friends popping in and out. There was someone with a camcorder to capture it all. Everyone wished us well and they were really excited for us. I kept looking at Becky; she loved every minute of it, all the fussing and pampering. It was lovely to see her so happy and engaged with it all.

The church bells rang out and the pews were packed with our family and friends. Everyone seemed genuinely happy for us. There was such a special atmosphere. Chief bridesmaid was one of Charlie's daughters, but I made sure Becky was by my side the whole time. She had never looked more lovely, wearing her green full-length taffeta bridesmaid's dress. She didn't stop smiling all day, it felt as much her day as it was mine.

After we were married Charlie sold his house and one of my step-daughters and Steven moved into my old house while we renovated the farmhouse. On Sundays we all came together as I cooked the Sunday roast, sometimes for up to sixteen or more. We had become one big family unit and it was so special.

Not long after the wedding, Charlie wanted me to give up work to take the pressure off that and running the home. It was true, bringing our families together did give me extra work at home and I was struggling to juggle the two. But equally I loved my job and relished the independence that brought. He did, though, have my best interests at heart and assured me he was there to look after us now. It was a hard thing to accept; I'd spent so long having to bring the children up alone. But now that had changed. After some resistance to the idea, I gave in and handed in my notice. I was now a housewife.

Despite our happiness, Becky continued to have problems at school. Thank goodness I now had Charlie to share this with. He was such a great help; when Becky broke down at school and became quite ill, he suggested we go and have a meeting with the education authority. During the meeting, we came to the conclusion that it would be best for Becky if she was home tutored. The school hadn't convinced me that they could keep Becky safe from bullies. She was still having a miserable time and it had to stop. We agreed with this course of action. At first, a tutor came to the home. She taught Becky a range of subjects, but her clear favourite was English and particularly poetry, which she had loved since primary school. Unfortunately, Becky didn't take to the lady at all. Then it was suggested that I tutor her. I seized on the idea. I drew up a timetable and we studied English, Maths and History. I was very strict, ensuring that she was under no illusion I meant business and she took this seriously. We would start our lessons as she would as if she was in school, finishing at the same time as the normal school day.

Becky was very happy with this arrangement. We made good use of the local library and she went swimming at the gym where I was a member. I loved spending time with her like this. I watched her and saw how she lapped up her studies. She had no worries and could focus at last. It was good to see her with a smile on her face. Life felt the best it had in years.

We also managed a few holidays, taking Becky with us to Spain, along with a chosen friend for company. Charlie knew it was important to include her in all we did and if taking a friend along too meant she enjoyed the holiday more, then that's what we did. Because we knew she would love it, we also took Becky to Disneyland, Florida. Tracey and Tony had already taken their children, Sam and Laura, out there for three weeks, so we joined them for a week. As a family we were lucky in that we all got on so well together. I knew Tracey and Tony treated Steven and Becky like their own as they were growing up and I felt the same about their children. Becky loved spending time with Sam and Laura; Laura, being that much younger, was in awe of Becky, but despite the difference in their ages – some ten years – Disneyland was somewhere they both enjoyed regardless.

Like millions of others, Becky loved the fairytale Cinderella from when she was a tiny tot and, along with Laura, would never tire of watching the film. Even then, in her teens, Becky would still rerun the film on the video recorder. We captured her excitement on seeing the real Cinderella Castle on a camcorder. Another favourite of hers was Winnie the Pooh, and she delighted in shopping for the largest cuddly toy she could find; a three-foot-tall Winnie stood in her bedroom on our return. They were magic times and it was so good to have these experiences and see Becky's delight. We wanted to distract her from her past troubles and hoped that this was a help to putting them behind her.

I look back on this period as such a happy time for us all. Becky was growing up fast; she was making grown-up choices. Due to her love of animals, she had decided she was now a vegetarian. Luckily, this didn't affect her love of Italian food, or her favourite pizzas. And no matter how old she was, she would always love her 'squashed fly' garibaldi biscuits and dolly mixture sweets. Becky was happy with life, and I felt her past troubles were behind her.

However, something was worrying Becky. She had been educated at home for quite a while when she began to ask about her exams. She wanted to be a vet or work with children and would be looking to go to university, so I approached the Education Board to ask them what she needed to do to achieve her aims. The answer was to go back to mainstream education. I rang several schools to see if they would take her but to no avail. Charlie suggested a private tutor, but that wouldn't work. The only option suggested to me was an interim school, to assess her before going back into mainstream education. At this point we were becoming desperate; time was marching on, so we agreed for Becky to go to Stratton Education.

Stratton Education was a school for children excluded from

mainstream schools and education, due to them having a range of problems, be that behavioural difficulties or health issues. Becky had never been a problem to educate, nor had she ever been excluded. She had been prevented from learning by bullies. She was no slouch; Becky was a bright girl who behaved in the classroom, but this school apparently was the route through which I was told she had to go. I wasn't enamoured of this; I didn't think it was the right school for Becky. She wanted to focus on her exams and I didn't want anything to get in the way of that, or set her back. She had been doing so well and was looking forward to further education. Tracey and Tony lived near the school, which was a bonus, so Becky knew that her aunt was at hand. I hoped this would give her the confidence to attend.

I took Becky to school each morning, picking her up at 3 p.m. unless she was going to Tracey's for tea. She would bring home-work back every night, which she completed straight away, ready to hand in the next morning. It wasn't long before the teacher commented to me that Becky was her star pupil. She sat at the back of the class and got on with her work. She seemed to be adapting to her new school. At last, it felt as though things were going her way. Unfortunately, this happy state of affairs was not to last.

The first thing to happen was that John had a baby with his long-term partner. It was a girl. Looking back, Becky so hankered after John's love and approval that the new addition to John's family was another blow to her and her relationship with her father.

It was at this time that Becky's behaviour suddenly changed.

She became erratic, she had mood swings and became very cheeky, answering back, which was so unlike her. Then she started staying out late with no explanation. I thought it was just the normal teenage hormones kicking in, just Becky growing up, pushing the boundaries. But soon I was left in no doubt about the cause of the change in her.

She had made herself a den in the top barn, where she would spend time when friends came over. One day, after some girls from her old school had been to visit, one of the dogs had gone missing so I went looking for him, thinking he was trapped inside the den somewhere. Still calling the dog, I went up to the barn and was shocked at what I found: lots of empty cans of aerosols, furniture polish, deodorants and air fresheners were strewn across the floor. Furthermore, the tops of the spray had been pulled off, leaving the thin tube sticking out. What on earth were a load of empty aerosol cleaning products doing here of all places?

I had recently noticed that various sprays had gone missing from the house, but had just bought more. As I stood there, looking at the empty cans, I put two and two together. Slowly, it all started to make sense. I thought about Becky's behaviour, how different she had become recently. I knew about kids embarking on inhalant abuse and now it seemed this had been going on with Becky and her old friends from school, here in the den. There was no other explanation for it. I was sickened. I slumped into a sofa, unable to believe what I was thinking. Why? Why would she do such a thing to herself?

I gathered up the cans in my arms and marched up to Becky's room. I was furious with her. It was so dangerous, what if they had harmed themselves? What would the parents of the other girls think? Becky was lying on her bed, drawing.

'Becky, what are all these empty cans doing in the den?' I asked her, doing my best to keep calm despite boiling inside. My heart was thumping, still hoping against hope she was going to give me an innocent explanation. But how could it be innocent? With the tops pulled off, the cans even looked sinister. I couldn't bear the thought of her inhaling solvents, damaging herself. Children killed themselves doing it. Why did she feel the need?

Becky shrugged at me without looking up, not wanting to answer.

'Becky, I'm asking you why all these empty cans are in the den?' I threw them on to her bed. Becky carried on drawing, ignoring me. I was frightened and angry at her behaviour towards me. I saw red at that point and lost it, grabbing a pair of plastic children's scissors from the side and pointing them at her. Quite what I was going to do with them I didn't know, it had been an instantaneous reaction to my fears and sheer frustration.

'Becky?' I barked at her, waiting for her to answer. 'Now,' I said, waving the scissors at her, 'you start talking.'

She continued to ignore me as if I wasn't there, wasn't speaking to her. This wasn't the Becky I knew – what was she playing at? I grabbed a box of pencils that were lying on her bed and threw them across the room. They ricocheted off the walls and windows, before I stormed out of the bedroom, crying. Becky was impassive. I didn't know what to do, I didn't know how to handle this, handle Becky for that matter. I had never had cause

53

to speak to her like this before. This Becky was a different girl to the one I knew. What on earth was I going to do?

Steven was in the garden, planting some trees and saw that I was upset. When he asked me what was wrong I couldn't speak. I didn't want to tell him what I'd found because I didn't want to believe it myself. Panic gripped me. I was crying tears of fear.

'I don't know what to do,' I cried. 'I've found empty aerosol cans in the barn and she won't tell me what she's been doing with them. She won't speak to me. What am I going to do with her?'

I must have scared Steven, because he rang Charlie. The next thing we knew, Becky appeared with a bag and a backpack over her shoulder, carrying her ghetto blaster in her hand.

'Where do you think you're going?' Steven called to her.

'I'm leaving,' she said, 'I'm going to my friend's.'

'Well, you know where the door is when you want to come back,' I shouted after her. I thought she needed some time to cool off. I was still crying when Charlie came back. I couldn't make sense of it. Surely she wasn't so stupid as to be using inhalants? What could she possibly get out of it? We started to discuss it when the phone rang. I thought it was Becky, wanting a lift back home, but it wasn't. To my complete surprise, it was social services; Becky had contacted them and reported me to them! I couldn't believe it.

'We have a report of you threatening your daughter with scissors,' they said.

I told them about Becky and her friends with the aerosol cans and how I'd approached her with them. Yes, I had picked up a pair of scissors, but they were plastic Early Learning scissors due to Becky's history of self-harming. I had no idea at the time what I thought I was going to do except point them at her in the hope of getting her attention.

After speaking to them further, they accepted my explanation and were fine, but I couldn't believe she would report me. It felt as though I was starting to lose her; I didn't recognise this Becky. This was my own child and it felt as though a distance was growing between us. I still didn't know how to handle it.

For a couple of days, Becky stayed with one of her friends who'd been in the barn with her. I rang her friend's mother and explained about the aerosol cans, hoping she would feel the same as I did and we could tackle the situation together, but she refused to believe her daughter would be involved with inhalants. When Becky returned home the atmosphere was a bit strained before things settled down again.

Unbeknown to us, while she'd been away, Becky met up with a friend called Holly from Stratton Education. Becky had first brought Holly home not too long after she had started at her new school, and at that time I was glad she was making friends. I used to pick them both up, bring them home for tea and then take Holly back to a pub, where her mum would be. I began to feel sorry for the young girl, who started to spend a lot of time with us at home. We even took Holly with us when we went away and invited her to a family Christmas in the hotel where we were married. When she racked up a room service bill and drank the minibar dry, we overlooked it, as Becky liked her a lot. But unknown to us, her influence over Becky was great and it would have huge ramifications. Holly had introduced her to a boy called Martin, who would soon play a prominent part in our lives. I had established that Martin had become Becky's boyfriend and, needless to say, I did not approve.

It wasn't long before Becky disappeared again and this time we had no idea where she was. We all went out looking but couldn't find her, so I called the police and a few days later she turned up with no explanation. Becky had quickly turned into a rebellious teenager and I had hit a brick wall with her. She was pushing all my buttons and I didn't know how to deal with it. I had never had any problems with Steven like this, so to have teenage troubles with Becky, my sweet little girl, was completely unexpected. Her behaviour was so out of character, I didn't understand it. I didn't know whether she was just growing up, or whether there was some more ominous reason for her actions. I soon had my answer.

4

CHASING THE DRAGON

I found it while doing a spring-cleaning session. I decided to start with Becky's bedroom, and had been in there for about half an hour when I pulled the bed out to hoover behind it. As I did, I saw a plastic bag on the floor. It contained cigarette papers, lighters and a ball of silver paper alongside a pet rabbit's water bottle. There was also a casing of a Bic pen taped to it. As I examined all this I wondered why such an odd collection of items would be together in a bag secreted under Becky's bed. What did it mean? I took the bag downstairs. As I turned it over, looking at each of the items, my initial curiosity suddenly turned to dread. This bag had been hidden, so I feared it had a sinister connotation.

There was only one way I could find out what it meant. I had to act fast while Becky was out. I rang my brother-in-law, Tony. I knew he had a friend, Ben, who he worked with, who was also a part-time bouncer at a local nightclub. In my mind, Ben might be just the person who could tell me what the contents of this bag were. Tony sensed my urgency and came and picked the bag up to take to Ben. Within a few hours, Tony returned. We went into the kitchen.

'You'd better sit down. Sorry, Ka, it's not good news.' He placed the bag back on the kitchen worktop. 'They call it "chasing the dragon" or "brown".' He hesitated, knowing I didn't have a clue what he was talking about. 'It's heroin.'

I gasped. '*Heroin?*'

I was so shocked. I felt as if all the air had been knocked out of me. What on earth was heroin doing in Becky's bedroom? This was alien to me; of course I knew drug taking went on, but not in my world, not in my family's world. We didn't know anyone who took drugs. I'd once told Becky that if I ever caught her smoking like her friends, I would ground her, but this, this was something completely different.

I had been worried sick about the aerosols, but this was off the scale. I was glad Tony was with me. We'd known one another for years, and as Becky's uncle he was, I knew, as concerned about this as I was. He'd watched her grow up; she'd spent so much time with him and my sister when I was at work as they'd looked after her. He was as puzzled as I was about why Becky would be involved in such extreme behaviour.

Tony explained to me that the contents of the bag allowed for inhaling the vapour from heating heroin. The heroin was heated on the foil and 'chased'. This was known as a 'fix'. I'd had a drugs lesson. I couldn't believe it. Had she been doing this in the den, in her bedroom? For how long? How come I hadn't noticed? But it explained her behaviour. I felt physically sick with worry. Heroin! The word kept going round and round in my head. This was hard drugs. In our house, in Becky's bedroom. How had this vile substance found its way into our home? It couldn't belong to *her* surely? Perhaps she was hiding it for someone? What on earth did she think she was doing?

I was furious. I immediately phoned Becky and told her I needed to speak to her and that I was coming to collect her. She was at Martin's house. Somehow I had to calm down. But calm was the last thing I was feeling; in fact, I didn't know what I was feeling apart from being so very, very frightened. I drove off to pick her up.

I said nothing during the journey home. All the time I was driving I was trying to work out what to do, what to say to her, how to play it. We arrived home and went into the kitchen, where I gave her a cup of coffee. It was just us two now, in the quiet of the house. I knew I had to keep a lid on my emotions. I was completely calm as I produced the bag with its contents to confront her. As soon as she saw it, she began to cry.

'Oh, Mum, I'm so sorry. My life is a complete mess, please help me.' She then told me how her friend, Holly, had introduced her to Martin, who had introduced her to heroin.

'I don't know what to do with you, Becky.' I was incredulous. 'You're taking heroin.'

'I only smoke it, Mum,' she said, 'I don't inject, you know how much I hate needles.'

'But it's heroin, Becky. *Heroin.*' I could hardly believe we were having this conversation at all. I couldn't believe heroin had become part of the vocabulary between us. She was sixteen and we were having a conversation about her taking heroin as casually as we might about her smoking cigarettes. I was in turmoil. Within about four months she had progressed from inhalant abuse to heroin in one terrible leap. My lovely, sweet, bright girl was disappearing before my eyes.

She started to cry again. I had expected her to give me lip, to shout, storm out, but her explanation and her tears took the wind out of my sails. I crumbled; now we were both crying and I hugged her close to me. We said nothing further to each other but sobbed. It was as if both of us knew it was a watershed moment in our lives, in our relationship. I was scared and so out of my depth I felt I was drowning. It was clear Becky needed help, but how could I help her through this if I lacked knowledge myself? I kept turning it round in my head; heroin. I hated the word. It struck absolute fear into me. I had no idea when or how this was going to end. Little did I know, it had only just begun.

I took to the internet. I had to do my research, I had to try and understand this new scourge that had now entered our lives. If I could understand it, I could deal with it. I put heroin and 'chase the dragon' into the search engine. I needed to find out all I could. I waded through pages and pages of stuff until my mind could take no more. There was so much information and the more I read, the more I was filled with dread. It was a minefield. I thought it would be easy to get her off it, but I now knew I had to get her help.

Why Becky? I started to ask myself. With everything she had already been through, why her? Why us? Why our family? I wanted to hit out at her so-called friends, at Martin, who she'd accessed it through. I hated him. She had to stay away from him. Becky needed help and I was determined that I would help her. Firstly, though, I had to tell Charlie and Steven.

As ever, Charlie was brilliant and practical. It seemed nothing could shock him. We called the doctor as a starting point and they referred us to Druglink. They contacted us a few weeks later, leaving a message on the answering machine. This wasn't good enough, so I went in person with Tracey to Druglink and made Becky an appointment. The soonest they said they could see her was in two weeks' time. This didn't feel immediate enough. What was I supposed to do with her for all that time? Becky needed help now, not in another two weeks' time.

The frustration in finding help for her was killing me. Becky continued to be a complete pain. The sorrow she'd previously felt when I held her in my arms was obviously for having been caught with the drugs in her bedroom. Perhaps she was even relieved that I'd found them. Her secret was out. She didn't have to hide it any more. In fact, she continued to leave home to be with her friends, where no doubt she was getting her 'fix'. I would go and bring her back, but she would go again and I would repeat the exercise. I couldn't get through to her. She wasn't interested in anything I had to say. It was like she was on a piece of elastic.

Her friends seemed to have such pull and influence over her, drawing her to them like a magnet, the lure of the drugs irresistible to her. Eventually, two weeks passed and finally Becky attended Druglink. They took a urine sample. They said would be back in touch in a couple of weeks' time, once the sample had been analysed. But two weeks was too long! I offered to pay, go private, but they told me it didn't work that way. They were a charity. I understood that, but I wanted to give them money to sort Becky out. They wouldn't have to use their funds, I would pay them. No, they said. There were others in line for treatment. Her turn would come. She couldn't jump the line. Everything was moving too slowly for me, Becky's life was becoming chaotic, as was mine trying to keep up with her. I was losing her and it frightened me to death. Taking a urine sample and asking us to wait was the extent of their help. We needed help there and then. I didn't want to *wait*. Who knows what could happen while we waited. Why would no one listen?

Becky's bad behaviour quickly got worse. She started to disappear for days, then weeks, without telling me where she went. Tracey and Tony would help in trying to find her. I tried to involve John in searching for Becky on these occasions. In the beginning, he would go out and look for her, but as she returned so regularly, he soon couldn't be bothered, saying, 'She'll be back.' Charlie showed more concern for her. We would be frantically ringing around her friends, trying to find her, or driving round to see if we could see her.

Each time we brought her home, I thought this will end now, this time I will get her sorted. But off she went again. We seemed to be on our own, there was nowhere to turn for professional help. The doctor referred me back to Druglink; Becky was on their 'list', but it was all too slow. There was obviously a very long list. When I rang them, all I got was an answering machine. I would leave a message. Could I just talk to someone, *please*? No, there was no one available as they were working on this or that project. Ring back. And so it went on. I contacted Narcotics Anonymous. It seemed no one cared. And no matter what we did, we couldn't stop her from running away.

Our life quickly settled into this miserable routine. She ran away to be with her friends to take heroin. Then, when she had her fill, she'd call me and I would go and fetch her. She was now clearly addicted. It was utterly heartbreaking. But at least she continued to come back and for that I was so grateful. Every time she returned was like being on a tightrope; each time, I had to try and keep her with us for as long as possible, so that at least we provided respite from the lifestyle she had chosen. It was important to me that she knew she could always come home, that she would always be welcome. It was tempting to give her ultimatums but I knew, if I did, I would lose her for ever. No matter what she did, she knew she would always have a home to come back to. She knew we would never turn our backs on her.

I was starting to learn about what heroin did to her. I could see the deterioration every time she came back. I was also learning how it made her behave, so I knew what to expect. The high of the drugs made her sleepless and stay up all night. During these times, she would eat everything she could lay her hands on, but she was starting to lose an alarming amount of weight. When she was 'high' her eyes would glaze over and, much like the smell of tobacco on cigarette smokers, there was a distinctive aroma when she'd had a fix. I could still detect it despite her efforts to mask it with perfume. Her hunger for heroin was, it seemed, relentless. I felt totally powerless.

Weeks passed into months and, before we knew it, Becky's drug-filled life became our new 'normal'. I kept the news of

Becky's addiction tight; Charlie obviously knew, as did Steven, but apart from them, only Tracey and Tony knew what was going on. We kept it from Mum and Nan and I put on a front to everyone else that everything was just fine, when it was far from the case. I didn't want people to judge her, to write her off. I still hoped that this was a blip, that she would come to her senses, stop as suddenly as she had started.

Little by little, the periods away had increased incrementally, until again, she made it seem normal for anyone's teenage daughter to go missing in this way. This is what we had come to: a reluctant acceptance of the way she had chosen to live her life. But I could not accept it. She was still my little girl. One day, I was helping Charlie out at work. He had just bought new premises and I was cleaning and sorting them out for him. It had been a long day and I headed off at 4.30 p.m. for a nice soak in the bath before Charlie came home at about 8.30. As I put the key in the front door, the phone started ringing. I ran to answer it. It was Becky. By now, she was in the habit of going missing for about a fortnight or more. I always thought she would see sense, let me help her. That it was only a matter of time, a phase she was going through. She knew I only wanted the best for her. Now, as I held the phone and listened to her, I couldn't believe my ears.

'Mum, I need £500 *now*.' She sounded strange, tense.

'Becks, love, you know we don't keep money in the house.'

'But I need it *now*.' Her voice was different, there was an edge to it. She was scaring me.

'You're in trouble aren't you Becky?'

'Yes, Mum.'

From the recesses of my mind I remembered an address in an area of Swindon that I'd heard her talk about and I asked her if she was there.

'Yes, I am.'

'I'm on my way, stay there Becky. Ring Aunty Tracey and keep talking to her and I'll be with you.'

I dialled 1471 and took a note of the telephone number of the phone box she had been ringing from. I had no idea where I was going exactly, but jumped in the car and headed towards Toothill in Swindon. I was in a blind panic and I was running on adrenalin. I turned down a road and seeing an empty phone box with the phone swinging off the hook, I got out of the car and checked the number. It was the same as the one I'd written down. So Becky had been here and now she was gone. What was she playing at, why hadn't she waited for me? Was she just messing me around? No, I had heard her voice, she was scared.

I looked around – there was no sign of Becky. I got back in the car and drove around the streets, looking for her. I was desperate, I couldn't see her and yet I knew she couldn't be far. I needed help, I couldn't do this on my own, so I went to get Steven who was at a friend's house. On seeing the state of me, he got in the car, along with his friend's dad, so now there were three of us, driving around looking for Becky. I was distraught. She could be anywhere. I'd heard the fear in her voice and she was in trouble. I had to find her and fast.

Suddenly, I saw a woman who I recognised as the mother of a boy Becky knew from school. She was walking across the green to the bus stop. I slammed the brakes on and ran over to her. I explained that Becky knew her son and that we were looking for her. I told her that Becky might be in trouble and asked if she knew anywhere local to the phone box where she might be. She gave me the name of a man and where he lived. I went back to the car armed with my information and drove in the direction of the property. Once there, the man had moved and so I was directed on to another property. There a man told me where she might be; he started to put his shoes on to come with me but his girlfriend stopped him, telling him he couldn't go because there were guns at the property.

I was filled with fear. I knew I was dealing with drugs – but guns? This was new. What sort of company was she keeping now? As we arrived at the place, Steven told me to stay where I was and was out of the car before I could say anything. I watched as he ran up a flight of steps up to the premises and banged on the door. Now both my children were in danger. When the door opened, Steven pushed himself forward. Steven's friend's dad had been watching with me and got out of the car, ready to intervene if he had to.

'Is Becky here?' he shouted. Looking beyond the door into the gloom of a dark room, Steven could see nothing but young boys off their heads on drugs, lounging around.

'No, she's not,' came the reply.

As the door was being shut on him and as he turned to go, Steven heard Becky calling out. She was inside and had heard his voice. He turned around, kicked the door in and re-entered the dingy premises. He called out to her.

'Becky, Becky, where are you?'

'In here.'

Steven went to a locked bedroom. Kicking at the door until it opened, he found Becky inside with another girl. By now he had been joined by his friend's dad and they both grabbed Becky, dragged her down the stairs and bundled her into the car. I'll never forget the sight of her. She looked like a rag doll, her legs lifeless and her head lolling around with the effects of drugs.

I put my foot hard on the accelerator and off we sped, but coming towards me was a large white transit van. I veered to avoid it but for some reason, the driver seemed intent on driving at me. I had to mount the pavement to avoid it. As we got to the end of the road, I was driving so fast, I had to swerve to avoid hitting a bus. All I knew was that we had to get away and out of the area.

We managed to get Becky to a safe place with a family friend, in case they came looking for her at home. As soon as we had her settled, I went home and called the police to report what had happened and the premises we'd been to. The scenario I described to them was familiar, they said. Young teens were plied with drugs to get them hooked; then they built up a drug debt which they would have to pay back, usually in the form of prostitution. They told me that the white van was probably going to collect Becky and the other girls for exactly that purpose.

I was stunned. I'd got there in the nick of time. Any longer and I'd have lost her for good.

With Becky in a safe place, we were able to nurse her back to as near normal as possible. Soon after she had returned home to be with us, we were warned by a young woman knocking on the door that she was worried for Becky. Becky's 'friends' obviously knew where she lived so we decided to install CCTV and put lights up outside. By now we also had three dogs. I felt outraged that they would come to the house – just let them try and take her.

The warning also made me realise that I needed to find a drug dealer so that I could manage Becky's supply of drugs, instead of her exposing herself to these lowlifes. I would buy Becky's drugs for her. My desperate reasoning was that at least she wouldn't be putting herself in danger any more. If she was getting her fix at home, from me, surely she wouldn't feel compelled to run away to get it? I felt more than up for dealing with these people. So that's what I decided to do. That was my plan.

With Becky back at home with us, at last I was able to make another appointment through the doctor for her to go to Druglink for professional help. As we were upstairs getting ready for the 4 p.m. appointment, I heard the front door shut. Looking out, I saw Becky disappearing into a taxi. I dialled 1471 to the taxi office to check where she was going. She was going back to her boyfriend, back to the drugs. I hadn't even had a chance to put my plan into action.

The next morning, Charlie left for work early. Around 7.30 a.m., I was disturbed by a loud, persistent banging at the front door. Still in my dressing gown I went to answer the door. It was Sue, the mother of Martin, Becky's boyfriend.

'It's Becky,' she said.

'What about Becky?'

'She's at my house. She's saying she's been raped.'

I ran upstairs, threw some clothes on and rang Steven, asking him to let Charlie know. I followed Sue back to her house. Becky was there with the police. They were gathering up her clothes. Unhelpfully from a forensics point of view, she had had a bath and with her hair in a towel, she was being put into a police car. I followed in my car as they went on to the rape suite at the police station.

I listened as she relayed what had happened. She had left Sue's house and had gone looking for Martin, who was a drugs runner. When she couldn't find him she went to see if he was at the dealer's house. She had waited there for hours and it was while she was there that she was raped by the dealer. He had trapped her in a room by shutting them in, barring the door from opening with a chair and threatened her at knifepoint to have sex. She was in a terrible state.

The police took her statement and did all the necessary checks and tests. It was heartbreaking to listen to her. We hugged and cried. Once again, someone had hurt my little girl. I couldn't bear it. I didn't know how much more either of us could take. When the police had finished with her, I took her home and nursed her. She was emotionally very frail. In the meantime, the police made an arrest.

Despite the challenges, we managed to put Becky back together again. It was a long process, but she showed enormous resilience. She was certainly a fighter. She was back with us and she was like my Becky of old. We even managed to find her a job in the office of *Reader's Digest*. Becky seemed to enjoy life at work and those months were the best I had known in a long time for her. I took her and collected her from work every day; she loved her office job and I felt terrifically proud of her. I'd have given anything for this not to have happened to her; however, bewilderingly, it had given us this upside. It was as if she'd re-evaluated her life. It felt like all the bad times were behind us. Only, we had the rape trial looming.

The police informed us that the man who had raped Becky had raped before but had never been charged. This time, they said, they were going to get him and bring him to trial. Becky attended court in a smart black trouser suit. I felt so proud of her and the way she had turned her life around. She had survived a very traumatic experience. She had a job and a new life beckoned. More than all of that, she was clean. Free of heroin.

The courtroom was small but intimidating. Tracey came with us. Becky stepped forward and was taken through her evidence by the prosecuting barrister. She was asked to identify the knife that was used and was able to do this by its distinctive handle, which had a piece missing from it. It all went well. Then the defence barrister started the cross-examination. Of course he was going to fight for his client, but as the questioning progressed, Becky became increasingly rattled. It was his job to cast doubt on her version of events, but eventually, she became annoyed with him and lost her temper. She'd had enough.

'He did this before,' she answered to one of the questions put to her, 'and he isn't going to get away with it again.'

Due to Becky disclosing that the man had raped before, the trial was stopped in its tracks. A new court date was set, with a new jury. However, the judge wanted to keep the case. When at last the day arrived, Becky went into court. She told the judge and jury what had happened to her. It was a harrowing thing to go through again. She was so brave. As well as Becky's rape, the man was also charged with possession of drugs. After going all through the prosecution and defence process again as a witness, we waited with Becky for the verdict. It came. The man was found guilty of possession of Class A drugs, but not guilty of Becky's rape. Becky was devastated by the verdict. Tracey and I cried; it was an outrage.

Becky felt worthless and as if she hadn't been believed. Twice she had had to put herself through the torment and trauma of telling her story to a court and for what? It tipped her over the edge and that night, Becky left home again and wouldn't answer our calls. She immediately went back to her old life, using the drugs to drive away the pain of the trial and the 'not guilty' verdict. She lost her job and disappeared. We couldn't find her. We spent hours driving around Swindon trying to find her without joy. I was sick with worry. I wanted her back; she should be with us at this time, with the people who loved her and who would care for her.

Becky retreated into her old life until one day Steven saw her on his way home from work. He dragged her into his car and brought her home. When I saw her, I'd had enough. She was in a terrible state. I marvelled at her tiny body's resilience to all the muck she put into it; she was certainly a survivor. But she couldn't go on like this. She looked so ill. I wanted her off drugs once and for all and decided that she had to go cold turkey. We had had to put locks on all the doors long ago, as Becky had taken to stealing things from the house to pay for her drugs. So I locked both myself and Becky in her bedroom. We would battle it out together, because that's what it felt it had come to.

We stayed locked in there for three days with just water to drink. When Becky needed drugs it was as if she was possessed by the devil. It was like being in a room with a wild animal and there were times when I felt sure she would have killed me for them. I lay on her bed with her, holding her as she fought against and held me in turn. I watched her face twist and contort with the pain of withdrawal. She pleaded with me to get her what her body desperately craved.

'Mum, Mum, please, come on, *please*, I'm tired. I'm tired, I can't do this.' It was like a mantra that she said over and over and over again. It was all she would say for hours to grind me down, to make me give in.

'Mum, Mum, *please, please*! Help me.' She shouted it, screamed it at me, raged. She went on and on, until my head banged with the noise of her screaming. On and on until I wanted to scream back at her, 'Just shut up, just shut up!' but I didn't, I couldn't show her any sign of weakness. I just held her.

I watched as Becky screamed, shook, sweated and shivered; she was physically sick and incontinent, but eventually, she came through. Once again, the poison had left her body. For three days it felt as if I'd been wrestling with a python; we were both utterly exhausted. Once again, she had some peace from the drugs and their wretched hold on her.

All the time we were locked in her bedroom together, the phone never stopped. It was Martin, ringing incessantly to speak to her. We took the phone off the hook. Then he turned up and sat outside the house in a car. He was waiting for her to come out. One Sunday morning I saw him. I ran outside.

'Go away, leave Becky alone.' I shouted.

'But I love her,' he said, pathetically.

'If you loved her, you would leave her alone. Let her get better.' I went mad at him and called the police. He was driving a stolen car, with no driving licence and they did nothing. Eventually, after I was very aggressive towards him, he left.

Months passed before Becky went off again. But she went all the same. The pull of the drugs and the boyfriend was too overwhelming for her. It broke my heart as I thought we'd made progress. Here we go again. But she came back. Steven saw her one night and brought her home to us. She was high, so Steven and I watched her through the night. Then Becky had to go to the toilet. She had been in the bathroom a long time before we realised she had in fact escaped through a window. We rushed outside and ran down the road, only to find Becky in a phone box at the bottom of the lane.

We brought her back home. Again she asked to go to the toilet and Steven told Becky not to try to escape through the window again, as he'd be waiting outside. She went to the loo. While she was in there, we suddenly heard a crash. The door was locked and Steven had to break in. We found her on the floor, with the thick cord of the light pull wrapped around her neck. She had stood on the toilet seat and tried to hang herself with the cord, but luckily the light fixing had not been able to bear her weight and it had been pulled from the ceiling.

We rang the emergency out-of-hours doctor at Redwood House, Swindon, and Tracey and I took Becky there to be assessed. All the way in the car Becky was screaming for a fix, she was like a mad woman. We got her inside and hoped that they could help her. However, Becky wasn't bad enough to be detained. They had to let her go with a referral back to her doctor.

Needless to say, Becky went off again and it was months before my next call from her. By now, the hopes and dreams Becky had once had – of passing her exams, of going to university, of becoming a vet or working with children – they all felt long gone. Her teen years were flying by and they were being lost to this senseless drug. Although I didn't know it then, the chain of events that would lead her to that evil monster Christopher Halliwell was already well in motion.

5

ON THE RUN

The next few years passed with Becky dipping in and out of our lives. I wanted to start up in aromatherapy again so took some premises. I expanded, took on a beautician, then offered Tracey the space to run a hairdressing salon. As and when Becky returned, I let her work on reception. I wanted her to share it, become part of it. I hoped it would stop her from running away, but she still took off at various times for weeks or months before returning again.

By now, Becky was 18 years old. One day I was at the dentist having a check-up when my phone rang. I couldn't get to it, but it wouldn't stop. Someone needed me urgently. It was Becky. She was at a bus station in Bristol. She wanted to see me. I drove home and as soon as Charlie saw me he asked me what was wrong. I told him.

'I'll drive,' was all he said.

Charlie had endless patience where Becky was concerned. He made no distinction between her and one of his own daughters. He was really concerned for her. Off we went to Bristol, arriving at the bus station as she had directed. It was starting to get dark by the time we arrived. We didn't know what to expect, as we hadn't seen or heard from her for months. She'd given us no indication as to what she wanted. I was hoping she wanted to come home.

As soon as I saw her, I was shocked. I barely recognised her. She was standing with her long hair wild, wearing a filthy long brown sheepskin coat and trainers. The coat was flapping open in the wind and I could see all she had on underneath was her underwear. I jumped out of the car and ran to her. There were people around looking at her, but she seemed oblivious. She looked ill, but was so pleased to see us. The next thing I noticed was the smell. She smelt putrid. I tried to button up the coat to give her some dignity, but she didn't seem to register what I was trying to do.

I ushered her into the car but such was the smell of her, we had to put the windows down. She wanted to come home with us, but before we left Bristol she wanted to go to St Paul's – an inner-city area notorious for drugs and prostitution. She needed to go there to buy more drugs. We had no choice but to find a supply for her; at least in St Paul's she might get more for the money and I knew £100 would tide her over for a while. She knew exactly where to go and directed us. The area was rundown and it was now dark. I was frightened for her as she jumped out of the car and disappeared around a corner with a hundred pounds in cash that we'd given her. She returned within ten minutes with her heroin and we quickly headed for home.

Once we were back, I ran her a bath and made her some soup. It was awful to see her in such a mess, but at least she was with me now. Once she had eaten a little, I helped her in the bath; she was skin and bone. She'd always been slim, but this was very different. I washed her hair, making sure one of the washes was with nit lotion that I kept for the occasions when she returned. By now, Becky had very long blonde hair. I don't know what had happened to it, but it took me three hours to sort it out. In between me coaxing tangles and matted patches, Becky continued to take her fix of heroin.

As Becky hadn't been home for a while, I'd tidied her room, packing away her excess clothes that couldn't fit into the wardrobe and putting them in the loft. Becky just had her underwear and coat on when we picked her up and would need some clothes. Right then, it was easier to shop than start sorting out what she might like or what might fit; besides which, new clothes might make her feel better. I quickly went into the local shopping mall and picked up some things I knew she would wear. She had become fussy over the years and would only wear certain labels. I'd left Tracey to sit with her while I quickly went shopping. I dashed back home, half expecting her to have left. She was still there, with Tracey, waiting for me to return.

It was lovely to have her home again and that night, I got into bed with her. I stayed awake all night, feeling her near me, listening to her breathing as she slept. I wondered why she had to keep pressing the self-destruct button. Why couldn't she give up the drugs, give up running away? Why couldn't we live peacefully like this?

Despite everything that had happened to her, I still recognised my little girl. She had never lost her infectious giggle that everyone knew. She still slipped her arm through mine and held my hand as she did when she was small and, as old as she was, she would still wriggle herself into my lap. Lying here with her was a rare moment of tranquillity. I relished feeling her so close to me. I smelt her clean hair and put my arm around her, holding her close as she slept. I could look after her now.

The next morning, the first thing she did was have a fix. I knew at this rate her £100 worth of heroin wasn't going to last long. If I was to try and keep Becky at home, I needed to get more. I knew what I had to do. Becky had split up with Martin, the drug runner, but he was the only person I could think of to help me. I went through Becky's diary and found his number, then arranged to meet him to get some more heroin. Charlie and Steven wanted to come with me, but I told them I was going on my own. If I got caught with drugs, or trying to buy them, at least it would only be me and not all three of us. I was the one with the least to lose as I saw it.

Before I set off, I called the doctor and Charlie and I decided to see Julia Drown, MP. I wanted her to know what we were going through, how long this had been going on and how difficult it was to find help. How bad did things need to get before you could access the type of help we needed? The doctor's appointment was a couple of days away, as was the appointment with Julia Drown.

In the meantime, I went off to buy Becky's drugs with Martin. I had to keep her at home and the only way to do that was to ensure she had a good supply. Martin said of course he would help me, but only if I paid for his drugs too, so with him in the car I drove off. I parked outside a phone box and along with many other addicts, we waited to buy heroin.

I looked at my fellow purchasers; I noticed how twitchy and fidgety they were as if there weren't in control of their bodies. I looked into their grey faces with their sunken eyes. They were like ghosts, ghosts of the people they once were, before the drugs, before the grip of heroin. Then the phone rang to tell me of a change of venue and off we went again. This time I was directed to go to the back of the civic offices. The dealer was there and I was able to buy Becky some heroin. Job done, I could now go back home and put my plan into action.

That night, as Becky slept, I sat with a tray and a small crafting knife in the kitchen. I opened each wrap of heroin and chipping away a little at a time with the knife, I took pieces off each 'lump' to reduce the amount. Then I wrapped each lump back up to make Becky think that this was the whole dose. While she was with me, I felt I had to try and wean her off but at the same time, give her enough heroin so that she didn't feel the need to leave and find more for herself.

I couldn't find the help I needed to wean her off, so I felt I had to work it out for myself. I would only give her one wrap at a time. I hid the rest in jam jars, burying them in flower beds around the garden. Then I put plant canes into the ground as a marker to myself as to where I could find the jars, when I needed to dig them up. The canes looked perfectly natural in the flower beds. It had come to this, I thought, looking out at the garden at all the canes; I was now a drug dealer.

I managed to get Becky to the doctor, who again referred

her to Druglink. At last, Friday arrived and I went with Charlie to see Julia Drown, while Mum and Tracey stayed with Becky. Obviously by now, Mum had guessed what was going on, but we didn't want her to know too much information. I told Julia that I had been out on the streets buying drugs for Becky to keep her safe at home. Julia was very helpful and gave us a list of drug organisations such as Hope House in London. I rang them, but they had no vacancies at this time and suggested I try again in a few months. As I sat going through the list, Charlie came to the rescue again.

'While we've got Becky at home, there's not a moment to lose. Let's just go private. Becky needs professional help now.'

I called the Diana, Princess of Wales, Treatment Centre for Drugs and Alcohol.

'We'll be able to take her next week,' they said. I cried with relief. At last, someone was going to help us. While we waited, I carried on buying drugs and administering them to her; I continued to cut bits off them, re-wrap and bury them in jam jars in the garden. My 'plan' was working as far as I was concerned, because all the time she had drugs, there was no need for her to run and she stayed with us, out of danger. During this time I managed to gradually reduce her heroin intake and substitute it for other 'softer' drugs, such as sleeping pills. To my mind, anything had to be better than heroin.

But it was a risky strategy and I was just waiting for her to run. We lived on eggshells. On one occasion Becky insisted on going with me on one of my 'buying' trips. It was in the evening; it was dark and raining. After making our purchase, such was her desperation I had to park in a side street where she had her fix right in front of me in the car.

It was such a sad thing to witness. It was such a hard thing to watch my own daughter, who I loved so much, dependent on drugs. It was as if she was in the grip of a dreadful sickness. It took every ounce of self-respect from her. She was utterly enslaved to it. As I watched her inhaling the vapour, I felt power-less and frightened. I also felt anger too, that our lives had been completely turned upside down for her addiction, for these moments. Why couldn't she stop? Before she finished, I suddenly grabbed her hand.

'No, wait. I want some,' I said to her, 'Let me have some. If it's good enough for you, it's good enough for me. I want to try it.'

She looked at me, wide-eyed. 'No, Mum!' she shouted.

'Yes, give it to me, let me try it. I want to see what it's like.'

'No, no, you can't, no!' Becky was screaming at me, totally freaking out at my suggestion. She was going mad at me. 'I won't let you.'

'Come on, we can do it together, we can both do it. Tell me, Becky. What do I have to do? How much do I inhale?'

'No, Mum, leave it alone,' she shouted.

'But I want to feel what you feel, I want to know why you have to keep taking this.'

'No, Mum, you can't, I won't let you. You're not getting involved in this.'

By now she was sobbing. Of course, I had no intention of trying it, but I wanted to scare her, frighten her like she fright-ened me.

'Becky, that's how I feel about you, that's how I feel when I see *you* take this.' I think she might have understood, just for a moment.

At last, the day arrived for Becky's admission. The night before, after having a fix, she had gone to sleep in the snug by the fire, wrapped in a white blanket. The tin foil she had used was lying on the carpet by her feet. With her blonde hair framing her face she looked angelic, just like she had when she was little. She was still my little girl. I reached for the camcorder and coaxed her to wake, calling her name. I wanted to capture her in that fuzzy warmth of waking. Like the Becky of old, before she had her morning fix. Before she went into the clinic.

Perhaps in a few months' time when she had recovered, we could replay it to show her how far she'd come. She was so thin, but still so pretty. She woke and immediately asked what time we had to be there. I whispered that I would ring them that morning to confirm. She had a fix, a bath and I washed and dried her hair for her. She knew where she was going and why, and seemed to accept the help being offered. Before we left she gave me a picture depicting a mother holding the hand of her little girl. She had written on it 'Our target starts from here and now. Becky and mummy in fourteen weeks.' I put it up in the kitchen and prayed it would come true.

We put Becky's things into the boot of the car and Charlie took us to Somerset. We drove through beautiful grounds to the building where Becky would be staying. It looked stunning as it came into sight. We parked up and I held Becky's hand as we walked through the door. Standing in a foyer we could see people skipping about, wandering around and looking lost. I started to feel uneasy about the place. Eventually, we were greeted by a friendly looking woman and then shown around. The building was huge and a little tired-looking.

We were taken to the room which Becky would be sharing with a few others. We were then ushered into an office to fill out forms. I had to tell them about the drugs and when Becky had had her last fix. My method of reducing Becky's heroin intake and substituting sleeping pills had apparently done her no favours I was told. In thinking I was helping her, I had made matters worse. They now had to wean her off sleeping pills before they could tackle the heroin addiction. It would slow things down. I was gutted.

They told us we would have no contact with Becky as it would upset the programme. It was based on the 12-steps model of drug and alcohol rehabilitation. We paid the money and signed the contract. It was at this point they indicated to me to leave the room. Becky started to cry and I hugged and kissed her. I stood on the other side of a glass wall when she suddenly threw herself to the floor and grabbed Charlie's legs, begging him not to leave her.

'Daddy, Daddy, please don't go.'

The tears rolled down my face and I turned away. We had no choice but to leave her. They lifted Becky off the floor and took her to a medical room. Charlie and I both cried as we walked away. It had been a heart-wrenching scene, the only comfort being the thought she was in a place with people who could help her. At least, I hoped so. Charlie and I held hands tightly as we walked back to the car. He was such a rock to me. We drove home in silence, both of us hoping we had done the best thing, both of us fighting the urge to turn the car round and get her. I swear if either one of us had said it, we'd have done it; but we could not say the words. We were now in uncharted territory.

Becky had only been there two weeks and had started the steps programme when we received a phone call from the Trust. Becky wasn't settling in and they wanted to move her to Norwich, where they had another of their establishments. We arranged to collect her from Somerset at 11 a.m. That morning was very foggy and damp. There had been an accident on the motorway, so we had to go on through the back roads. They told us they would be giving Becky her meds at 11 a.m. so we knew we had no time to waste.

We had set off in plenty of time but had only got as far as Malmesbury when a Mercedes SLK car rammed into the back of us. The restraining bars shot up through the back window of our vehicle. Within seconds I was out, shouting hysterically at the driver, who was shaking like a leaf. I knew we had a deadline to meet to pick Becky up and we would be delayed. We assessed the damage and exchanged details. We taped up the back window so it was safe to drive and continued on to Somerset. We were late when we eventually arrived; Becky had been given her medication and was ready to go. We made good progress, but on reaching the M11, the traffic was moving slowly.

With the traffic stacked up, we were going nowhere fast. Becky's medication was wearing off and she was going crazy in the back of the car. Eventually, we arrived at Norwich at which point Becky was screaming for her meds. Before she could be given anything, she had to provide a urine test to make sure she hadn't taken or been given anything en route. When she had been checked in, we left her to stay overnight in a hotel nearby. Again, I hoped that this time she would settle and they could complete the treatment programme.

The next morning, before we had even left the hotel, my phone rang. It was the staff at the treatment centre. We had to go and take Becky away.

'She's trouble,' came the explanation. I was distraught. We had travelled all that way and now they were refusing to help. 'We can't keep her here. She's aggressive, too much trouble. If you don't come and get her we will put her on the next train.' I started to cry in despair. If they couldn't help her, who could? Charlie took the phone from me.

As he spoke to them he walked through the automatic doors and out of the hotel foyer. I watched him as he paced up and down outside, the automatic doors opening and closing as he walked in and out of their range, with me catching snippets of his conversation as the doors opened.

'We know she's trouble, of course she's trouble, that's why she's with you. I've signed a contract. You can't just put her on a train. If you do that, I'll sue you. I'll have you closed down. You're there to help.'

They kept Becky for a few more weeks. A week before Christmas, we picked Becky up. She was clutching a large folder; part of the therapy was writing and it was this she now carried with her and that would stay with her in her bedroom at home.

She looked wonderful, the best I'd seen her in years. Whatever it was they'd done, it seemed to have worked. On the way home as a treat, we called into a mall. Becky wanted to go shopping and have a meal. I felt so proud of her and Charlie and I treated her to some new clothes, some in her favourite designer brands. For the first time in ages, I felt really relaxed in her company. I had my old Becky back. It had all been worth it to reach this point, to see her looking so well, so healthy.

We had Christmas at home with all the family, but it was strained. It had been a hectic day; my nan was ill and the paramedics were called, and there was an argument between the kids which had upset Becky. It felt as if I was asking too much for a nice, calm Christmas. Charlie went to bed with a migraine. I sat up on my own eating a heated-up Christmas dinner while I opened my presents. The following afternoon I took Nan home. By the time I got back, Becky had gone.

Becky disappeared back and forth during 2001 and 2002. One day I received a phone call from her. She had taken an overdose of paracetamol. I picked her up from the bus station at Swindon and took her to A&E. She had a medical assessment and blood tests. It took four of us holding her down for the blood to be taken, as she didn't like needles. From here we went into a side ward, where she could be monitored through the night. They recommended an assessment by the duty psychologist.

As we waited for him, it was clear that Becky was becoming agitated; she needed a fix. I went back home to get her pyjamas, dressing gown, slippers and a warm blanket. I knew I had some heroin left so I dug up one of the jam jars in the garden. I also took some tin foil and called at the garage for a lighter. On my arrival back at A&E Becky was waiting for me. She knew what I'd gone to get for her. We got back in the car and I drove to a quiet corner in the car park. I sat in the car with her as she chased her dragon. The smell was absolutely foul. I opened the window and all you could see was the glow from the lighter and 'cigarette'. After her fix, we went back into A&E. She reeked of heroin and it was quite obvious what she had been doing.

After the psychiatric assessment, it became clear what had prompted Becky's overdose. She had caught her boyfriend with another girl. I was hoping that Becky might be admitted but no, she was duly discharged and I took her home. It was a matter of weeks before Becky left again. This time, we heard that she was renting a caravan to live in near Lechlade with her new boyfriend, Lee (by this point Martin was in prison). She had been to see John, as she did now and then, to get him to help her with a reference to vouch for her rent.

This was a chaotic time and, before long, Charlie and I had another call from Becky. She had been arrested for her part in a burglary at a pub in Lechlade, Gloucestershire, and was in Stroud Police Station. When we got there, she told us that her boyfriend owed drugs money. Someone had turned up at the caravan looking for him. She'd told him that he wasn't there, so he said he would take her instead. He was going to burgle a pub and he took her as a lookout. Becky said she had no choice but to go with him and had stood outside chain-smoking, while the man burgled the pub. She had been caught because her DNA was on a cigarette stub she had left behind. She was released on bail on condition that she came home with me, which she did. Her bail conditions were that she had to report to the police station every week. There would be a court hearing imminently.

To help with her court hearing, we employed a psychologist to prepare a report on Becky for her solicitor. My fear was that she would incur a custodial sentence for the burglary and the psychologist knew Becky, as he had treated her before. His psychological assessment said Becky, despite being 20 years old, had the emotional age of a 12- to 14-year-old, believed to be due to drug use ultimately suppressing her emotions. We were surprised; she certainly showed no obvious signs of being anything other than very savvy.

However, bail conditions did not deter Becky and she went off again. Letters arrived from the court and I put them in her room unopened. She continued to come home and disappear. Eventually I discovered that she was on the run and a warrant had been issued for her arrest. During this time she didn't come back. She probably knew if she did, I'd have taken her straight to the police station to sort everything out. It was a long time before I saw her again. Despite this, she didn't forget me on Mother's Day, when, having been out all day, I came home to find that she had been in and left me a card, along with a box of wine and three little figurines with 'mum' written on them. I loved the fact that she hadn't forgotten me, but, equally, I wished she'd stayed so that I could see her. Later in the year, we received a phone call from Becky at a police station. She had been arrested and was in custody; this time there was no bail. She was being sent to a female prison in Gloucestershire for three weeks until her court date, as she was considered a flight risk.

She sent me a letter and a visiting order. Of course I had to go to her. I had never been in a prison before. I took a suitcase full of clothes for her, along with chocolate, stamps, paper and envelopes. I took her ghetto blaster, tapes and even some cigarettes as she had requested, but when I got there I was not allowed to give them to her. I was searched on arrival and had to use a locker for my bag and phone. I felt like a criminal myself. At last I was shown to a large room with lots of plastic orange chairs in pairs, facing each other. A buzzer sounded and Becky came in. She was wearing a sash across her. We were not allowed to touch one another, but we talked. It was heartbreaking, seeing my own child sat in this room; but she looked surprisingly well.

'Becky, you've really got to sort yourself out now,' I told her. Prison was a new depth she had sunk to and I wanted her out of there. 'You've got to get help now, when you come out . . .'

'It's alright, Mum,' she said, 'I'm clean, I haven't had anything since I've been in here. I went cold turkey.'

'Then we've got to get you home.' I just wanted her back with us.

'I'm alright. I know people in here. It's not so bad.'

Becky wrote to me and rang me regularly and I sent her a postal order every week. I kept all her letters to me.

On 16 December 2002, Becky was due in court in Swindon. We managed to get her a good solicitor and I asked if he could ask for her to be tagged to avoid a custodial sentence, but this was not an option. She was called into the courtroom and I was sitting in the gallery on my own. I saw her walk in. She was dressed smartly, as she had requested new clothes for court. My stomach was turning over as she was looking up, trying to find me. She looked so tiny. She saw me and we exchanged air kisses. The process was over very quickly and I was relieved when Becky was fined, with conditions that she had to attend probation and go back with me.

I paid the fine and while I was waiting for her I was handed a bright orange bag containing her things. The court usher must have sensed my embarrassment and offered me a black bin bag which I accepted. After seeing the solicitor I put the bin bag in the boot and set off home with Becky. I suggested a nice bath and then some food, whatever Becky wanted to do. However, she had other ideas.

She wanted me to take her to another new boyfriend, Jason, who lived in Swindon. I told her I wasn't happy about this, but if I didn't take her to see him, I knew she would just leave once we arrived home. She told me where to go and I drove her there. I was annoyed with her.

'Just half an hour and then we go home,' I said to her as she got out of the car. I watched her walk over to a maisonette and disappear inside. I sat in the car to wait for her to come back out. After a while, she came out and walked towards me.

'Can I stay a bit longer, Mum?'

'We agreed half an hour, Becks,' I said. The sooner we were home, the better.

'You could go to the shop and get a chocolate bar, Mum? Then I'll be back.'

'I know what you're doing in there,' I told her, 'You told me you were clean.' She didn't answer.

I drove to the shop, but I didn't go inside. I went back and parked facing the green so that I could see the property. The urge to knock on the front door and drag her out was overwhelming, but I sat and waited. I was confident. It was nearly Christmas and Becky would naturally want to be at home at this time. She never missed Christmas with us. Eventually, after half an hour, Becky came back out. At last, we could go. I watched as she walked towards me. I put my window down, as she approached.

'Ready, love?'

'Mum, I'm staying with Jason,' she told me.

'No, Becky, come back with me. *Please*.'

'No, I'm staying with Jason,' she told me. 'I love you so much, Mum, I can't keep putting you through this. I can't keep doing this to you. I'll come home when I'm clean.'

She meant it. She kissed me on the cheek, walked to the boot and took out the black bag. I watched her walk away; she didn't look back. The drugs had taken their hold once again. There was nothing I could do. As I sat there, I felt powerless. I had nothing left in my armoury to fight the pull of the drugs. I'd run out of ideas.

The feeling in my chest was heavy and I couldn't stop the tears from rolling down my face. I'd been defeated yet again. I sobbed as I drove away, I felt so sad and hurt. I had lost her, and right then I'd lost hope. I thought prison would have shocked her, brought her to her senses. She had been clean but within an hour of leaving court she was back to her old ways. I'd so wanted to get her out, but now I wished she was still in prison. I'd prefer that to where she was now. I drove home. As I pulled up on the drive I felt as if all the life had drained out of me. I badly needed Charlie.

Perhaps my despondency came from somewhere deep in my subconscious. Perhaps I knew. This was the last time I was to see Becky alive.

6

WHERE'S BECKY?

The police were trying to establish exactly when Halliwell killed Becky. The policewoman was curious as to why we hadn't reported Becky missing, given that we hadn't seen her for years. Halliwell couldn't remember if he had killed her in 2003, 2004 or 2005 and the police had knocked on the door in 2011. It was a fair question. I explained to the officer, from the time I'd last seen her in December 2002, up until a few months before the police came, different people had told me of their encounters with Becky.

It seemed a lot of people saw and spoke to Becky during the years when we hadn't seen her. During that time, I thought she was staying away from me deliberately. People would tell us about her; some of these sightings had even been from members of John's family. I wasn't in a position to challenge people, as each seemed genuine enough, although, as much as I was glad to hear what they had to say, it hurt to think she would talk to others and not me.

I therefore didn't consider that she *was* missing, she just didn't want to see me, or come home for whatever reason. Becky's last words to me had been 'I can't keep putting you through all this, I'll come home when I'm clean.' As I explained to the policewoman, I assumed she was living up to her word. As the years wore on and we didn't see her for ourselves, we did go to the police station, twice, to see if they could help us find her, but they directed us to charity websites.

The last time I saw Becky was when she walked away from me into her boyfriend Jason's house, on 16 December 2002. Following that, Becky had had a letter which, without even opening it, I could see was from her probation officer. I had put this to one side, waiting for her to open it when she returned. Although I had left her with Jason, I was sure Becky would be home with us within a matter of days, as she loved Christmas. But Christmas came and went. There was no Becky. Her letter remained unopened and her presents were still under the tree, waiting for her.

We had gone to Tony and Tracey's for Christmas lunch, fully expecting Becky to turn up at the door for her dinner, but she didn't. It was the first Christmas in twenty years that I hadn't seen her.

It hurt dreadfully not to see her during such a special time of year. Despite all her problems, whatever difficulties she had, prior to 2002, she never missed a Christmas before, so it made me angry to see that she would do this, as she would know how much we'd miss her. During the years I didn't see her, I continued to buy and wrap up her Christmas and birthday presents every year and this year was no exception. Whenever she decided to return, I wanted her to see that she hadn't been forgotten. I had every hope that she would turn up. I kept thinking of her last words, that she would come home when she was clean. She was obviously still on heroin and felt this promise prevented her from coming home.

In March 2003, I relocated the hair and beauty salon and again, expected Becky to hear about it and reappear. We had a grand opening, but there was no sign of Becky. I'd been hoping she would turn up and that I might be able to persuade her to take an interest, find work for her, like I had before. It would have been lovely to share it with her.

At this point, a client came in for a facial. We started to talk and somehow we got on to the subject of drugs. I confided in her about Becky, and during our conversation she told me about a drug she had heard about called naltrexone. This could be used in the form of an implant and she told me that it helped to manage drug addiction. I made a note of it, promising myself that as soon as Becky came back, we would try naltrexone to see if it would help her.

As the months went by, several customers came into the salon who knew Becky, or whose family members knew her. I was always asked, 'Have you heard anything from "our Becky"?' Most of the time the answer was no. But some came in and told me they'd seen her, or spoken to her. I had people saying that she was living in Bristol and London. She knew Bristol and she had visited London for the tourist sites in the past. Another came in and told me she was abroad, in Spain. Even this seemed to make sense; I knew she liked Spain, we went there when she was young and it had been where Charlie had taken us on holiday. I could understand her being there.

I held on to what people were telling me, imagining her in these places. I had no reason to doubt them. As time passed by, I then heard more news about her, but this time it was through messages passed on to Steven. He had been told by his cousin from the Godden side of the family that Becky was living in Bristol and he had been to visit her. She was running a nightclub with her boyfriend and had given him money. I took this as being completely genuine; this was great news, as it certainly didn't sound as if she was on the streets. On the contrary, it sounded as if she'd landed on her feet. I heard other similar such stories and every time, I would ring my mum and Tracey to reassure them that Becky must be OK.

After a while, as these comments and messages were passed on, I became increasingly annoyed with her. How was it that she felt able to speak to her cousin and others but not me? This started to bug me, so along with my friend Shirley, I decided to research nightclubs in Bristol in an effort to find her so I could go and see her. I wanted to confront her and ask her why she hadn't come back. As I'd been told she was the manager of a nightclub, we rung around clubs in Bristol, posing as reps to make appointments to see the managers, but we drew a blank. We didn't find her.

About the same time, our family doctor rang me at the salon. It was about my nan, Iris. He had visited her at home as she had not been feeling well the day before, but it was not good news. He'd had to call an ambulance as Iris had had a stroke. My mum and Tracey met me at the hospital.

Nan spent long months recovering as best she could, but it

was clear she would never return to her former independent way of life. On her return home we devised a rota to help with her care, which meant Mum and I stayed overnight. Along with Tracey, between the three of us we made sure that Nan was looked after around the clock.

Like a ray of sunshine through the gloom, one day Steven met his future wife, Kelly, while she was working at the salon. They secretly dated for a while before announcing their engagement. Kelly quickly fell pregnant with our granddaughter Chelsie, followed by Chanel. My grandchildren brought me huge joy during what was otherwise a very stressful time. In 2005, Steven and Kelly were married in a registry office in Jersey. At the time, I took some delight in helping with the arrangements, not least because I thought it would be good practice for when it came to helping Becky in the future.

As Nan's ill-health continued, the pressure on me was immense, with a business to run and the problems that went along with it. And of course, I still hadn't seen Becky. I needed to get a message to her about Nan, as I knew she would be devastated about her having a stroke. When Nan had a second stroke, we feared for her life and again I wanted to find Becky to tell her. Nan pulled through and we carried on looking after her in her own home for the next five years, but when she had a further, final stroke which left her partially paralysed, blind, deaf and unable to speak, this time she ended up in hospital. After a short time, we were told that we would have to find alternative provision for her as Nan was bed-blocking. Social services were insistent this time she had to go into a nursing home.

Even with Nan in a nursing home, we continued with our rotas, visiting her every day and ringing each other to keep up to date with her care. We had looked after her for so long, we couldn't stop just because she was no longer at home with us. The nursing home might be able to provide the expertise, but they could not supply the love we felt for her.

We quickly arrived at the conclusion that the situation at the nursing home wasn't right. Nan wasn't checked on properly and we started to log details of incidents we witnessed. It started to take over our lives and was very wearing. One afternoon, I received a call from my sister to say that Nan had been rushed to A&E. She had been vomiting blood and was covered in bruises.

This now involved the police as the circumstances were investigated, but it was not straightforward. The police wanted to close the case, but after a battle we managed to get the case reopened. It took a long time to investigate, with the care home being taken over in the meantime. It was an extremely anxious time for us all. Eventually, it took its toll. I drove to work one morning feeling unwell and a member of staff called an ambulance for me as she thought I was having a heart attack. It turned out to be stress.

My body was obviously telling me I needed to rest, but with staff on maternity leave and sick, I had to cover their hours. During this time, people continued to come into the salon telling me they had seen Becky around. Birthdays and Christmases came and went and still there was no sign of her or any word. She'd never missed Mother's Day before but now she was missing one after another. What was going on with her? It was odd behaviour even for her to stay away without being in touch for so long, especially with Nan being so ill. I felt sure Becky would have heard about that by now.

According to Charlie, I was becoming paranoid. I'd started to get out of bed in the middle of the night and go and drive around looking for Becky. When it was Becky's birthday, I would go to areas where people had told me they'd seen her, or thought she might be. On her birthday, I walked the streets, peering through the windows of houses, particularly looking for Winnie the Pooh bears, as he was her favourite. I told myself that if I saw one, this might indicate she was there. Between visiting Nan on the rota and running the salon, the middle of the night was the only time I had to look for Becky, but I had to do it. I felt compelled to find her.

But I couldn't make sense of her absence. Normally, she always got in touch; she only stayed away at most for a few months, and it had never been more than a year, but by now, I hadn't seen her for several years. Something in the back of my mind was always saying things didn't add up. I kept asking myself why she would see these other people and not me. We hadn't fallen out, and there was no bad blood between us. I was always her backstop; the person she called in times of trouble. She never called John to help her when she was in trouble, always me. Even though she knew she would get some straight talking rather than easy answers, it was me she turned to time and again.

Our personalities were very similar. Sometimes, we would clash and go up against each other, especially when I could see she was harming herself and she wanted her own way. I only wanted the best for her and could see her as she couldn't see herself. I could see the potential in her, if only she'd give up the drugs. Sometimes I got through to her. She told me once that when she was clean, she wanted to go into schools to talk about her experience to teenagers. She didn't want others to make her mistakes. I knew teenagers would easily relate to her; she was smart, she was pretty, there were times when she dressed up she could look a million dollars. If her experiences stopped only one teenager from falling into drugs, it would be worthwhile. But her addiction prevented that from happening.

I had always been the one person she could rely on, no matter what she got herself in to. I had never once refused to help her and always told her that I would be there for her no matter what. Perhaps the fact she hadn't made contact was, by definition, a sign that she wasn't in any trouble. I wanted to believe that. So things went on much the same; we carried on looking after Nan and I would continue in my efforts to find Becky. Also around this time, Charlie's uncle fell ill, so we nursed him and supported his wife as well. Life was pulling me in all directions.

With all that was happening, I came to a decision. The salon was going to have to go. It was just too much with everything that was going on and family had to come first. The salon was sold. Then, sadly, Nan died. It was such a bleak time. I knew Becky would be so upset to hear about Nan, but there was no way to get a message to her.

Charlie and I often speculated about the reasons for Becky's absence, as it continued to both worry and annoy me.

'What if something bad has happened to her?' I would ask.

'If anything has happened, the police would be on the doorstep,' Charlie typically tried to reassure me. I suppose that was true enough.

'But why won't she come and see me? Why will she see others but not me?'

In a new bid to find Becky in 2007, I posted a message on a missing-persons website. It was a large local charity that I thought would have the best chance of reaching Becky or people who knew her. I wrote:

Karen Edwards is trying to trace the location of Becky, she has been missing for 5 years and I need to contact her urgently or just to know she is OK! Can anyone help? She could also be in the Bristol area.

Despite my plea, I recieved no information from this request.

Out of the blue, in 2010, Charlie answered a knock at the front door. It was a man who had done a bit of gardening for us when we first moved here, who we hadn't seen for years. He wanted to talk to me but I was out so Charlie took his phone number for me to ring him when I got back. When I did so, he gave me information concerning Becky.

'I thought you'd like to know. I saw Becky the other day.'

'Where?' I asked him.

'I gave her a lift to the Abbey Meads pub. She told me she lived in a flat nearby.'

'Thanks for telling us. I'll see if I can find her.' I was so grateful. It was kind of him to think of us and come round. The pub was only about an eight-minute drive away. She was that close.

'Yes, she would appreciate that. She's pregnant, told me the baby was due in December. She'll need you then.'

I was shocked into silence.

'Perhaps I could mediate between the two of you?' he said.

'I don't need a mediator,' I told him, 'I never have where Becky's concerned.'

I explained that we had never fallen out with each other; she told me she would return when she was clean and I took her at her word. Now all I wanted was to see her. More so if she was indeed pregnant. I couldn't imagine anything more lovely than my Becky with a baby. It would change her perspective. It could be the making of her. I needed to see her, clean or not. He was right about one thing; she would need my help.

I drove round the area looking for her. All I could think was if Becky was pregnant I definitely had to find her. I took my most recent photo of her into a Tesco Express near to where she had been seen and asked if anyone knew her. She was petite, pretty with long blonde hair, expecting a baby, I told them. They had never seen her. I walked away feeling deflated and upset.

Night and day, I continued to go out and look for her, but there was no sign of her. Then, two weeks later, we received a letter asking for a reference for our old gardener. He was having to reapply for his job as a car park attendant. I was gutted. We could only assume that he had used the story about giving Becky a lift to re-establish contact for the purposes of the reference.

The following January, in 2011, I was dropping off my two granddaughters, Chelsie and Chanel, as they had stayed with us overnight. As I approached the front door to their house, I saw my ex-father-in-law, Pete Godden. I stopped to talk to him and asked him how the family were. I asked him if he had seen anything of Becky.

'The last time I saw Becky,' he said, 'was about two years ago, at Stratton crossroads. She saw me, got off the bus and came running across the road. I was just picking up my prescription from the chemist. She put her arm through mine and said, "Hello, Granddad", putting her head on my arm. I asked her what she was up to and she told me she was running a nightclub with her boyfriend in Bristol.'

There it was again, the story about her being involved in a Bristol nightclub. We'd first been told this years ago. This really annoyed me; what on earth was she playing at, staying away for so long? To hear Pete talking about her so casually it felt as if she was deliberately choosing to stay away from me. After all we'd been through, after all the times she'd come to me for help, she was talking to everyone except me. I told Steven of my encounter with Pete, but he was sceptical.

'I don't believe a word of it,' he said.

'Well, why not?'

'They're liars, all of them.'

Because I hadn't seen Becky for myself for so long by now, I went to the police station with Charlie. In the eight years that Becky was missing, we did this on two different occasions, showing them a photo of Becky, asking them if they had seen her, but without luck. They gave me the contact details for the Salvation Army and the Missing People charity. Of course, by this time, Becky was an adult and because we told them there had been sightings of her, she was not deemed missing in an official way. Nevertheless, I wrote a letter to the Salvation Army, asking them if they could help me find Becky.

Becky had been troublesome and a drug addict. She had a conviction for burglary, but for very many years now there had been no record of her being in trouble. We'd had no calls from police stations, no visiting orders from prison. Becky seemed to be off the police radar. I'd checked hospitals over the years and once I was told she was pregnant, I even checked with her own GP to see if she had made any appointments to see him. I didn't know what to do or who to believe.

'So you see,' I explained to the policewoman, 'this is why Becky wasn't officially reported missing.'

When I heard of the body found in the field, although my gut instinct was telling me that it was Becky, there was enough evidence to the contrary for Charlie and Steven to tell me I was being paranoid. We had been told of so many sightings and there were the conversations people had told us they'd had with her over the years, since I last saw her. Were all those people liars? Apparently there was a girl in Swindon who looked very much like Becky, which might explain some of the sightings, but we had been told of meetings and conversations from people who knew her, people from John's family too. *Why?*

Now we were being told Becky might have been dead since 2003. When I was first told this, I thought there was a glimmer of hope. It meant the police were wrong, it couldn't be Becky! Pete had spoken to her just two years before, so it couldn't be her in the field. Pete would know his own granddaughter. Becky must be alive.

But the police were sure that it was Becky. One of the first things they had done when they discovered the remains was a DNA check against their database; they had Becky's DNA on file and it was a match. When detectives spoke to Pete, he admitted that perhaps his memory wasn't as good as it had been. No, it turned out he hadn't seen Becky two years ago; we now knew it was much longer than that.

As we discovered, no sightings of Becky after 2003 were genuine. I had last seen her on 16 December 2002. A local beat officer for Manchester Road, the red-light area in Swindon, had last seen Becky on 27 December 2002, when he had made a note of it. He knew her, but had not seen her since. Results of police enquiries suggested that 3 January 2003 was the last known sighting of her, by a friend who was with her in a nightclub. There was no trace of her from that date to when her remains were found in April 2011.

I'd spent all those years being cross with her when she'd missed her birthday, Christmas and Mother's Day. It hadn't been because she didn't want to be with us, or see me as I'd thought. It was because she couldn't come and see us. How could she walk through the door when she had been taken from us by an evil and callous murderer, who then buried her in a shallow grave in a remote field. She had lain there for years while I wondered where she was.

PART TWO

7

OPERATION MAYAN

Halliwell was now in custody, under arrest for the murders of both Sian and Becky. We were told we would be updated on any developments in the investigation, but at this stage, it was all one way. The police continued to come to the house, and helping with their enquiries was something I was naturally happy to do. We all were. We couldn't give them enough information, it seemed.

They now had Becky's story; her struggle with drugs, their magnetic pull and where that had taken her, on to the streets, where she had sold herself to pay for them. I went over the information we had received trying to make sense of it. She had last been seen by a friend in the early hours of 3 January 2003, which meant she could have been lying in that field for eight long years.

As I recounted Becky's life to police officers, it of course made me reflect. Could I have done more? Had I done the wrong things? Had I made a bad situation worse through the choices I'd made? If this or that hadn't happened, would the situation have been different? This was my fault, surely? I should have done more. I sent myself half mad as my mind ran wild with recrimination. If I'd tried harder to stay with John, would that have made a difference? If I had just accepted him for what he was, been happy with the life he had offered us and not wanted more, would she still be here? I should have kept us together as a family. I should have stayed at home, not gone to work. What if I had spent more time with the children, with Becky? I kept analysing how this could have happened, searching for the exact point in our lives at which I could or should have done something different. Searching for the *one* decision I should have taken that could have given a different outcome to this horror.

Moreover, I'd spent the last eight years feeling angry and annoyed with Becky. Why hadn't I had more faith in her? Of course she wouldn't have stayed away from us for all those years. What was I *thinking*? Why had I trusted the word of others? If I hadn't listened to people telling me they'd seen her, I would have reported her missing earlier. If I'd dragged her out of Jason's that day she'd wanted to stay with him, would it have prevented her from running into Halliwell's path only two weeks later?

The regrets, the 'what ifs' and 'maybes' took over as I tried to come to terms with Becky's death. I already knew I never would. The very thought of her coming into contact with Halliwell and being buried in that field for years would never lose its impact on me. I would never be able to control the emotion it made me feel. It still didn't seem real. I couldn't accept that I would never see her again. There was still time for this to all have been a terrible nightmare from which I was yet to wake. But every morning it was all too true. And this was about to be brought into sharp relief.

I asked if we could visit the field where Becky had been found. I thought it might help if I saw it for myself. Her remains had been removed for pathology tests but I wanted to see where she had been buried. Even in my fragile state, what I wanted now above all was knowledge. I had given our life story to the police, now I wanted to know everything they knew, no matter how painful I realised it would be. I had been living in a vacuum for years concerning knowledge and whereabouts of Becky and now I wanted to be told everything. I was dealing with the police now, not random people telling me they'd seen her. I could believe what I was shown and told from now on. I would be able to get to the facts and I was hungry for them.

The visit to the field was arranged. Three days had passed; it was the first time I had been outside since I'd been told Becky was dead. It was a beautiful sunny day and yet the brightness seemed to magnify my sense of raw grief; I was strangely aware of the colours and sounds around me, as if we were all living in some kind of vivid technicolour. The outside world seemed intense, a cruel place now, where bad things happened. I felt grateful for the presence and protection of the two Family Liaison Officers (FLOs) we had been assigned.

They drove us in unmarked police cars with the family and friends following behind. We had asked the vicar, Simon Stevenette, from our local church to come along to bless the ground. Driving through the Gloucestershire countryside we got lost; not surprisingly as there were many single-track roads en route. I struggled to keep up with where we were, as one unsigned road looked very much like another, passing in a blur. I didn't care that we got lost; I almost didn't want to arrive. I wasn't sure I wanted to go to the field after all.

Eventually, we stopped in a quiet lane. We were told the press were at the site, but in light of our visit the police had asked them to respect our privacy, which they did. We got out of the car; the FLOs walked towards where there was a drystone wall. There was an opening into the field, which we went through. The farmer who owned the field, Mr Kinch, was also there waiting. He looked a kindly man. I felt sorry for him, all this horror being brought to his door. As we walked into the field, I started to sob. I was acutely conscious of my feet on the soil, of not losing my footing on the uneven ground. As I walked towards the spot where Becky had been buried it felt surreal. Over the last few days my world had suddenly become a series of almost out-of-body experiences. And Becky was central to them. This was another such experience. Just a few days ago, I didn't even know this place where we stood existed.

Becky had been here all these years and I was just catching her up. I wanted to go everywhere she had been and yet, as I walked in the field and looked around, I wanted to run. I couldn't help but stray into that dark place in my mind that held such horrors. How had she come to be there? What had happened to her? Had she been murdered here? What had she suffered at the hands of the vile creature who had killed her? How could a human being murder another?

As I walked across the stony earth I wondered how she could be dead and I still be living. I was her mother, this wasn't the right way round. It should be me in the ground, before her. And since this was cruelly not the case, I wanted to be with her. I wanted to die there and then. I wanted to be with my little girl.

The field was deathly silent. My friend Gladys had come with us, and as she held my hand she gently pointed me towards a pair of lapwings nesting in the middle of the field. It was like her to seek out the beauty of nature among the sadness. I watched them; they were a welcome innocent distraction from the horror. It was a comfort to know nature could still be attracted to the field in spite of the grim significance it now had for us. And Becky had so loved animals and nature. As we approached the place Becky had been found it all became horribly real. A wooden cross had been placed by the police, bearing the words 'For an unknown lady'.

Now she was no longer unknown. Becky was ours, she was very much loved and wanted and we'd come to claim her. We hugged one another and cried. I felt the physical pain of my broken heart. Flowers had been laid on the ground and Steven and Kelly placed a white teddy there. Becky so loved her teddies. As I laid my own bouquet of flowers, I sunk to the ground sobbing. I knew her remains were no longer there, but if I had been offered the chance to melt through the soil to be with her, I would have taken it. I made sure the card I'd written on with the flowers was straight. The words blurred through my tears, but I had to tell her how I felt:

When you were born and put into my arms I cried with joy. I love you so much. But today I am crying for you, my beautiful girl. I loved you the day you were born and I love you even more today. I was always there for you, my baby girl, words can't be said about how I feel. Sleep tight my darling. Love Mum and Charlie.

We all stood and looked at the place where Becky had been found. I was trying hard to get it to sink in, but it was as if my mind refused to process it. My head started to bang with a terrific headache. The hatred I felt for the man who had done this bubbled inside me. He had prevented Becky from coming home to those who loved her. He had murdered her and left her here. I couldn't take any more. Suddenly, I didn't want to be there. I wanted to go, get away. I wanted to scream. I didn't know it then, but this would be the first of many visits. The field in the middle of nowhere would be for ever referred to and known to us now as 'Becky's field'.

The journey home was a long and silent one. My mind wandered back to when Becky was growing up. I saw the images of her like a kaleidoscope running through the years. *How had it come to this?* Why did it have to be *her*? I wanted to cuddle her again and make it all go away. Neither could I stop crying due to the sheer and utter sadness that racked me. The crying was constant, the tears just would not stop. By the time we arrived home, all I wanted to do was lie down. I was utterly exhausted.

I lay down but I couldn't sleep. It was all too overwhelming. My mind swirled with images of the field. I knew what it looked like now so I'd be able to recall it at will. There was still a large digger in the field when we arrived. This had been used to uncover Becky. As I lay there, I started to piece little bits together. Halliwell had led police to the field, pointed out where he'd buried Becky, then they'd dug and found her remains. But what had they found? I needed to know. How had she died? I wanted to know that too. Moreover, thanks to the local press, I also knew what he looked like. I now had the image of the man who had murdered Becky. There were two photos; one quite a demonic-looking photo of him with his shirt off, grinning into the camera, while in another photo he had the sun on his back, cigarette hanging out of his mouth, presenting a fish, his catch, to the photographer. Ordinarily, he wouldn't deserve a second glance. To me, now, he was a monster.

The police returned again the next day. They told me I had been appointed a homicide counsellor and we were introduced. Rosemary Waterkyne, a volunteer, would become a very valuable person in my life during the weeks and months ahead. Nothing was too much trouble for her as she listened to me, visiting as much as I required. She was an incredible lady.

Today the police suggested one way of controlling the media would be to give a press statement. They were still hungry for information regarding Becky, so this was generally a way of giving them what they wanted in order to maintain privacy going forward. I said I would do it, for as much as I didn't want to, this was another thing I could focus on. I sat down to draft what I would say.

Police took us to Gablecross Police Station for the press

conference. I felt anxious when I arrived. I wasn't sure I could do it after all. I wasn't sure I could hold myself together long enough. We were shown into a room and briefed on what to expect. We were then shown into another room, where we sat behind a long table with microphones and recording devices. In front were chairs neatly arranged in rows, full of representatives from the various media outlets with their recording devices.

My heart was thumping. I had to try and deliver this statement. Sat with me were Charlie and my sister, Tracey. I had to do this, despite it being so hard. It would give us some respite from the press:

My daughter has been murdered and to be given the news on what would have been her twenty-ninth birthday, we can't believe it, after everything she had been through in her troubled life. Life was hard before when she was living the life of an addict, but we really did think she was alive and that, one day, she would come back home. Becky was a very beautiful, intelligent girl. She was loved by all her family and we all loved her with all our hearts; our loss is so unbearable.

Becky gave me so much love and joy as a child. However, as a teenager, she got involved with people who introduced her to drugs. She left school and her life spiralled into some very dark places to feed her addiction. She became a very, very different person. Following a conviction for theft, Becky made a choice to leave home rather than stay where we could care for her once again and try to rehabilitate her.

She once told me that she loved me so much, she couldn't keep putting me through this hell and she would not come back to me until she was clean. I never saw her again but I thought she was living in Bristol, she'd lived there before.

Over the years I have tried to find her through the police, the hospital and other organisations that trace missing persons but to no avail. I was told by sources close to the family that they had seen Becky during the missing years, so I had a strong belief and really did believe that one day she would come back home. I continued to buy her birthday cards, Christmas presents and cards so that when she did come back home she knew I had been thinking of her every year since she left, hoping one day that I would be able to give them to her. If anyone has any information, anything at all – no matter how small – that may help the police to establish when Becky was murdered or to fill in those missing years, we plead with you to come forward. I would like to take this opportunity to thank Detective Superintendent Fulcher and all his team, and all the well-wishers for all their help and support they have given us through this terrible time.

Somehow I managed to pull myself together and muddle my way through it, pushing on through the tears. It was over and we were led back into a side room. We could now go home.

The next few days were taken up with visits from Mark Hillier, an undertaker, and the vicar. We had to think about arranging Becky's funeral. In order for this to happen, I had to be issued with a temporary death certificate, as without one there couldn't be a burial. Again, I couldn't believe I had to engage in such conversations, it didn't seem real, or right, talking about Becky in this way, in the past tense. We discussed what we wanted. A traditional wooden coffin didn't seem right for Becky. She was such a tiny, slight little girl that a white wicker coffin seemed more appropriate and gentle, as her nature had been. When I saw the coffin at the funeral directors for the first time it suddenly felt very real. I had learnt that when Becky was found, just her skeletal remains survived, so I never had the chance to see her face again, or kiss her goodbye in the chapel of rest.

As we prepared, there was a delay. It was Halliwell. Having been given several funeral dates, we were then told police could not yet release Becky's remains after all. Halliwell's barrister had requested further forensic tests to be made. This was utterly heartbreaking. I just wanted to put her to rest in a proper and dignified manner. She had been through enough. I couldn't imagine why this would be required; it seemed wrong that after all this time Halliwell could still delay a proper burial. How was it that his needs were given priority? Here we were, now waiting on him and his legal team to finish with Becky's remains. No one seemed to care about my feelings or those of our family. It was all about him. And so we waited in a terrible limbo.

The days rolled into weeks. The police came most days, continuing to go through Becky's belongings, looking for clues. They went through her diaries, notebooks and letters, some of which had remained unopened, waiting for her return. The FLOs were brilliant; they cut through all the jargon for us and explained what was happening, although information about the investigation was slow at this early stage. But still my mind continued to work overtime. I wanted to know how Becky died, what had happened in that field. I wanted to know what remains of her had been found. As distressing as I knew it would be, I needed to know the facts. I took my chance when the FLOs came one day.

'I need to know the answers to some questions,' I told them tearfully. They looked at one another. 'I need to know about Becky, how she was when she was found. I want to know what was in the grave. I need to know whether Becky was "complete".'

Again, they looked at one another.

'Are you sure you want to know?' they asked.

'Yes, I *have* to know.'

There was silence.

'I really do have to know,' I insisted.

One of them spoke. 'There's no nice way of telling you.' She paused. 'Her skull was missing. We don't know why.'

Her head was missing? I don't know what I'd been expecting, but it wasn't this. I couldn't understand. What? Not there? Where was it then? *Her head was missing?* They explained that they couldn't be sure why Becky's head was missing. I listened intently.

'Because of the shallow nature of the grave, there are three possible scenarios; her body was attacked and disturbed by animals, or the farmer disturbed the body by ploughing. A third possibility is that Halliwell deliberately removed it.'

Halliwell deliberately removed it?

'Why would Halliwell have taken it?' I asked dumbly.

'Because, sometimes, murderers take things when they kill. It's something they do, it gives them a kick. Sometimes murderers take "trophies".'

Trophies? I didn't stop to let that register. If I didn't ask now, I feared I never would. It was now or never. I needed to know.

'How did she die?'

Again, the two FLOs looked at one another.

'I want to know,' I said. And I did. As bad as I imagined it would be, I still needed to know.

They told me they thought Halliwell had strangled Becky. This wasn't because he had suddenly opened up and was now talking to officers. Since his arrival in custody, Halliwell was saying 'no comment' in interview to any questions detectives put to him. He had also refused to sign a copy of notes that had recorded his confession to DSupt Fulcher. Having confessed to two murders, Halliwell was now saying nothing.

But while he had been in DSupt Fulcher's company, before going to the police station, he had told him that he had picked Becky up one night from Swindon. She had been working as a prostitute, he said. He said he'd had sex with her and then strangled her.

Now I knew the horror of Becky's last moments. But there was more. Halliwell told DSupt Fulcher that, having killed Becky, he then took her clothing from her, leaving her naked body hidden by bushes at the edge of the field. He returned the next evening and dug what he described as a five-foot grave where he'd put Becky before covering her in soil. Furthermore, Halliwell had said he had last returned to the site three years ago, in 2008. *He returned to the site? Five years after? What for?*

As I listened to this, my tears fell. I now knew what the bastard had done to her. There were now facts for me to take into the torture chamber. I didn't have to guess, or imagine, any more. *But why had I asked?* It was so brutal, but I knew it was going to be. Now, I couldn't bear the images that sprang into my mind. This was worse than I'd imagined. Much worse. Becky called me whenever she was in trouble and I went running. It didn't matter what she did or where she was. *Had she called out for me in her terror as he strangled her, as she'd fought for her life?* The thought crucified me.

I was numb, I felt sick. There was a lot of information to take in. They had given me the information I asked for. I'd made them tell me. Words kept ringing in my ears – no skull, strangled. They were talking about my baby. My beautiful Becky. She was small, slight, she would have been no match for Halliwell. The hatred I felt towards him was something I'd never felt the like of before.

The FLOs also told us that the murder investigation was called Operation Mayan. We learnt there was something called an incident room where statements and evidence were entered into a computer program called HOLMES2 (Home Office Large Major Enquiry System). They told us there were also officers from Avon and Somerset and Gloucestershire police forces working on the case. Everyone was working flat out gathering evidence to make the case against Halliwell.

I clung to the vision of a room full of police officers, busily ensuring Halliwell would be brought to justice. We had every confidence in them. From what we'd already seen, the police were doing a very thorough and methodical job, particularly in relation to gaining an understanding of Becky and her lifestyle. It certainly was a comfort in the utter misery of it all.

They had answered a lot of the questions I had at this point. However, I now needed to go away, to be alone and retreat to my bed to digest it all. It's not that I wanted to sleep. How could I? I couldn't help but imagine what Becky had gone through, the absolute terror she must have felt. But I needed to curl up and somehow deal with this in private. Through the torture chamber, I relived the things I had been told. I had to deal with it, try to process it.

What they'd told me about her remains went round and round in my mind. Her head was missing. Was it still in the field? Why couldn't they find it? I wanted to go and dig the field myself. If they couldn't find it, I would. I'd dig up every inch. It wasn't right that her beautiful little face might still be in the field. Would they ever find it? *Trophies*, they'd said. *Returned to the grave*, they'd said. *What sort of monster was he?* I couldn't get the visions out of my mind. I cried endlessly for days, tortured by thoughts.

We continued to receive fantastic support from family and friends. They came in every day, keeping us all going, bringing food and cakes, trying to get me to eat, but I didn't feel like eating. I couldn't after what I'd been told. I was just about managing to get through each day and friends and family helped enormously at that time, the worst time.

By the end of June, we were at last told that we could go ahead with her funeral. When Becky's remains were returned by the police, they said not to look inside the box they had left with Hillier's. Why had they said this? What could possibly be in there that they didn't want me to see? Perhaps they were referring to the fact her head was missing. It would be many years before I had the answer to this question.

Charlie, Steven and I decided to have Becky back at home rather than lying in the funeral parlour, so we arranged with Hillier's to bring Becky back to the house. We used the snug, a nice room that Becky spent a lot of time in. When Hillier's arrived and brought Becky back into the house, the pain in my chest intensified. It seemed my heart wasn't done with breaking. When they left, Charlie poured me a glass of whisky and we sat with her.

So many times she had left this house and so many times we had brought her back to it. It was a large and happy home, but it hadn't been enough to counter the pull of the drugs. Now she had been brought back for the last time. I couldn't bear the thought of her leaving and never coming back home again. The family arrived the next day and we all sat in the snug with her. Every night, I slept on the sofa next to her. I didn't want to leave her alone. I cherished this time with her now.

Charlie suggested we should invite John and his family over. It was a lovely gesture; I hadn't been in contact with John for years. Becky was his daughter too and, despite everything, I knew she loved him. Charlie was right. I was unsure how John would take it; we hadn't so much as been in the same room together for decades and, after all, he had been the one who'd left us. But John and the rest of his family did come over to see Becky a few times during the time we had her. We were united in our grief.

Whenever I had to leave Becky, to sort out the funeral and the catering, I asked my mum, my sister or John to sit with Becky as I didn't want her to be left on her own. I sat night after night with her, talking to her, playing her favourite R&B music. I guess I was making up for all the time she hadn't been here, all the time she spent away from us. And I knew the time would come when I wouldn't be able to do this, when she would have to go and never come back.

I realised that some people might have viewed having Becky at home with us all that time as strange or even morbid. But the time I spent with her in those three weeks was a time I always look back on as being very special. Everyone got a chance to say their goodbyes before the day arrived to put Becky in her final resting place.

We sat and reminisced, looking through Becky's school books. She had been such a bright little girl in infant and junior school. We looked through her written projects, at her neat handwriting where she'd used an ink pen, re-read the poems she had written. Her teachers always heaped praise on her at parents' evenings and in school reports. Sometimes Mum and Tracey had had to go when I was working, but I managed to go to most of them. So we sat and talked about what the teachers had told each of us.

We looked through all our photos of her, from when she was tiny to a teenager. Some made us cry and some made us laugh. They stopped abruptly when there should have been more. There were no photos of Becky's wedding, of her children – her future had been rubbed out. Despite all her troubles I felt sure Becky would have come good. She was only twenty when I last saw her, so there was plenty of time for her to turn her back on drugs, get her life back on track. We talked of the things she did and the things she said. And we wondered what she would have thought of this or that. We celebrated her.

I hadn't slept at all the night before Becky's funeral. We had spent the day making wreaths and flowers for her coffin. Family and friends were helping with the flowers and catering. On the day I was finding it difficult to function. I couldn't so much as drink a cup of tea. Today I would have to say goodbye for the last time. My mind had gone blank. I didn't want to get ready. Each hour and minute ticked by and the moment when we'd have to leave the house got closer. I vaguely remember being in the bath and then someone dressing me and drying my hair. Then I went back down to sit with Becky.

The house was full of people, family, friends, caterers, setting out food and getting things ready. We had a marquee erected in the garden. Charlie and I had talked about the sort of wedding we would have given Becky if we'd had the chance. Since that would never be an option for us, we decided to give her a grand send-off. Her white wicker coffin was draped with pink stargaze lilies. Becky had chosen those for my wedding bouquet. Every car had a pink ribbon – pink was the theme for the day.

Eventually, Hillier's arrived to collect Becky and family members. I made sure I had every last second with Becky before she went. So many times she had left us here when I hadn't wanted her to. So many times we had brought her back, or she had returned herself, only to go again. Now she was being carried out in her coffin. I said my last words to her as they put her in the hearse: 'Well, Becky, Mummy loves you so much, but it is time for you to go now; this time it's my decision.'

We had a police escort to the church; the media were set up along the street when we got there. I suppose it was understandable as Becky's funeral was the second in months after Sian's, and the murders had been big news in Swindon.

The service passed in a blur. As we followed Becky into the church, I was totally oblivious to what was going on. My mind was elsewhere, in a torment of different images. We'd last been here with Becky in a different and happier time. Fourteen years ago, she had been my bridesmaid; she had walked in her bridesmaid's dress where she was now being carried in her coffin. It had been such a happy day then. We had stood side by side, smiling, laughing to one another. Now we were here with her again for a most wretched day, filled with tears. I should have been able to look forward to Becky having her own wedding here, but instead we were watching her white wicker coffin being carried down the aisle. The music playing was 'Fix You' by Coldplay. The words resonated with me; we'd lost Becky, despite guiding her home so many times and like so many of us there, I had tried so hard to help to fix her.

I was worried for Mum; she kept herself so contained, but I knew she was hurting too. Despite our efforts to shield her, Mum had witnessed Becky's decline; she wasn't stupid, she knew what was going on and, like us, she continued to love and support Becky. Becky had spent such a lot of time with her when she was small, as she had with Tracey and Tony. We simply couldn't believe we were here, burying Becky. During the service, my niece, Laura, read a beautiful poem she had written, and my friend Shirley and her daughter, Sarah, who I'd seen grow up from a little girl, delivered the most wonderful eulogy about Becky as she was growing up.

As we left the church and followed Becky's coffin, it began to rain. I remember crying out; I didn't want Becky being buried in the rain. I didn't want her to get wet. We followed the hearse back to the cemetery for the private burial. We stood around the freshly dug hole in the graveyard; I remember feeling I wanted to be lowered into the ground with Becky. My friend Jenny comforted me. She had been such a good friend to me and the children over the years when I was on my own. She knew Becky and we cried into each other's arms.

I have been told that I knelt down on the ground and cried, 'Not my Becky, not my little girl.' I don't remember; perhaps it was my mind's way of coping. Shirley and Sarah could feel my pain and anguish. After the burial, walking away from Becky was the hardest thing to do, but she had been laid to rest. She was no longer in a remote and lonely field where she had been left naked to rot. She was free of her demons and she was, at last, in perfect peace. She no longer had that savage hunger for drugs that took her away from us, and, most importantly, no one could hurt her any more. She was no longer in harm's way. That was my only comfort.

We made our way back home for the wake. It didn't seem right to be eating and drinking after we had just buried Becky but I guess it had to be done. I was in a complete fog of grief, but somehow we got through the day. By the end we were all drained, physically and mentally.

One thing I remember I was told during this time by a friend was that Sian's grandmother had come to Becky's funeral.

'That must have been a hard thing for her to do,' I acknowledged, especially with Sian's funeral being such a recent event.

'Apparently she knew you,' my friend said.

'She knew me?'

'Yes, she knew you.'

I racked my brains, such as they were. I wasn't able to think straight. I spoke to Tracey and eventually, we worked it out. Sian O'Callaghan's grandmother was a woman called Fran Logan. Her daughter, Debbie, Sian's auntie, had been friends with Tracey and Tony. I used to go with them round to Debbie's house and Fran used to take Steven and Becky down the garden to feed the hedgehogs and the birds. As Becky loved anything to do with animals, she would have so enjoyed Fran showing her how to feed them. How strange that our lives had linked together then, and now, years later, they were linked together in such tragic circumstances.

It was summer and Steven's son Nathan, my grandson, wanted to stay with us for the rest of the summer holidays (Steven and Nathan's mother's relationship had ended long before Steven met Kelly and Nathan lived away). As far as I was concerned, this was a blessing as it made me get up in the mornings. Nathan was nine years old and a very active and intelligent little boy, who seemed to have a mind older than his years. He loved spending time with us and we loved having him. We planned some days out with him and on the days we had appointments with the police, my mum or sister would entertain him, or, rather, spoil him.

We talked about Becky to him; he couldn't remember her, but Becky had doted on her nephew as a baby as they shared the same birthday. All the grandchildren used to come to the house to see Nathan when he was with us and although it seemed like a madhouse some days, it was nonetheless a welcome distraction from what was going on.

We took Nathan back at the end of August; he had enjoyed himself so much he wanted to spend Christmas with us, so that's what he did. That year, we had Christmas with Tracey and Tony. Mum was there too with Nathan, who was thoroughly spoilt. Steven, Kelly and the kids came over in the evening and we had a quiet gathering. Last year, like the years before, we had had the expectation of Becky knocking on the door. I thought again how annoyed I was with her when I thought she had deliberately stayed away from us. I remembered all the Christmases I had been angry at her for missing. Now, of course, I knew better; she had been gone all those years.

With everything that had happened and with Becky very much in our thoughts, having Nathan with us made it all a little easier to bear. But when it was time for him to go, a heavy feeling settled on me again. He'd been such a comfort and I wanted him to stay with us, but I knew he couldn't.

Charlie and I never usually celebrated New Year. We used to have the grandchildren while their parents celebrated but this year it was different. Steven and Kelly gave a little tea party for their daughter Chelsie, as it was her birthday on New Year's Eve. It was lovely to see all the kids having fun; I wanted to wrap each one of them in cotton wool to protect them. My mind instantly wandered back to seeing Becky play when she was the same age. I couldn't help but wonder how she had gone from that beautiful innocence I now saw in my grandchildren to that shallow grave in the field we had visited. It felt like we lived in such an evil world.

On New Year's Day we visited Becky's grave. It was cold and miserable, but we laid fresh flowers and I told her I loved her very much. We stayed a good while, talking to her, telling her things about everyone as if we were having a catch-up. We cried as we thought of her and then left to go home.

Throughout all this time with family and friends, the murder investigation continued and remained in the background. Police officers had carried on with their questions and visits, or occasionally we would go to them. On one such visit, officers spoke to Steven and Kelly, showing them a number of items that had been found in Halliwell's car. These included a cannabis crusher found in the glove box, a necklace with a shark's tooth that had been wound round the rear-view mirror, as well as a perfume bottle, a bra, a lighter and a lipstick. They wanted to know if any of them could be identified as Becky's. They asked us to scour our photographs for Becky wearing items of jewellery. They asked me if I could identify a plastic tan-coloured handle from a handbag. It was constant.

Our FLOs were amazing people; they updated us on the court

processes and asked their endless questions in such a gentle way, always respectful of our grief. By now, we had been told that DSupt Steve Fulcher had left Wiltshire Police to work for the National Crime Operations Support Team, so was no longer in charge of the investigation. It was eight weeks since he'd knocked on our door, when he left the enquiry.

As news wasn't given to us on a weekly basis, what with the regular visits from the police, we assumed everything was progressing to the natural conclusion that would result in Halliwell going to court to be tried for both murders. We had heard that he was pleading not guilty, which seemed utterly laughable given his confessions. I couldn't understand how he could be defended when he had taken officers to the sites where Sian's body and Becky's remains had been found.

But, behind the scenes, events had been happening that we weren't aware of. Eleven days after Becky's funeral, Halliwell had appeared at Bristol Crown Court via video link from Long Lartin prison. It was a Plea and Case Management Hearing and, although it was simply a preliminary stage in the process, Halliwell's defence team, led by the barrister Mr Richard Latham, QC, had laid the foundation to challenge the circumstances of Halliwell's arrest and right to a fair trial.

Now, several months later, police were warning us that things would not be as straightforward as we had assumed. We were told Halliwell did indeed have a very capable defence team; they were asking for a judicial ruling to be made on the admissibility of his confessions, and to determine whether the Police and Criminal Evidence Act (PACE) had been breached.

This, we were told, took the form of a court process known as a '*voir dire*', a special pre-trial legal hearing, where a judge was going to hear defence arguments on behalf of their client, Halliwell. There was also a second aspect which Halliwell's defence sought a judgement on; this was that the force had released too much information in the public domain, meaning, they would argue, their client could not receive a fair trial.

As Charlie said, it was a joke, right? Man commits two murders. Man confesses to police. Man takes them to where his victims' remains are. Man is arrested. Man goes on trial. It seemed simple to us. What on earth was there to argue about? Everyone has a right to a fair trial, but what was fair or right about him taking two women off the streets of Swindon and murdering them? What was *fair* about that? The *voir dire* was set to take place at the end of January 2012. We thought he didn't stand a chance.

8

A BOMBSHELL

The first two weeks of January dragged by. The weather was as miserable as we were, hanging around like spare parts, waiting for news of the *voir dire*. A call from Charlie's cousin, Michael, tried to put us in a better frame of mind; he asked us if we'd like to go away to Mexico for two weeks. With the *voir dire* looming, we were not sure if we should go. I telephoned one of the FLOs and asked her advice. She said she would get back to me once she'd made some enquiries of senior officers. The *voir dire* would only last a couple of days we'd been told. There didn't seem to be any sense from the police that it was anything other than another administrative process.

The FLO rang back; we didn't have to be there, so it was OK to go. God knows we needed a break and a change of scene. We made the necessary phone calls and we were booked on a late deal to Mexico. However, in the following days, a nagging doubt sprouted in the back of my mind as to whether we were doing the right thing.

Before we left, I received an email from Cathy, one of the FLOs. She told us that Mr Lawrie, QC, who was the prosecuting counsel, wanted to meet with us before the *voir dire* process. It was due to take place on 31 January 2012, and he wanted to meet with us on the 23rd, shortly before we left. Cathy came and picked us up and we went over to Chippenham to meet him.

On arrival at Chippenham CPS offices, we signed in at the desk and waited to be collected. We were taken to a large room where Mr Lawrie was with his legal team. They shook our hands and we sat down with them around an enormous table. I found it very hard to follow what Mr Lawrie was saying; there was a lot of legal jargon, but he explained the *voir dire* process was going to examine DSupt Fulcher's actions during his interaction with Christopher Halliwell.

Apparently the defence were taking great exception to the way Halliwell's confessions had been elicited. So much so, they were seeking for them to be inadmissible in court. The presiding judge would then make a decision on what had happened which could have many consequences.

We were asked if we had any questions, which we didn't. How could we, when we weren't knowledgeable in the ways of a *voir dire* process and the law? We still didn't see the significance of what was being said and we made our way back down in the lift, signed out and Cathy took us back home. If I'd had had any idea of what was to come, I would have gone straight back in there, much less gone away.

The next day I was contacted by the local media. We'd had regular contact from a few journalists since Becky had been found. Now they asked if we would be at the *voir dire*. I told them we wouldn't, as we were going away for a much needed break. Why had they asked us that? Were they subtly trying to tell us we ought to go? Again it was there, that nagging doubt as to whether we had made the right decision to leave the country.

On 26 January, we flew out of Heathrow for Cancun. I was uneasy. I was trying to look forward to spending some time in a warm climate, on a beach. But as the plane took off I felt strongly that we had made the wrong decision, and yet I didn't know why. I'd tried to ignore my feelings in the days before, but it hadn't worked. I looked at Charlie: he already had his eyes shut. I knew he could do most things, but even he couldn't stop a plane; by now, we were soaring into the sky. I fidgeted in my seat. I couldn't settle. The only thing I could do now was take a sleeping pill to give myself some peace from my thoughts. I slept for eight hours. When I woke, we were nearly there.

I hoped I'd feel differently, but I still felt the same. We should be back at home, so that we could go to the *voir dire*. This was a mistake.

Despite being in the sunny climes of Cancun, I continued to feel as though we shouldn't be there. I tried to put these thoughts to the back of my mind – after all, there was nothing I could do, we were here now – but they persisted. We should be going to court. If nothing else it would have shown our support for DSupt Fulcher. He had, after all, brought my baby back to me, for which I would be eternally grateful.

As far as I was concerned, Halliwell and his legal team could moan all they liked about his confessions; I thanked god DSupt Fulcher had done what he did in talking to Halliwell. What continued to surprise me was that Halliwell pleaded not guilty. What were his defence team thinking?

Tuesday, 31 January, arrived and, sitting on the beach, I checked my emails. I received an update from Cathy, my FLO. She told me that a number of people were lined up to give evidence at court alongside DSupt Fulcher. These included Police Sergeant Ed Strange, the police officer to whom Halliwell had given directions to drive to the sites where he had left the bodies of Sian and Becky. DSupt Fulcher's personal assistant, Deborah Peach, who had also been in the car and had taken notes of the conversation between Halliwell and DSupt Fulcher, would also give evidence. Deputy Chief Constable Pat Geenty, who had been the Gold Commander at the time of the investigation, had also been called.

I took comfort from Cathy's email. With so many people lined up to give evidence, surely this didn't have a chance in hell. It was them against Halliwell. Them against a self-confessed murderer. Perhaps I could relax now, calm my over-active imagination. Perhaps I was being too sensitive. But why had Mr Lawrie asked to see us? Why hadn't I asked more questions at the time? I still didn't understand what was at stake and try as I might, I couldn't shake off a feeling of foreboding.

As I sat on the beach, thousands of miles away the *voir dire* process began in a small courtroom at Bristol Crown Court. Elaine O'Callaghan, Sian's mother, attended and listened as the defence outlined their legal argument. They sought to have the confession evidence given by Halliwell excluded from a jury, due to the breach of PACE by DSupt Fulcher. In addition, they said the confessions had been obtained by oppression. They further sought to argue that Halliwell could not receive a fair trial due to the information released by police at the time of his arrest, because it was now in the public domain.

Halliwell had been arrested in the north Swindon Asda car park for Sian's abduction, using an 'emergency interview' provision of PACE. This was because DSupt Fulcher considered that Sian could still be alive and wanted to ask Halliwell to disclose her whereabouts. Halliwell had been cautioned on initial arrest by a uniformed officer, then further cautioned when interviewed under emergency provisions by two detective officers. He gave 'no comment' answers to their questions.

Once told of Halliwell's 'no comment' response, DSupt Fulcher directed his officers to take Halliwell to Barbury Castle, the place where Sian's mobile phone last had a signal and where it was thought she might be. He wanted to meet Halliwell there himself in a last-ditch attempt to get him to reveal Sian's whereabouts. If she was alive and Halliwell had kidnapped her, she would be dependent on him for food and water. If Halliwell was held in custody for up to 96 hours, continuing to refuse to answer all questions, she could die during that time. If she was still alive, he had to try to save her.

Halliwell arrived at Barbury Castle with Deborah Peach on hand to keep a record of their conversation. DSupt Fulcher faced Halliwell and asked him to tell him where Sian was. Halliwell requested a solicitor. After DSupt Fulcher repeatedly pleaded with Halliwell to reveal Sian's whereabouts, Halliwell asked for a car to leave the site. This was provided. Once in the car, Halliwell directed the driver, Police Sergeant Strange, into the

Oxfordshire countryside. During the journey, he revealed to DSupt Fulcher that he had killed Sian and told him where her body could be found. After Halliwell had taken the police officers to Sian's body, DSupt Fulcher told Halliwell he would be taken back to Swindon Police Station. However, he asked for another 'chat' in private.

Finding a suitable location, DSupt Fulcher asked Halliwell what he wanted to say. Halliwell revealed that he had killed previously and asked if DSupt Fulcher 'wanted another one.' He described what he'd done and said he could take officers to the exact spot where he'd buried the body. They all got back into the police car and this time Halliwell directed the driver into the Gloucestershire countryside, where he revealed the location of Becky's grave. After all this, he was then taken to Swindon Police Station.

Barristers for Halliwell argued that DSupt Fulcher had failed to give Halliwell a police caution before the start of his questioning. Halliwell had repeatedly requested a solicitor and DSupt Fulcher had ignored this while asking him to reveal Sian's whereabouts. He had also told Halliwell that he would be vilified by the press. This, they said, amounted to oppression. Furthermore, they argued that upon revealing he had killed Sian O'Callaghan in the car on the journey to Oxfordshire, Halliwell should have been cautioned and immediately taken to a police station to be given access to a solicitor. This they said, should have happened before he had revealed the whereabouts of her body.

The defence also said that upon Halliwell telling DSupt

Fulcher of a further murder he had committed, Halliwell should have again been cautioned. They said that he should have been taken to the police station immediately, which would have prevented him from revealing the whereabouts of the body in the field.

DSupt Fulcher was called to the witness box to make his case. He said that in all conscience, as the person charged with the investigation into Sian's disappearance, he felt compelled to look Halliwell in the eye and ask him to reveal Sian's whereabouts. He said that until he knew otherwise, he thought she might still be alive and sought to save her life.

After Halliwell's initial refusal to answer his questions, DSupt Fulcher said he persisted because he believed Sian could still be alive. He was well aware of a suspect's right to silence, but he said he was balancing Halliwell's right to silence over Right to Life, under Article 2 of the European Court of Human Rights. In his mind, Article 2 – Sian's Right to Life – took precedence over a suspect's right to silence under PACE. He was, he said, also following the instructions in the police National Police Kidnap Manual in prioritising finding Sian.

He said he purposefully didn't caution Halliwell, as to tell him he did not have to say anything was contrary to what he wanted him to do; he *wanted* Halliwell to speak, he *wanted* him to tell him where Sian was, so giving him a caution telling him not to would not serve that purpose. This, he said, he had done quite deliberately.

At the time they had set out on their journey, Halliwell had given no indication Sian was not alive. That only became clear when Halliwell had directed them out of Wiltshire and into the Oxfordshire countryside, where Halliwell indicated Sian was in fact dead and the general location of her body. DSupt Fulcher explained he only had Halliwell's word that Sian's body was in the vicinity, and only when he found her could he be sure Halliwell was telling the truth.

With regard to Halliwell's revealing he had murdered before and wanting to take officers to the exact spot where he had buried the body of a young woman, Fulcher argued that he felt he had no choice but to let Halliwell lead him to that site.

Halliwell's defence team were having none of it. There was a clear breach of PACE they argued. Furthermore, DSupt Fulcher had told Halliwell he would be vilified in the press. This, the defence argued, was evidence of oppression on DSupt Fulcher's part, despite him explaining that this was a direct reference to the murder investigation of Joanna Yeates, in Bristol, where three months earlier Christopher Jefferies had been wrongly suspected and arrested. Halliwell's legal team said there was no indication that Sian O'Callaghan was still alive, therefore Halliwell should have been taken straight to custody and to legal advice after the initial emergency interview upon his arrest at the Asda car park. Following DSupt Fulcher's testimony, Deborah Peach was dewarned, meaning she was no longer required, so her evidence was not heard. The evidence of DCC Pat Geenty, however, was heard. He told the court that he totally supported what his officer had done.

'There may be occasions where police officers have to make a decision in terms of saving a life to step outside the rules. I think the decision he made was, to use slang, a gutsy decision, a brave one. I would like to think I would make a similar decision in his circumstances, bearing in mind what we'd been through to find Sian alive.'

The defence also argued that information put into the public domain precluded Halliwell from receiving a fair trial. This included the press statement following Halliwell's arrest that had stated two bodies had been found, one of which was suspected to be Sian O'Callaghan.

Judge Cox listened to the arguments. Instead of the two days it was expected to take, the *voir dire* lasted four. Judge Cox made her ruling on the case on Friday. Unable to be there, I was left to imagine what was occurring at court. Not in my wildest dreams could I have come up with what happened next. It was a stunning narrative.

That morning Charlie and the rest of the men were going zip wiring. Charlie had said he would stay with me; he knew my mind was elsewhere, back at home with the court process, but I persuaded him to go. I wanted him to enjoy himself; he had been such a rock for me and he deserved to have a good time. It was his holiday too, after all. I would stay on the beach with Carol, Charlie's cousin's wife.

I received the news via mobile call from Cathy, my FLO. I was on the beach alone, as Carol had gone to get some drinks. When she told me Halliwell's defence were successful in part one of their argument, I leapt to my feet, pacing up and down on the sand. I couldn't believe what I was hearing. As Cathy told me what happened I started to shout.

Judge Cox ruled the confession evidence would not be heard by a jury. Despite the prosecution barrister, Ian Lawrie, QC, arguing that DSupt Fulcher had 'had to balance the defendant's right to silence and Sian's right to life', in the judge's view Halliwell's confession to the murder of Sian and taking officers to where he'd left her was due to oppression and had incurred 'significant and substantial breaches of the code in circumstances deliberately designed to persuade the defendant to speak'.

She also deemed that when Halliwell confessed to Becky's murder, the police should have taken Halliwell to the police station and not allowed Halliwell to point out where he had left Becky. This confession, she deemed, was also inadmissible. On the issue of whether or not Halliwell could receive a fair trial for both Sian and Becky's murders, there would be a further hearing in April at which she would make her judgement.

What it amounted to was that when Halliwell went on trial, a jury couldn't be told that he had confessed to both murders and revealed the bodies. It was utterly ridiculous. I was sickened. I was raging inside. If this was justice, it was cruel. If these were PACE codes of practice, they were being used to protect a self-confessed murderer. What were the defence barristers thinking? What was the judge thinking? Halliwell hadn't made a confession as a lark. He had produced two bodies as evidence to back up what he said. And now we had a judge saying that because the *rules* had been broken, we had to ignore these two bodies and the confessions. It seemed to me they were making the rules more important than the crime that had been committed. Our lives had been broken by Becky's murder, her life had been taken, and they wanted to talk about broken rules!

I was grateful for the actions DSupt Fulcher took that day, despite barristers saying what should and shouldn't have happened. I *wanted* my daughter back, as no doubt did Sian's mother, Elaine – what mother wouldn't? What if it had been *their* child they were saying shouldn't have been found? *Their* child that should have been left lying in a field, all for the sake of a breach of PACE?

Justice was being treated like a game. Well, it wasn't a game, it was real, it was Sian and Becky's lives. What's more, they were playing with the truth. Halliwell *had* confessed to murdering Sian and Becky. To back up his confessions, Halliwell *had* taken officers to both their bodies, and a judge had decided that a jury could not be told that had happened. It was the *truth*. What right did the law have to play with the truth?

I was in shock; not for the first time I felt betrayed and angry at the justice system. I remembered Becky's rape trial. She was being let down again. This wasn't justice. I was in total disbelief. Carol did her best to comfort me, but suddenly so many emotions came at me at once and I started to cry in anger. I phoned Steven; he too had been told the news and was angry and upset. I should never have come on holiday, I should be there with Steven. I rang Tracey and asked her to go to him.

We went back to the hotel. I was inconsolable. Charlie arrived back and I told him the news. He too couldn't believe they would make such a ruling. We couldn't understand it. It didn't make any sense. I felt totally useless. How was this justice? I thought that was the point of a court process. How could the justice process come out in favour of a murderer? In favour of the adherence to rules over the actual crime itself? This was murder, for god's sake, two murders. Rules were making a mockery of justice. All I could do was stride around our room and fume. I vowed to Charlie that we would never again miss another court process after not attending the *voir dire*. I didn't sleep at all that night; what had happened just kept going round and round in my mind.

The next day the FLO rang. She felt the full force of me venting my anger and disbelief at the justice system. I think I heard her mention something about an appeal. I hoped so. There was little we could do from this distance and we were no longer good company for our travelling companions. The holiday was over as far as we were concerned, but we couldn't find an earlier flight. Every day passed in the miserable agony of putting on a brave face until finally we went home.

The day of our wedding anniversary arrived – 19 March. This had been when Sian O'Callaghan had gone missing, and in the current circumstances we certainly didn't feel like celebrating. We were in sombre mood during those weeks. We visited Becky and I told her what was going on. There was nothing we could do. We were in a legal process that was yet to finish, and so the weeks rolled by as we waited for the second part of the *voir dire* procedure in April.

I hoped that somehow the system would see us right, that this was just a blip. That someone, somewhere, would suddenly wake everyone up and turn things around. I somehow had to trust the justice system to come good. It had to, didn't it?

On 4 April – Becky's birthday – we were back in court for the second part of the *voir dire* to hear the defence case for Halliwell not receiving a fair trial. We turned up in force, there were Charlie and I, along with Mum, Tracey and Tony. My homicide counsellor, Rosemary, was also with us. Halliwell appeared via video link from Long Lartin prison. This time, I would see the justice system enacted for myself without relying on others to tell me what had happened.

I was now able to see Judge Cox and all the barristers. I was able to put faces to people who, until now, had only been names we had heard when updates were given to us. The police and FLOs talked about these people so casually, but I found it easy to confuse them. I captured the photographs of all of them on my mobile from their profiles on the internet so I didn't forget who was who. Judge Cox was a small, attractive, light-haired woman, cloaked in red robes. Mr Richard Latham, QC, leading the defence team, was a tall, lean man, with a stern demeanour. By contrast, Mr Ian Lawrie, the prosecutor who we had met before, was shorter and rounder, with a beard.

Judge Cox kindly acknowledged that it was Becky's birthday and apologised to us that the hearing occurred today. It was certainly a terribly cruel twist. Exactly a year ago, we had been told Becky had been discovered buried in a field and now we were sat facing the man who had taken her life. On today of all days, I had to sit and look at the evil monster who had murdered her. More than that, I had to listen to barristers trying to stop him from going to trial. Furthermore, I had to sit in front of the judge who'd said Halliwell's confessions were inadmissible. It was unbelievable. I sat and quietly seethed with anger.

We listened to all the legal jargon. Then Halliwell's barrister, Mr Latham, described how there had been 'saturation coverage' of the case in March 2011, as the media had been actively engaged by police for their help in 'flushing out' the suspect. In making his point, we watched as Mr Latham had boxes and boxes of newspapers wheeled into the courtroom. He picked one off the pile, then another. Holding them aloft, he asked how his client could receive a fair trial when everyone knew of Christopher Halliwell, the taxi driver.

How, he said, could a juror fail to recall the story of Halliwell leading police to two bodies, evidence that was now inadmissible? The story, he said, 'went viral' and was reported up and down the country, not just in national and local newspapers, but also regional publications. There was also widespread TV coverage. It would, he said, 'be engraved on the consciousness of the average juror'.

I couldn't believe this was happening in front of us; was this clearly intelligent man asking a judge to feel sorry for his client being branded the murderer he so clearly was and that he wouldn't receive a fair trial? Again, this was a *fact*, due to his client's confession and him locating his victims' remains. Besides which, what was fair about a trial that would not allow a jury to hear his confessions to two murders?

We broke for lunch and discussed Halliwell's barrister over a coffee. I'd discovered that Mr Richard Latham, QC had successfully prosecuted the infamous murderer Ian Huntley. It was inconceivable then that he didn't know the pain we were in. This was even more reason I couldn't understand how he could defend Halliwell. Despite the theatricality of his gestures, we all concluded that he was being extremely clever. Given what the judge had ruled in February, we were really worried. Her specialism in human rights and Latham's theatrics could swing it for Halliwell. Would she really find in Halliwell's favour and dismiss the case of a double murderer?

We went back into court. There would be a further hearing for Judge Cox's decision on the matter, possibly at the end of April. Deflated, we went home. We would have to wait. The tension during these weeks was almost unbearable. It consumed me, it was all I could think of. I wasn't sleeping well; I'd taken to pacing around the house as I continuously went over what was happening, trying to make sense of it all, trying to think of what to do. I was very bad company and poor Charlie took the brunt of this. I think he feared for my sanity.

On 4 May, the FLO rang to say we were back in court for the conclusion of the second part of the *voir dire*. The hearing was in Preston, so we decided to stay overnight at a Travelodge to be ready for the morning. I couldn't eat much that evening, I was so tense and uptight. I did, however, manage two glasses of wine, which left me a bit light-headed. We headed back to our room, and after making sure we were organised for the morning, I took a sleeping pill.

Next morning, we dressed, packed, checked out and drove off to the court. Walking to the building, I saw the press were already there. I was sick with nerves, the pressure of the last few months mounted inside me. We had waited weeks for this moment; whatever the judge decreed today we would have to live with. *Would today be the day that Halliwell went free?* I felt I was going to explode.

We joined a queue to get inside. We hadn't expected there to be one – the court would sit at 10.30, and it was now 10.10. We couldn't be late. The palms of my hands were clammy and my heart was banging so hard I could hear it thumping in my ears. The people in the queue were talking, some laughing as if we were queuing for the cinema. I felt like screaming. I wanted them to shut up. Didn't they realise how important today was?

Eventually, we got inside and saw the cause of the queue: tight security. Charlie went ahead of me. I went through the motions like everyone else and placed my handbag through a scanner. At least we wouldn't be late. From somewhere, someone's voice spoke.

'Do you have any aerosols in your bag?' The question was levelled at me.

'Sorry?' my heart continued banging in my chest and beating through my head.

'Do you have any aerosols in your bag?'

'Pardon? I might have,' I answered, distractedly, confused by the question. What did it matter?

'Can you remove them.'

The demand was simple enough, but it was like lighting the touch paper. I exploded. All the endless weeks of waiting spilt out in a misdirected tirade.

'An aerosol? A bloody aerosol? I could understand if it was a gun. I wish I had a gun and I would shoot the bastard who murdered my daughter. There! That's what you want. Take it,' I handed a security guard my hairspray. I was given a receipt for it and asked to collect it after court. I was fuming.

Charlie had been waiting for me with our FLO. Both had seen my outburst and said nothing. Our ever-patient FLO guided us to the courtroom. By now my legs were shaking. As we sat down, the room closed around me, as if I was in a tunnel. Halliwell appeared via video screen from Long Lartin prison. As Judge Cox sat, I focused on her intently, trying to see if she gave anything away that might help prepare me for what she had to say. There was nothing. My stomach churned in anticipation of bad news. I had to try to prepare myself for what I didn't want to hear.

She thanked everyone for coming and turned to the screen. She asked Halliwell to confirm his name and address and he spoke. She then turned to the court.

'I have given a lot of deliberation to my decision.' She paused. I was hanging on her every breath. My heart was pounding. 'I have decided that this case will go to trial.'

I wanted to scream with relief. I wanted to shout at Halliwell, 'You're going away for a long time, you bastard' but instead my tears choked me. At last, justice had arrived. We were so pleased, we even smiled. It really did feel like a small victory for common sense. Halliwell would be put on trial, despite the efforts of his barrister and legal team. What would they have done if the ruling hadn't gone against them, if they'd won – patted themselves on the back to see a murderer go free?

Following her decision, Judge Cox ordered that all information regarding Halliwell be removed from the internet with immediate effect. She wanted to limit what was out there so that future jurors couldn't be influenced.

This burnt in my mind all the way home. As soon as we stepped in the door, I started to print off all the information I could find on him on the internet. There was so much I ran out of paper and ink, so at 1 a.m. in the morning, I drove to Asda to buy some more. They might be able to wipe the internet of traces of him, but I would make sure I kept a record of what had been there. I made sure I kept every newspaper reference to the case and the pile was growing.

At a further hearing, the trial was provisionally set for January 2013. That came as some relief; now we had an end in sight. But there was still no word on an appeal process for Becky from the *voir dire*, which would determine the admissibility of the confession evidence at the trial. I was still hopeful for this. I had to be.

We didn't have to wait long for the next court appearance. A further date was set, at Preston on 31 May, this time for a Plea and Case Management Hearing where Halliwell would again appear via video link from Long Lartin prison and we would hear whether he intended to plead guilty or not guilty.

We drove up to Preston with Tracey and Mum, but this time, before we went into court, we were asked if we could see the prosecution barrister, Mr Lawrie, QC. Charlie and I were shown into a small room. Mr Lawrie sat us down and explained the reason he wanted to see us. I can still remember his words:

'It has been decided that Becky is going to be officially withdrawn from the indictment. Halliwell will not be charged with her murder.'

The words ricocheted around the room. It was an absolute bombshell. Mr Lawrie explained that there wasn't enough evidence to proceed to trial. I was in shock; I wasn't expecting this. What I *had* been expecting was news of an appeal; I had clung to that ever since it had been mentioned by my FLO. But that had never been an option, it seemed. I didn't understand; how could Halliwell murder my daughter, bury her in a field leaving her to rot and, because he confessed to police and took them there, be allowed by our justice system not to be prosecuted?

How were we supposed to understand that? *How were we supposed to accept that?* Well, I wouldn't. I would do everything in my power to stop this. I would go up and down the land to tell people what had happened, because it didn't make sense. It was ludicrous.

But there was more they wanted; could we please, asked the police, not tell anyone that Becky's name had been removed from the indictment. The reason behind this was to keep Halliwell out of the press, in case this prejudiced the case for Sian. My head was absolutely spinning. Now what could we do? Of course we wouldn't jeopardise the case for Sian. But at least there *was* a case for Sian. *What about Becky?* Didn't she count? Why was this happening?

'This is a joke, right?' asked Charlie, directing it at the blank faces looking back at us.

I thought I was going to pass out. We left the room. The court was sitting in just ten minutes' time. I was utterly despondent.

What was it with the justice system and Becky – why did it keep letting her down? We walked out in a haze of disbelief. Tracey and Mum approached us – they could see by the looks on our faces that something wasn't right. Quietly, we told them.

They were as shocked as we were. It was in this state we shuffled into court to hear Halliwell's plea. It was predictable, he pleaded 'not guilty' to Sian's murder. The vile monster was going to ensure he caused the O'Callaghans the maximum distress. We left the court, but not before the judge announced Becky's official removal from the indictment and put a gagging order on the media and us as the family.

I remember my emotions overwhelming me as we were ushered into a family room. I felt hysterical. This was my daughter they were talking about. All I could think of was that they must think Becky was worthless, not worth fighting for. Where was the outrage from the prosecution? Why was I not seeing police officers' faces red with anger? Where was the *fight* in these people? There seemed to be dull acceptance.

Audrey Carsons from the Homicide Counselling Team was brought into the room and was shocked to see me in such a state of distress. A call was put into the surgery and an appointment made with my doctor on our return. She also arranged for me to see a trauma counsellor, as well as arranging for my homicide counsellor, Rosemary, to come and see me. Somehow, I pulled myself together and we all made the long drive home. But we were in a state of shock and disbelief. This shouldn't be happening.

My good doctor saw me and prescribed me some diazepam. I

confided in him what had happened earlier and he was wonderfully supportive. Like the rest of us, he couldn't quite grasp what had happened. Nothing made sense to me. All those learned men and women with all their training had ensured that Halliwell would not be charged with Becky's murder – even though he had confessed to killing her and located her remains. What sort of perverse game was this? I thought I'd entered a parallel universe.

9

GUILTY

Our bruising experience of the justice system so far had left us despondent. We found ourselves in a nightmare and knew that a long wait was still ahead of us. Until the trial for Sian's murder was heard, we wouldn't be able to say a thing.

Then things then went from bad to worse. I took a phone call from the Independent Police Complaints Commission (IPCC) asking me if I wanted to make a complaint against DSupt Fulcher. They informed me that my ex-husband, John, had made a number of complaints to them, one of them being that DSupt Fulcher's actions had led to the charge against Halliwell for the unlawful killing of Becky being dropped. It came completely out of the blue.

I thought John's complaint was bizarre. The searches for Sian had taken place in Swindon, so how on earth would we have found Becky in Gloucestershire without the intervention of DSupt Fulcher in getting Halliwell to talk? We hadn't even known she was dead. What's more, Halliwell had remained silent ever since his confession. DSupt Fulcher had obviously tapped into something that others had failed to and in that one moment Halliwell had opened up to him. Without DSupt Fulcher breaching PACE, I would still be driving round at night trying to find Becky, thinking she was alive. I would have continued to look for her until my dying day, but I would never have found her. I couldn't understand how John didn't see this.

The question from the IPCC was, did I want to add my complaint to his? I told them, no, I did not. I was immensely grateful to DSupt Fulcher for his actions that day and always would be. I was very clear where my support lay; in my eyes, DSupt Fulcher could do no wrong and I certainly would not be making a complaint against him. It was the justice system John should be directing his anger at, but this seemed not to compute with him.

As far as I was concerned, DSupt Fulcher was the only person who so far hadn't let us down, let Becky down. He was the only person who had actually done his job. In the strangest set of circumstances, he had used his judgement and had caught a killer. More than that, he had returned two beloved daughters to their families. This was so important to us as a family – to any family whose loved one is missing or murdered. We had been spared the unending torture of never knowing where Becky was. And now I was being asked to make a complaint about the one person whose actions made any sense at all. Had our world gone completely mad?

As a family I think we were just going through the motions that summer. We felt utterly helpless. Charlie's natural instinct was to try and do all he could to protect us as a family. Like me, he wanted to fight the iniquity we now faced. So we discussed trying to bring a private prosecution against Halliwell. Charlie was keen to start this, but on researching what it would entail we decided it would be sure to bankrupt us, without our being certain of the outcome. It was crushing. It seemed all avenues were closed.

We had a family gathering for Steven's birthday, my lovely son who I was so proud of. But recent events tainted our celebrations. It was all we could do to put on a brave face in front of the children. He was born on 3 June; Mum pointed out that he had the same birthday as Sian O'Callaghan.

With the passing of Steven's birthday, I found myself wishing the months away to Halliwell's trial. I couldn't find any peace of mind. We were in turmoil for the most part, not really knowing what to do. I couldn't just let this go. I couldn't leave it like this. There must be something I could do. I couldn't let Halliwell get away with Becky's murder. I was angry, I wanted to kick the world up in the air most days. My wonderful husband coped well with me for the most part, but I even stretched his limits and, at times, he knew he just had to leave me to myself.

As ever, our family and friends did not desert us, they were wonderfully supportive. Later in the summer we were invited to a wedding. We decided to go, if even for a short while to be in the company of others and take our minds off events. However, when people asked how everything was going with the trial, we were dumbstruck by the constraints of the court order; we couldn't explain what had happened. It was so hard not to talk about it. I couldn't even explain it to my closest friends.

Nevertheless, friends would take me for coffee, lunch, to visit

Becky or even just for a drive; nothing was too much trouble. Just going about our daily routine was proving difficult. As we went shopping, or collected the grandchildren from school, people asked me how I was, how it was going? It was so difficult – I hadn't actually worked out a stock answer, as the question always seemed to catch me unawares.

Our FLO, Cathy, was also a massive help in supporting us. She was the only one I could talk to about this, as she knew what the situation was. I bombarded her with questions; what other evidence was there, what other avenues could they explore? I pressed her continuously. I had always wondered: why Becky? Had Halliwell chosen her randomly or did he know her? On one of her visits, I asked Cathy about this and she told me that Becky had used Halliwell as a taxi driver to get her to Bristol to buy her drugs. I was astonished. So she had known him and he had known her. What's more, Halliwell used Becky for sex. He had been one of her 'clients'.

It was during this miserable period that I also found out a little more about Becky in the time she had been away from us. I'd found a letter among her things when police were looking through them. It was from the One25 charity in Bristol, which provides support to sex workers. At some point, Becky had gone to them during the day, had a bath, food and clothing, and help with self-esteem. They had written to Becky some time ago to ask how she was getting on.

I wanted to thank them so I got in touch and travelled to Bristol. When I arrived, I spoke to a woman called Josie. She remembered Becky and showed me into a room with a sofa where we sat and talked. She told me that both she and a former colleague, Isla, had worked with Becky. It had been Isla who had written the letter I'd found. Josie said she'd had long conversations with Becky, who told her she had been beaten up by her boyfriend and needed help. She also said Becky mentioned me, telling them both how I'd always been there for her and how much she loved me. She said Becky wanted to make her family proud of her. Hearing that we had such a good relationship, Josie had encouraged her to get in touch with me, which I think she had when we picked her up from Bristol. They were of course very saddened to hear what had happened to her. I couldn't thank them enough for helping Becky. I asked them where they would have spoken to her, as I felt compelled to go where Becky had been, hence my visit. We were, in fact, she said, in the same room and sat in the same place where she had spoken to Becky. It was a very surreal moment. All these years later, I was where Becky had actually sat. I took such comfort from this and hearing Josie recounting Becky's words, finding out all these years later she had said she loved me.

I had been told that DSupt Steve Fulcher was back in Wiltshire. He had left the force less than three months after the arrest of Halliwell to work as a national advisor to other senior investigating officers around the country. Twelve months later, because of the fallout following the *voir dire*, he had been recalled to the force. Although he was no longer working on the case, I wanted to meet him in different circumstances from all those months ago when he had first turned up on our doorstep. I felt that I had never had the opportunity to properly thank him for what he did for us. He kindly came round to see us. As soon as I opened the door, I could see how apprehensive he was. After inviting him in, I made him some tea and we sat and talked.

'We just wanted you to know that we fully support everything you did.' I could see he felt relief at my words. I continued: 'I think it's really important for you to know how grateful I am. You can't know how much, you really can't. I *know* I would never have had Becky back if it wasn't for what you did that day. I get so angry when people can't see this.'

I told him I was sickened that Becky had been dropped from the indictment. It was clear to me that he blamed himself for this. He'd hoped that he could have persuaded the judge he had acted with the best of intent. To an extent she'd agreed, stating in her ruling that he had not acted in bad faith. I hoped I was able to put his mind at rest, especially with regard to John's ridiculous complaint; as far as we were concerned, he had nothing to reproach himself for.

We kept ourselves busy through those summer months by choosing Becky's headstone. It allowed me to focus on something that I had some control over. Charlie and I found ourselves walking around graveyards, looking at other headstones to find ideas. It was strangely grounding reading the inscriptions, some tragic and moving. It served the purpose of bringing me out of my own circumstances to thinking of other families who had had to cope with tragedies.

As we walked round I knew what I wanted, but I couldn't see it, so I went to the internet. I wanted a material that would catch the sunlight. I found a company based in London who worked with black granite with gold flecks. I decided to go up to meet them and see it for myself. They were fantastic and so helpful. I'd spent months working out exactly what I wanted. I'd spent a lot of time going over every detail, as I wanted it to be perfect for Becky. I wanted an angel and a heart, and all the companies I'd approached said they could do either one or the other but not the two together, due to size restrictions at the cemetery. However, when I told the London-based company what I was hoping for, they helped me to design it exactly as I wanted. Their service and workmanship were exceptional; as I saw it, Becky deserved nothing less

The summer passed and we entered into a different phase. From the unending drag of hearing no news for weeks and months, suddenly things started to happen. But we continued to be surprised at the turn of events. We were informed in September 2012, by our FLO, that DSupt Steve Fulcher had been suspended. Since his return, he had been contacted by an ITV news reporter, Rob Murphy, to explain the nuances of the *voir dire*. Rob had been at the *voir dire* himself, but much like the rest of us he wanted to try and understand what on earth was going on, and as a result of Steve Fulcher's attempting to explain this to him, he had been reported for speaking to a journalist. Now he found himself suspended. I couldn't believe it. But there was more to come.

Halliwell had at last bowed to the weight of evidence against him and pleaded guilty to Sian O'Callaghan's murder. It was ironic; DNA evidence had been retrieved from Sian's body which was irrefutable proof that linked Halliwell to her. According to the powers that be, the recovery of Sian's body – DSupt Fulcher asking Halliwell to reveal its whereabouts – should never have happened. They would rather that crime scene had not been discovered. Now it proved Halliwell's guilt.

I was in no doubt that had Sian's body not been recovered when it had, the DNA evidence would never have been retrieved. I remembered the thousands of people who had turned out to search for her in and around Savernake Forest. She had in fact been found in a different county entirely, no doubt destined for the same fate as Becky. Halliwell would have returned to bury her, but thanks to DSupt Fulcher's actions he had been stopped and would now be imprisoned.

On Thursday, 18 October, we were asked to attend Gablecross Police Station. It was the evening prior to Halliwell's appearance at Bristol Crown Court. Because of his guilty plea, Sian's family were saved having to sit through a trial in January. We would be attending of course. I wanted to see the monster sentenced. The police briefed us on what to expect, going into detail regarding Sian's murder and what Halliwell had done. She had suffered stab wounds to the back of her head and had been strangled. I sat there totally numb; it was too awful. All I could think of was Sian and her family.

Sian, the beautiful girl whose life was halted merely for walking down a street at the same time that Halliwell was driving by in his taxi. It had been that random, that opportunistic. It could have been someone else that night. It still didn't fail to shock me. Her family had been through so much to get to this point.

But there was more. We were also told that the judge might

not lift the gagging order yet. This set alarm bells ringing for me. Still, I sat and listened and at the end we were told the FLOs would see us at court in the morning. We headed off home. During the journey I mulled over what had been said about the gagging order. I discussed the situation with Charlie; for months and months, we had been unable to say anything about what had happened to Becky's case. We had done as asked and kept this out of the public domain. Nothing had been mentioned in order not to affect the case against Halliwell for the murder of Sian. This had been torture for us, as friends or strangers asked how everything was going in relation to the case. They would ask what was going on, why they hadn't seen Becky's name in the newspapers. We hadn't been able to risk telling anyone anything in case something was posted on social media. People reasonably expected to hear of a trial for Becky's murder. But we'd had to remain tight-lipped and not say anything.

As far as I was concerned, this had been a parallel process with Sian and Becky, where Becky had been treated differently. Like Becky, Sian had had a good upbringing and came from a good home, but let's face it – Becky was different. Becky was rebellious, she was the naughty girl, the drug taker, the sex worker. But she was also a brave girl, who'd been through a lot. Becky had been bullied; she had self-harmed, attempted suicide as a cry for help on more than one occasion. Becky had experienced things no mother wanted her child to experience. Becky had been harmed by others; Becky had been raped, beaten up, exploited and exposed to hard drugs. Becky had been convicted, Becky had been to prison. But Becky was resilient, she had come through all this. She deserved a chance to build a new life, as I am sure she would have, if her life hadn't been so cruelly taken.

Becky was also my daughter, a granddaughter, a sister and an aunt. She was a girl like any other. At her best, Becky was a very gentle girl, who wouldn't harm a soul. She was pretty, with long blonde hair and a liking for nice clothes. She had been studious, she loved to read, loved poetry, had wanted to be a vet or work with children. She loved her R&B music, loved to laugh, loved to dance and go to nightclubs. She loved life like any other young woman her age.

Who had Becky ever harmed but herself? I don't count the pain that she caused me; that goes with the territory of being a mother. Looking back, as I did often, I knew Becky's insecurities and feelings of rejection had had an impact on her that affected her sense of self-worth, which bullies ruthlessly exploited. It sowed a destructive seed, so that when she made the wrong friends, who introduced her to the world of addiction, she was so desperate to fit in with them that she went along with them. Becky had survived all this. Until, like Sian, she had crossed paths with Christopher Halliwell and got into his taxi.

Sian's family were about to have their justice. But I wanted justice for Becky too. I couldn't let it go, I wouldn't let Halliwell get away with it. Becky had as much right to justice as Sian. I didn't exactly know what I could do, but I did know there was one thing I *had* to do. I was going to write to the judge. I sat all through the evening and into the night composing my letter.

On arrival the next day at Bristol Crown Court, I said hello to my FLO and to Detective Inspector Matt Davey, the officer in charge. I asked them to excuse me for a moment, as they wanted to show me to the family room. Charlie got us the lift to the second floor, where we acknowledged the press, not answering any questions. As we approached the courtroom, I saw Mr Lawrie, the prosecution barrister. I told him that I had a letter for the judge. He offered to take it to her, but I refused; he didn't fill me with confidence. I needed to make sure the judge would get it, so I gave it to the usher. I had printed the letter on dark cream paper and put it in a matching envelope. I had told the judge what a torment the gagging order had been and asked for it to be lifted.

We returned downstairs and I explained to the FLO what I had done and why. We went inside, taking our place in the viewing gallery with our family and friends. My homicide counsellor was also with us. Behind us sat the press and Halliwell's ex-wife and two daughters. Unknown to me, also present was Anna Proctor, the IPCC investigator who was going to investigate DSupt Fulcher for John's complaint.

From our vantage point, we watched through the glass window down on to the courtroom. Halliwell sat to the left, behind a screen. When we finished hearing what the barristers had to say, the judge left to go and make her decision regarding Halliwell's sentencing. When she returned, she made her sentencing remarks. The mood was sombre as the details of Sian's abduction and death were read to the court. A young girl, just 22 years old, who intended to walk home from a nightclub, got into Halliwell's taxi, was violently assaulted and murdered. As the judge read out Sian's horrendous injuries and described the fear she must have

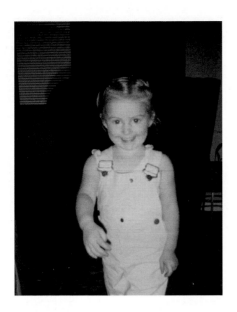

My beautiful girl Becky and her big brother Steven (*above right*).

My husband Charlie and I on our wedding day with bridesmaid Becky (*below right*).

Becky was such a happy child but as a teenager she struggled with being bullied at school. She made friends with the wrong crowd and suddenly started to go off the rails.

When a boyfriend introduced Becky to drugs, it didn't take long for addiction to take hold. We desperately tried to get her help and I took this video the morning before we took her to rehab, to show what effect drugs were having on her.

Shortly after this video was taken, Becky disappeared.

Detective Superintendent Steve Fulcher (*left*), the man in charge of the investigation into the disappearance of Sian O'Callaghan in 2011. After closing in on taxi driver Christopher Halliwell (*right*), he was able to persuade him to reveal where Sian was buried.

Halliwell then made a shocking confession about a second victim, and Becky was found in a remote field. She had been there for eight years.

(*right*) 'Becky's tree', planted in her memory at the location where she was found.

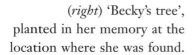

Above: Halliwell's mugshot and under police questioning.

Below: in a strange coincidence, my sister Tracey (*circled right*) discovered she had once attended the same wedding as Halliwell (*circled left*).

When justice for Becky was denied and Steve Fulcher instead was punished, I campaigned day and night for a change to police rules and to keep pressure on the case against Halliwell.

Above: collecting signatures for our petition which we delivered to 10 Downing Street (*below*) with our MP Robert Buckland.

Left: with Steve Fulcher on the set of the ITV's *A Confession*.
Right: Actress Stephanie Hyam who plays Becky.
Below: Imelda Staunton who plays me in the drama.

felt, I couldn't control my sobs. It was too much. My mum was sat next to me; I wished she'd stayed at home. I didn't want her to hear such gruesome details. I looked across at Halliwell. He was sitting with a smug look on his face, completely unmoved by the details the court was hearing. He was utterly evil.

Of course, visions of Becky came into my mind. How much fear must Becky have felt? Was it similar to what Sian had had to endure? What kind of monster was he to do this to young women? A taxi was a trusted source to get from A to B, except when it was driven by Christopher Halliwell. Being a taxi driver had given him licence to drive around, on the prowl, night after night, in plain sight of everyone. Sian had trusted him to take her home that night. Becky had got into a car with him. How many other women had done the same and not arrived home? We had heard too much.

The judge continued, business-like. She explained how she calculated the sentence. I listened avidly. She started at thirty years' imprisonment and took five years off for Halliwell's guilty plea. From his now 25-year sentence she also deducted 571 days that he had already spent in custody.

By my reckoning, he was already down to 23 years and seven months. He had been sentenced to one year for just over every year of Sian's life. It didn't seem very much to me. It was conceivable he could be released. In fact, the judge then said if eventually he was released, he would be on licence for the rest of his life. So it was possible! I knew I had to do all I could to make sure that never happened. I looked down at Halliwell as she delivered his sentence. At least in the meantime he would be incarcerated.

'He's not smirking now is he,' said Charlie, with his eyes on Halliwell at the same time. Halliwell had gone pale, probably with shock.

'No, he isn't,' I replied, through tears. 'But it's not going to bring Becky back.'

I was pleased. At last, Sian's family had justice. Mr Lawrie made a representation about the length of Halliwell's sentence, asking if it had been correctly calculated; he wanted more. So did I. In the event he lodged an appeal which would invoke a further legal process. I looked across to the judge as I wanted her to say something regarding the restrictions that had been placed on reporting on the case; there on the desk in front of her was my letter. She had received it. I listened as she confirmed that she would lift the gagging order. I felt such relief.

As they led Halliwell away, it was a strange feeling. As I watched him I felt a wave of evil and revenge come over me. I felt like shouting to him, 'You killed my daughter too and I won't let you get away with it.' My eyes didn't leave him until he disappeared to be driven back to his cell. I had never felt such pure hatred. Poor Mum hadn't stopped sobbing.

'All rise,' came the call from the usher.

As we turned to go, I caught the eye of one of Halliwell's daughters. I felt so sorry for them, I truly did. They were brave to sit with us in the gallery. Halliwell had made victims of Sian and Becky as the result of his actions, but his ex-wife and daughters were victims too, in a way. I approached them and told them that none of what we had heard related to them as people, for them not to think any of this was a reflection on them. The girls were so young.

Before we left, Cathy introduced me to Anna Proctor, from the IPCC. In the haze of loathing I felt for Halliwell and the bewildering spectacle I had just witnessed, I politely shook her hand. She said words to the effect that she could now begin her investigation. I suddenly realised who she was and what she meant. She was going to begin investigating DSupt Fulcher following John's complaint.

It was a strange sensation leaving court. I was very pleased for the O'Callaghans. They had had justice; Halliwell was going to have to get used to the monotony of prison life for a long time. But we were leaving with nothing for Becky. That left a very bitter taste.

Outside court, Sian's family made a statement to the waiting press, speaking of their feelings on the sentencing of Halliwell. It was an incredibly emotional time and they showed such dignity. Then it was my turn to face the cameras. I seized the opportunity, just about managing to hold my emotions in check. I had written my speech on my iPad and now I stood, clutching it in my hands to steady them. I spoke to the waiting journalists.

'Today, Sian's family have had justice for their beautiful daughter. But my journey to justice has just begun. I am asking each and every one of you to help me get this justice.'

My restraints were gone; the fight was on.

10

THE FIGHT

Throughout the last eighteen months I had hoped that, somehow, some way would be found by the CPS, or police, to cut through the legalities of a system that said a murderer's confession could not be heard in a court of law. Naively, I thought the justice system would come through, that at the last minute common sense would prevail. That somebody, somewhere in the system would say, 'Hang on, what are we doing here? This isn't right.'

It felt that as a family we'd been collectively holding our breath, constantly on tenterhooks, treading on eggshells. There was no way we would have jeopardised Sian's case, but it had been hard. Not being able to voice our concerns when we knew Becky was being dropped from the indictment was crucifying. I wanted to shout about it, about how wrong it was, about how we were being denied justice.

In all this time, with this on my mind, I hadn't really had a chance to properly grieve for Becky. Yes, I'd certainly cried for her; my tears were seemingly unending, they came when I least expected. But I hadn't really had enough space and peace to sit quietly, to contemplate all that had happened. To remember Becky as I wanted to, to focus on our happy times, without this in the background. Neither could I do that now.

Now, I had to fight for her. I would never accept Halliwell not being held to account for her murder. And I had to use all the means at my disposal; which included the press. I had meant what I'd said on the steps of the court – I was addressing the media as much as the public. I had made a few media contacts during the course of the murder investigation and I saw how they could be used to deliver messages. I very much wanted to keep Becky's story in the public consciousness. I quickly realised, if she was ever to receive justice, her story needed the oxygen of the press.

Following Halliwell's trial, there was a media frenzy; not only were they reporting on Halliwell's conviction, but news had leaked of DSupt Fulcher's suspension. For many days, the stories appeared side by side, with lots of commentary. Depending on what you read, the 'red tops' reported it as 'police bungle', with reference to DSupt Fulcher breaching PACE, and the broad sheets ridiculed the justice system and praised him for taking the steps he had to catch a killer. A whole range of people had opinions; typically, there was condemnation of Steve Fulcher from the legal profession, while others decried a system that allowed a murderer to get away with killing his victim. Journalists waded in, Richard and Judy gave their opinion. There was though, overwhelming support for the actions of DSupt Steve Fulcher, and sympathy for the predicament he was in. I added my endorsement of him too in a statement to the press: 'Steve Fulcher is a committed and dedicated police officer and family man. As far as I'm concerned, he is a hero and I just want to give him a big hug . . . it's an absolute disgrace.'

The next day, the *Swindon Advertiser* ran an article stating 'Police vow to find justice for Becky'. It quoted Detective Chief Superintendent Kier Pritchard saying that there would be a new senior investigating officer and the investigation would remain live. They intended to seek justice for us as a family. I took heart from this public declaration to continue the investigation. Thank god they were not giving up on Becky.

The IPCC review of the complaint that John had made was still ongoing. I remembered shaking hands with Anna Proctor at court; I didn't want to take part in any investigation that criticised the actions of DSupt Fulcher. I wanted to tell them that I was completely happy with him breaching PACE. Without his actions, we would still be under the illusion that Becky was alive, much less have been able to bury her with dignity.

I was still extremely annoyed at John for taking this line. He appeared on the ITV *Daybreak* programme, sounding off about the police. I couldn't watch him. They also spoke to one of Halliwell's daughters on the same day, who publicly asked Halliwell to do the right thing and confess again to Becky's murder. She wanted us to have justice and hoped her plea might persuade her father. The plea fell on deaf ears.

Following Halliwell's conviction, the newspapers continued to leave no stone unturned. The headlines were bold and lurid. Among all the stories about his past was that of Ernest Springer, a former cellmate of Halliwell's when he'd served a term of impris-

onment for burglary at HMP Dartmoor in 1986. Springer said
Halliwell had displayed excessive anger and aggression towards
women. He said Halliwell talked of strangling a woman while
having sex and asked Springer, 'How many do you have to kill
to be a serial killer?'

This was awful to read. Not only did it demonstrate Halliwell's
seeming hatred of women, but it described a method and mindset.
I quietly sobbed, thinking of Becky. She had been strangled by
Halliwell in 2003 and here was a former cellmate saying that as
long ago as 1986 he had described that taking place. It seemed
he'd also aspired to be a serial killer. Was that question to his
cellmate a hint to murders he had already committed by then?
Was it a statement of his intent to be a serial killer? By his
own admission, he'd strangled Becky. Apparently, Springer had
answered Halliwell's question. 'At least three,' he told him. We
know he murdered Becky and Sian; could there be a third victim,
or even more, given that he'd asked the question so long ago?

I cut out and kept all the newspaper reports on Halliwell,
devouring every bit of information they contained. They printed
details of Halliwell's conversation with DSupt Fulcher following
his confession to Sian and Becky's murders. 'I'm a sick fucker,'
he admitted, 'I know you're not a psychiatrist, but what the
fuck's wrong with me? Normal people don't go around killing
each other. What caught me? The gamekeeper at Ramsbury?' It
was chilling. There were comments from the police about him
having owned eighty cars over the years. Eighty cars! Of him
having a narrowboat, about him travelling widely around the
country as a driver and construction and groundworker, about

him being forensically aware, of him keeping work diaries. I read details of Halliwell from people he worked with in Dalbeattie, Scotland, where he grew up. At sixteen, he was apprenticed to a butcher, who said, 'He did the sweeping up and cleaning, along with basic butchering tasks, such as paring bones and helping to make pies and sausages.' This was utterly chilling, as we knew he had used a knife to kill Sian. I looked across his life through the newspapers: he was skilled with a knife; he was an experienced groundworker; he was forensically aware; he was a taxi driver. It seemed to me that Halliwell had been equipping himself with the skills and abilities to become a killer for years.

Even Halliwell's sister was quoted in the newspapers as saying that he was 'an evil manipulative bastard' who would 'believe he had won' after getting away with Becky's murder. She said, 'He's done two murders and probably many more.'

I took a call from Cathy, my FLO on Monday, 22 October 2012. She said that DI Matt Davey wanted to come and see us. He was the 'fresh senior investigating officer' referred to in the *Swindon Advertiser*. Although I had met him before, now he would be leading the investigation. Charlie and I decided we would go to Marlborough Police Station to see him instead, as Cathy had said he wanted to explain about Halliwell's sentence. I was eager to meet.

When we arrived, DI Davey confirmed he was now the SIO for the case. We learnt there was now a new operational name; it had changed from Operation Mayan to Operation Manilla, as the focus was now on Becky. There was also a new team, with all the investigators from Operation Mayan now stood down.

He said that they had been pleased with the sentence as they had been expecting Halliwell to be sentenced to fourteen years' imprisonment. DI Davey went on to explain that there was not enough evidence to charge Halliwell for Becky's murder but now they were satisfied that he would be locked away for a long time.

Then, quite extraordinarily, he asked me if, given the sentence had been higher than expected, would that satisfy me in terms of Becky's murder.

'No, *no*,' I told him. 'How could I be satisfied that Halliwell had got away with Becky's murder? No, I will never be satisfied with that.'

Rather than leaving the meeting confident that the investigation was in safe hands, we felt totally confused and let down. My mind was in a whirl. We went to the Castle and Ball in Marlborough High Street for a coffee and discussed what Matt Davey had said to us.

We had taken heart from the *Swindon Advertiser* piece as a positive sign that the investigation would be kept alive, but now we were less sure. The same article had quoted Nick Hawkins, the chief crown prosecutor for the Crown Prosecution Service Wessex, as saying the most likely way of catching her killer would be if he confessed. But Halliwell *had* confessed and this had been rejected. Well, then to my mind, the Police and Criminal Evidence Act was wrong and needed to be amended. How could it be right if a killer's confessing to a murder and revealing the whereabouts of a body could not be accepted in a court of law?

No matter how much Charlie and I chewed this over, we

couldn't seem to get it to make sense. It kept coming back to the same thing. How could breaching PACE be prioritised over *truth*, over *actual fact*? It didn't make sense; in fact, it went against all common sense.

Ever since he'd confessed, Halliwell had remained silent. To our minds, this gave even more importance to what DSupt Fulcher had done that day. It told us that if Halliwell had indeed been taken straight into custody, as the barrister and judge had said he should have been – as PACE decreed – there was no way we would have had Becky back. He would never have revealed where he had left Sian and the O'Callaghans would never have had the satisfaction of seeing Halliwell convicted of her murder. It seemed as though the barristers were arguing Halliwell had been disadvantaged by his own confessions and they were effectively standing up for him. But he was *a guilty man*! Who was standing up for us – for Becky – in all this?

As we sat there, talking this through, we decided that the one thing we could do was to start a petition, to change PACE, so that Halliwell's confession could be put before a jury. PACE seemed to be the obstacle, so that's what needed our focus. We didn't know it at the time, but amendments to PACE regularly occurred over the years. PACE was guidance to police officers, and, as officers on the streets applied it, there had been many aspects of it that needed to be amended.

We started by meeting with our local MP, Robert Buckland; we were going to need all the support we could get. We discussed the idea of a petition and made a further appointment to see him to discuss PACE and the aspects of the case. Robert

Buckland certainly had sympathy with our cause. I felt galvanised and empowered.

In addition, the next day, the *Swindon Advertiser* reported that officers would now comb through the last thirty years of Halliwell's life to see if there were more victims. 'There will be extensive research into his lifestyle and background and we will start to cross-reference his movements against other unsolved crimes.' Well, while they did that, I would fight for Becky.

But there was another thing I needed to do. Unless I did, I would never know if it would have worked. I wrote an open letter to Halliwell to ask him to confess again to Becky's murder. My letter was published by the *Daily Mirror*:

> I know you were responsible for the cruel and savage death of my only daughter Becky. My every waking moment is filled with the horrific thought of her terrifying, frightening moments as she suffered her death at your hands. The nightmare never ends. Please could you find it in your heart as a father to tell us the truth about my beautiful girl. I'm begging you, please admit Becky's murder.

This was followed by an article in the *Daily Mail* the next day stating, 'Halliwell has written to his family saying he is ready to talk about Becky.' Nothing came of this. In my desperation I even asked Wiltshire Police if I could visit Halliwell. This was something I wanted to do, as there were still things I wanted to know that only he would know. I knew from what he had told DSupt Fulcher that he had strangled Becky. Now

I had had time to adjust to that, there was more I wanted to know. I wanted to know why – why Becky? He knew her, so why had he wanted to kill her? I wanted to know how he had killed her – I wanted to confront him with what he had done. I wanted to know where he had killed her. There were still so many unanswered questions for me. And only he could answer them. However, the police told me that it wouldn't be helpful. It would be helpful to *me*, but this avenue was closed, it seemed. Predictably, I never had a response from Halliwell to my letter.

As the days went by, the newspapers continued to pick up on the absurdity of DSupt Fulcher solving a double murder case but Halliwell's confession not being allowed. The Prime Minister, David Cameron, had made a speech on crime, saying that he wanted 'no-nonsense policing'. Well, here was no-nonsense policing and the justice system had rejected it. There was no shortage of press coverage and I made sure that I used all the opportunities I could.

Andy Davies, the home affairs correspondent from *Channel 4 News*, got in touch, requesting an interview. He came to the house with a small camera crew. It was one of the better interviews, allowing me some seven minutes' air time to talk about Becky and show footage of her. The video that I'd taken of Becky before she went to the Diana, Princess of Wales, Treatment Centre was shown, along with footage of Becky at Disneyland. Despite her problems, the drugs, she'd still managed to look so pretty. My heart broke again to see it now.

When we met Robert Buckland we went through the case. He

advised me how to begin a petition, directing us to the government's petition website. This was something that I could focus on. If I could get 10,000 signatures the government would respond. One hundred thousand signatures and it would be considered for debate in Parliament. I thought I would aim for 10,000.

On 5 November 2012, we officially launched the 'Justice for Becky' petition on Facebook. I had spent hour upon hour emailing the link to friends to sign the petition. Everything seemed to be moving so fast that I sat up night after night working out how I could push the petition and get it into the wider public domain.

Slowly, as they heard about it, I started to be contacted by members of the media; I was asked to do a radio interview for 5 Live, which I did, then the *Swindon Advertiser* called me to say they had received a message from a lawyer – people seemed to be listening. Then Swindon 105.5 radio contacted me for an interview. *LINK* magazine also asked for an interview – news was travelling fast. Then interest was shown nationally and I did a double-page interview for the *Sunday People*. It was well written and I was pleased with the response from it.

The Home Affairs Select Committee took notice of the situation. Then, on 21 November 2012, Robert Buckland raised the matter in the House of Commons at Prime Minister's Questions:

The person responsible for the murder of Becky Godden-Edwards, whose mother is my constituent, has not been brought to justice because important incriminating evidence was excluded from the court process. Will my right honourable Friend join our cause in calling for a thorough review of code C of the Police and Criminal Evidence Act 1984, so that such a terrible situation will not occur in future?

David Cameron responded:

I will look very carefully at what my right honourable Friend raises and the specific case he mentions. I will also look at the issue of the Police and Criminal Evidence Act. It is always important that all information that possibly can be put in front of a court is put in front of a court, so that it can reach the correct decision.

This spurred me on. It was a glimmer of hope. I had to capitalise on this and keep the momentum going.

In the meantime, the prosecuting barrister, Mr Ian Lawrie, QC, had launched a challenge to Halliwell's sentence; he had calculated that it should be 30 years. It was due to be heard by the High Court in London on 13 December. Of course, we had to be there. We travelled up by train and jumped in a taxi to the Strand. I was glad we went; it was like no other court we had been to so far. The High Court is a huge and immensely impressive Victorian edifice. It was cathedral-like, with a labyrinth of courts and rooms running through it. It was busy and noisy with the business of the day, and we found ourselves being shown to an oak-panelled courtroom with uncomfortable upright oak benches that creaked every time we moved.

The judge's bench was long and high up. To the side was a secure area, with metal bars to the ceiling for the prisoner to stand behind. The call went for 'all rise'. Sat with us were DI Matt Davey, Detective Sergeant Pete Ritson and barristers from either side. Three judges sat high up in their robes. The verdict was delivered quickly. They were satisfied that Halliwell's sentence of 25 years was correct. I was disappointed; I would have liked to have seen a further five years added to his sentence and claim it for Becky.

As we left the courtroom through the crafted oak doors, someone opened the door for me. It was Halliwell's barrister, Mr Latham. As I thanked him, he went to say something to me, but then seemed to change his mind. I have often wondered what it was he was going to say. 'Nothing personal' perhaps, or 'I was only doing the bidding of the law.' I'll never know.

Outside, the press were already waiting. I was surprised, but again knew I had to take every opportunity I could to speak to them. I was getting used to talking off the cuff. I needed to use every opportunity to gain maximum exposure for the petition. This was the focus for us, this is what drove the family on. Before we left, I reflected, looking back at the magnificent building. There we were, at the highest court in the land, having to fight for justice. As Charlie held my hand, he remarked, 'Those scales of justice are not balanced, are they?'

The online petition was gaining signatures but then, at Christmas, my mum asked if there could be a paper version, as many of her friends didn't have computers or email addresses. I contacted Robert Buckland for advice; yes, that could also work, it could run alongside the e-petition; this was fantastic news. I started putting together petition packs, each containing a front cover which had a photo of Becky, the Justice for Becky petition and columns where people could sign. I was being asked for packs by people for their families to sign and for them to take to work for people to sign. I couldn't believe the response. My small printer was now in full production.

Printing paper copies meant we could also go out on foot. Along with my sister, Tracey, and niece, Laura, we knocked on doors asking if people would sign. It was hard work and a slow process; there was certainly no lack of interest – people were keen to sign but they also had lots of questions which took time to answer. We were finding we could be out all day to only collect a hundred or so signatures simply because we were having to tell the story of what had happened to Becky every time. As soon as people understood what we were trying to achieve, they were really supportive.

One day, Tracey was contacted by an old friend who was interested in signing the petition. She did though, have some news to impart, which Tracey found really disturbing.

'Oh, Karen, I have to tell you this, but I feel so sick about it.' Tracey looked shaken as she directed me to sit down. 'Back in 2008, Tony and I were invited to a wedding in Swindon. My friend has found photographs of us there. At some point, a group photograph was taken. Among the guests was Halliwell. I was standing a few feet away from him. I can't believe it.'

She explained that it had been Halliwell's partner who had been invited to the wedding and had taken Halliwell as her 'plus one'. Tracey showed me the photo. Sure enough, it showed her with Tony and stood at the back was Halliwell.

It was awful to think that my sister had been in close company with Halliwell all that time ago. He'd murdered Becky and there he stood, at a happy occasion, like any other person, just a few feet away. Like me, Tracey's heart had broken when she was told of Becky's death. And there she stood, unknowingly, near her killer. I was mesmerised by the photo. It was unbelievable.

'I must have seen him.' Tracey continued to look at the photo with me. 'I might have spoken to him. The thought turns my stomach.'

Strangely, in that moment I recalled Fran Logan, Sian's grandmother, attending Becky's funeral because she'd known her as a toddler. Our two families had been in contact all those years ago. Now, with Halliwell in a photo with Tracey, it struck me we had all been in contact by degrees over the years.

Wanting to take advantage of any opportunity that came our way, we asked Tracey's friend if we could give the story to the media; she agreed. It would be more oxygen for our cause of Justice for Becky, and the *Sunday Mirror* picked it up. The number of signatures continued to climb. Locally, the *Western Daily Press* picked up the story and they too asked for a change in the law.

I found all the relentless activity incredibly tiring. Sometimes it was a struggle just to get out of bed. When I opened my eyes each morning, staring back at me would be an image of my little Becky, with her infectious smile. I would force myself up, into the bath or shower, I would get Charlie some breakfast and a coffee and off I would go again, touting for signatures. It angered me at times that I had to take this on, but I couldn't think of anything else to do. I couldn't contemplate the alternative: people just thinking that, with Halliwell now sentenced and behind bars, justice had been served. It hadn't. There had been no justice for Becky.

It occurred to me that to make real progress I'd need to centre myself where there was a good footfall, somewhere there would be no shortage of people. One day, I was shopping in Asda for milk and something for dinner when I suddenly had a thought; I asked to see the store manager. I explained to him about the petition and asked him if he would allow me to stand outside to collect signatures. He gave me the head office number to call. Astonishingly, they said yes, they would support me. I was prepared to stand outside in all weathers, but they would even provide me with a table at the entrance, not outside, so I would be sheltered. I was so grateful for their kindness. It was a fantastic boost.

I knew I would need to up my game now. I bought packs of white printing paper and some more ink for the printer. I designed and ordered a pop-up banner with a photo of Becky on it and our strap-line 'Justice for Becky'. I cut out and laminated the newspaper reports on Halliwell to put on the table, along with maps showing where Becky had been found. I also used the headline news report, quoting Halliwell's words to his cellmate, Ernest Springer, 'How many do I need to become a serial killer?' All night long I printed out sheets for signatures, not sure of what the response would be. Would people just view me as a nuisance? Someone who couldn't accept what had happened? Would I get abuse?

I needn't have worried. People recognised me and had no hesitation in signing. Tracey joined me in the afternoon, as did Laura, bringing me a sandwich and a cup of tea. Before the end of the first day, I had to ring Charlie to ask him to bring me more copies of the petition. I stayed out there until 9 p.m.; the day had gone so well.

Things started to gain momentum and I began to be approached by different organisations, such as Rotary Clubs, to attend events as a guest speaker. This brought even more invitations. Word was spreading fast and the signatures were growing. My granddaughter Chelsie volunteered to make up packs and came out with me whenever she could. It became a full-time job. TV companies started to approach me, as did radio stations – Charlie drove me around the country to the venues. We were working flat out.

At the same time, it was starting to take its toll. I was running out of energy. I wasn't sleeping well as I was spending long hours campaigning. It had taken over our lives, I hardly saw Charlie and the grandchildren. The most time I spent with Charlie was when he was driving me to Manchester, or Bristol, or London, for TV and radio interviews. Anywhere I wanted to go, he would take me without question. Adrenalin and determination were all that was keeping me going at this point.

My friends would come and help on the stands whenever they had any spare time. I was truly blessed at having such a good network of family and friends. They understood what I was trying to achieve and wanted to help me in that endeavour. One day, while I was in Asda, a woman came up to sign the petition.

'Would you like a hand?' she asked.

'I could do with some help,' I replied, not knowing what to expect.

'My name's Sandy,' she said, 'And I just have to pop home, but I'll be back.'

Sandy did indeed come back and from then on, she became my wingwoman. During a conversation with her, I worked out that we had actually worked together when we were in our mid-twenties. Sandy had worked in the Debenhams cosmetics department for Lancôme, at the same time as I had been there working for YSL. We hit it off straight away and Sandy helped me whenever she could.

One day, the e-petition received a huge boost: Ed Sheeran had retweeted it. This was absolutely amazing! In addition, the One25 charity in Bristol, who do so much for vulnerable young women, also offered to help. A local BBC crime correspondent, Steve Brodie, knew of the charity and offered to do an interview with me while I was there.

Whenever we could, we took the petition to car boot sales, Blunsdon market, Swindon Speedway at the Abbey Stadium, supermarkets, bonfire displays, the Swindon half-marathon – anywhere there were large gatherings. We did this in all weathers. This included Swindon Football Club and a derby match between Swindon and Bristol. We had a small stand with the petition which went well to start with, but soon descended into a mini-riot when we found ourselves dodging flying beer bottles and caught up in running battles, involving police dogs and horses, between the two sets of supporters. It was my first experience of a football match and something of a baptism of fire. We all got separated during the incident but we weren't frightened. Despite the trouble, we still managed to get 700 signatures. And it didn't put us off; we went back three days later, for another match, Swindon and Chelsea. This time, it was different, much calmer, with fans willing to give their support and queuing to sign the petition.

We were starting to make good ground but we still had to maximise every opportunity. I would even go out late at night and approach people queuing to go into nightclubs. Most times I didn't need to explain what it was about as they remembered Sian and Becky's case.

Our MP, Robert Buckland, was also continuing to be a great help. He had arranged for us to have an update from the Policing Minister, Mike Penning. Robert had listened to my plea for a change to PACE and he had written amendments as requested by Damian Green, then the Justice Minister. Robert had suggested two small amendments to both Code C 6.6 and 11.1 (a) to add: '*hinder the recovery of important evidence connected with the commission of a serious offence*'.

Mike Penning asked a Chief Constable responsible for serious crime to comment on the amendments. I was frustrated but not surprised by the message that came back: the police response was that PACE didn't need to be changed or amended. It was a blow to me, but I wasn't going to give up. After everything we'd been through, I wasn't going to let the knock-back from some distant Chief Constable deter me; I wanted this raised in Parliament. I continued to petition.

There was, however, an unexpected by-product of promoting the petition. As I stood at all these places, talking to people, explaining why I was there, what had happened to Becky, telling them about Halliwell, people started to give me information. In the beginning I never took a great deal of notice; after all, I wasn't there to gather information, but to gain support for Justice for Becky.

As time went on, some of the matters I was being told alarmed me to the point where I felt I had to write them down. I told the girls helping that if people started to give information, to put an asterisk by their name and make a short note of the conversation. I started keeping a notebook. I would write the details down and forward them to my FLO or DI Davey, in order to help police with their enquiries into Halliwell.

On one occasion, a mother came to see me with her son. They showed me a photograph of her daughter, who looked very much like Sian O'Callaghan. She had been on a night out and decided to get a taxi home. She had been drinking, but she immediately sobered up when she could see she was being driven in the wrong direction. She saw they were driving up a hill.

She said that when Halliwell locked the doors, it frightened her. He parked up in a forested area and she panicked.

She screamed as loud as she could which alerted someone nearby, who shouted out. Halliwell sped away, dumping her back in Swindon, where she called her mother to collect her. Her mother called the police, but they showed little interest. This had been a week before Sian O'Callaghan's abduction, she said. Her mother said her daughter had since been severely affected by the ordeal. I continued to hear numerous accounts of Halliwell and young females in taxis, and it was forming a very disturbing pattern.

11

STEVE FULCHER

Since John's complaint against DSupt Fulcher, the situation had deteriorated between us. When we arrived at Oxford County Hall for the coroner's inquest into Becky's death at the end of April, John and I were given separate family rooms to wait in. Today wasn't a day to fight about Steve Fulcher; today was about Becky.

We were shown into a courtroom and Charlie and I sat in the front row, with Tracey and Tony right behind us. The coroner, Darren Salter, entered the room and sat in a chair in the centre like a judge. There was a witness box to the side of him. It was clear he had great empathy for us as a family as he started proceedings, being very mindful of our wellbeing.

Despite his care, he could not shield us from what we were about to hear. As witnesses were called, we learnt the grim detail of the discovery of Becky's remains. We'd already been told that when her remains had been discovered, Becky's head was missing. I thought that was bad enough. Now we sat and learnt that when her skeleton was first revealed, weeds were growing up through her ribcage. I found it so upsetting to hear this. Then, unexpectedly, there was more; there was a question over a chip found on one of Becky's ribs.

The coroner was saying that it had not been established whether this had been done with a knife. This was new. I tried to process what he was saying. We knew Halliwell had carried a knife. He had used it to kill Sian O'Callaghan in the most dreadful way. We'd been told that he had confessed to DSupt Fulcher to strangling Becky; but what if he'd not told him everything? Had he used a knife on Becky too? My mind was drawn back to the press report following Halliwell's conviction that he had worked in a butcher's. A knife! This was something I hadn't contemplated. I felt sick and choked on my sobs.

The coroner checked on our welfare several times throughout the inquest, which was very kind of him. We found it a very traumatic process to sit through, especially as the cause of Becky's death could not be established after all this time. The coroner said that she probably died 'an unnatural and violent death, caused unlawfully by a third party'. With an ongoing criminal investigation in the background, he had to be cautious. At the end, the coroner recorded a narrative verdict (which sets out the factual details of a death rather than a short form verdict such as 'unlawful killing'). This appeared on her death certificate under cause of death. It felt wholly unsatisfactory, as the one thing we did know was that she had been murdered. It had been harrowing.

We left the courtroom and were escorted to a comfortable family room, unlike the ones I had been in at Preston and Bristol. I was asked by a police press officer if I would like to make a statement on the steps. This was unexpected and I hadn't prepared anything, but I knew, since I had been offered the opportunity, it would be a chance to bring the case to public attention. I knew I had to keep Becky in the public consciousness, but I was shaken by what I'd heard in the inquest. Once again, there were unanswered questions.

I took the opportunity offered to address the media and quickly gathered my thoughts. The best plan was once more to request Halliwell to do the decent thing and make a further confession, of Becky's murder:

'I feel that as her mum, I will get to the root of this, even if it's with the last breath in my body I will get a conviction of some description. And I'd also like to appeal to Christopher Halliwell. This is your chance now, come clean, please, please, what have you got to lose?'

The journalists were very patient and this was duly broadcast. When we arrived back home, I had to go to bed. It had been another long and sad day and I felt thoroughly worn out. A few days later, I sent off a letter of thanks to the coroner for his kindness and consideration during the inquest and a cheque for Becky's death certificate, which would replace the temporary one I had when we buried her.

I had hoped that Becky's headstone would have been erected in time for her birthday, but there was a delay which was entirely my fault. I couldn't find the wording I wanted and was also hoping that I might have had a date for when Becky died to put on there. We couldn't know for sure when that was, so we instead settled for the date when she had been returned to us.

Charlie and I went to the cemetery to see the new headstone. It was truly beautiful, more beautiful than I had remembered when we had been designing it. But I wasn't quite prepared for seeing it with Becky's name on. It was quite a reality check and it shook me.

I'd made some white flower arrangements to lay at the foot of the headstone. With the flowers in place, we stood back in each other's arms and cried. The sight of Becky's headstone made me even more determined. I knew I had to get justice for her.

The next day, I went out again for more signatures. That evening, I had been asked by a Rotarian group if I would be their guest speaker. The response was simply wonderful. They took packs to get signatures for me, as they wanted to help. One of the members offered to assist with the costs of printing, which was very kind, but I did not feel I could accept. I had never asked for financial help, just for people to understand my cause and give me their support with their signature. I arrived back at home to Charlie at 11 p.m. It had been another evening that he had had to spend at home alone, but, as ever, he totally understood.

All the time I was campaigning, the IPCC continued their investigation into the actions of DSupt Fulcher. On 29 May 2013, I received an email from Anna Proctor, the IPCC investigator, who had been told to let me see the IPCC report. This contained the conclusions to John's complaint. Nearly a month later, I had still not received the report so I emailed Anna Proctor and also made a request to see Rachel Cerfontyne, who was head of the

IPCC. There were a number of matters that I was not happy with, and on 15 August I met Rachel and Anna at home and outlined my concerns.

Chief among these was that they had conducted the investigation into DSupt Fulcher without taking a statement from me, or any other member of my family. This would have given a counterbalance to John's complaint. I told them both that we were very happy with the actions taken by Steve Fulcher. We were quite clear; if he hadn't breached PACE, Becky would still be lying in her remote grave and would most likely never have been found. During their visit, I discovered the report had already been published on the internet and they therefore said there was nothing they could do to change it. Rachel apologised for this and said she would see that a paper copy was sent to me. This was little comfort.

Even though Anna Proctor said she should have gathered more information from us as a family before coming to her conclusions, she offered no apology for not doing so. The conclusion she had come to was that DSupt Fulcher had a case to answer for gross misconduct. It was now down to Wiltshire Police to decide what action to take. I felt very angry at this; I was Becky's mother and I should have had a say. Why were they only prepared to listen to John?

I needed to do something, I needed to try and redress the balance. I decided to write to the Chief Constable, Pat Geenty, via letters to the editor in the *Swindon Advertiser*. The newspaper had already run its own poll in light of the recommendations of the IPCC report: 'Did DSupt Fulcher do the right thing?'

From nearly a thousand people, the poll came out with 88 per cent in favour, with only 12 per cent saying he should have followed the rules.

Pat Geenty had stood by Steve Fulcher at the *voir dire*, and I had been told by numerous people that the Chief was a decent man. I put pen to paper and wrote to him, asking him to take into consideration my feelings concerning Steve Fulcher. I sent my letter both to him and to the *Swindon Advertiser*, who published it. The reason I wrote it in this way was to ensure he would see it. I had no way of knowing whether, if I sent it to his office, it would be passed to him. By publishing it in the local *Advertiser*, even if he didn't buy the newspaper, I knew the force would pick it up through its press office. There was no way he would not be made aware of it. I had, in fact, addressed my letter to the wrong person: Deputy Chief Constable Mike Veale was in charge of discipline for the force. Whilst they didn't have to follow the recommendations of the IPCC, they did. DSupt Fulcher would face a misconduct hearing. But I was glad to have made my support of Steve Fulcher public. Since the IPCC had published their report online, I wanted everyone to be in no doubt of my support of him.

We stopped petitioning on 23 December to have a break over the festive period. I imagined what sort of Christmas DSupt Fulcher and his family would be having, as his misconduct hearing had been scheduled for 20 January 2014. Early into the New Year, I was contacted by Steve Fulcher's solicitors asking if I would write a statement so they could use it at the misconduct hearing. I was only too pleased to be able to help and wished there was more I could do.

We were really keen to show our support for DSupt Fulcher, so Charlie and I attended the hearing. Our FLO, Cathy, was waiting for us when we arrived at Police Headquarters in Devizes and we signed in. Cathy took us to the canteen for a coffee and just as we were about to sit down, a woman approached me. I had no idea who she was. She introduced herself as Yvonne Fulcher, Steve's wife. She gave me a big hug and thanked me for supporting him. She said it meant so much to them both. She was such a lovely lady that when we saw her over the coming days, we would have a chat. Yvonne also had the force chaplain with her for moral support. It was clear there was a lot of support for DSupt Fulcher from his police colleagues.

We were assigned a room in another building, where the misconduct hearing was taking place. It was somewhere we could at least be on our own. Before the hearing started, we were escorted over there to take our seats. As it was a private hearing, the windows had been completely blacked out so that the media couldn't see any of the proceedings. It felt grim.

The room was arranged like a courtroom. Cathy left us, as she was not allowed to stay. Neither for that matter was Yvonne Fulcher allowed in to support her husband. We decided to sit near to where DSupt Fulcher's team were setting up. On the other side of the room were John Godden, his brother, David, and Anna Proctor from the IPCC. A long table was ready for the three members of the panel.

When DSupt Fulcher came into the room, I could have cried for him. I barely recognised him as the man who had knocked on the door nearly three years ago, much less when we had last seen him some eighteen months ago at home. He looked so ill and had lost weight. He had the demeanour of a broken man, as if he was already defeated. My heart went out to him; I wanted to tell him that it would be OK, but I didn't know that it would.

We had been told that we were not allowed any contact with Steve whatsoever; we couldn't talk, or even make eye contact with him. It was ridiculous. But he knew we were there supporting him. I started to feel angry with John and angry with a system that had brought us all here. Following close behind Steve was his barrister, Mr John Beggs, QC.

The hearing started with the prosecuting barrister dramatically withdrawing one of the charges; this had been in relation to mishandling of the media. I took heart from this and John Beggs's withering response to the prosecutor that the charge 'should never have been brought'. There was further back-tracking on a charge of breaching a judicial order of meeting journalists – this had prompted his suspension. It was now apparent there had been no such judicial order. However, it was reworded to meeting journalists without permission. These aspects out of the way, the hearing proceeded.

Over the next three days we sat and heard a number of witnesses as they were called, the first of which was DCS Kier Pritchard. This was the officer who had spoken out after Halliwell's conviction stating the enquiry into Becky's murder was still live. Now he was here giving evidence against the man who had brought Becky back to us.

As the hearing proceeded, it became clear there seemed to be some dispute over whether or not he had specifically given

DSupt Fulcher an order not to conduct an interview with the journalist Steve Brodie, before the case had reached court. DCS Pritchard said he had spoken to DSupt Fulcher telling him not to do it, but it wasn't on a list he'd written of other issues he'd discussed with DSupt Fulcher over the phone. Steve Fulcher said there had been no such conversation regarding the Steve Brodie interview and neither had he been given any such order. It would be down to who the panel would believe.

The next witness was the Chief Constable, Pat Geenty. He had been the Gold Commander for the enquiry and had worked closely with DSupt Fulcher during the most crucial aspects of the enquiry. He had been forthright in his support for what DSupt Fulcher had done that day when Halliwell confessed and he had said as much at the *voir dire* back in 2012. He said then it had been a 'gutsy decision' to take. He told John Beggs that he still held this opinion; however, today, at the misconduct hearing, he added something more, something different.

His stance remained the same, up until the discovery of Sian's body; after that, he now said, he did not agree with what had happened. He said his own thinking would have changed at that point. He was basically saying Halliwell should have been taken into custody before he confessed to killing Becky. She would never have been found. I sniffed into my hanky. So much for my letter to him. From what he had said, that had just proved to be a waste of time.

Another issue that came up at this point was the whereabouts of a Gold Policy book. I learnt this was where the decisions of senior officers were recorded during major investigations.

Chief Constable Pat Geenty had kept such a Gold Policy book for Operation Mayan. DSupt Fulcher's barrister wanted to see what he had recorded during the course of the enquiry. It could demonstrate what he had thought about the decisions taken by DSupt Fulcher and whether they had been endorsed. But when it was requested, it couldn't be produced. John Beggs questioned Chief Constable Pat Geenty as to its whereabouts, but it was for all intents 'lost'. It was very odd.

I tried to keep notes where I could; Charlie and I found the atmosphere in the room oppressive and looked forward to the breaks, when we could breathe different air. I was filled with foreboding. I stole looks at the panel members, who sat impassively, not giving anything away.

Then it was the turn of DSupt Fulcher to give his evidence as to what happened the day Christopher Halliwell was arrested. Over several hours, John Beggs took him through the evidence and he was cross-examined by the force barrister. DSupt Fulcher explained his thought processes when conducting the emergency interview with Halliwell. He explained how he thought Sian O'Callaghan's Right to Life trumped Halliwell's right to silence.

This, he said, was the basis on which he carried out the emergency interview. Then Halliwell had confessed and revealed the whereabouts of Sian, then Becky. The force barrister was seemingly unimpressed, as were the panel members. As I looked at the three of them, sitting in judgement on their colleague, I so wanted to ask them how many murderers they had caught during their careers.

John Beggs then read out a nomination for DSupt Fulcher

for a Queen's Police Medal. This had been submitted by the force in the months following Halliwell's arrest in 2011, but following John's complaint it had been withdrawn. The text of the nomination was a glowing testament to DSupt Fulcher's abilities as a detective, praising him in the highest terms for his work, which, ironically, also included the actions he had taken during Operation Mayan. There was more; he also had commendations for past work. Until this point, his service had been exemplary. Well, it still was to us.

I found it deeply upsetting to listen to this in these circumstances. He clearly was a very good detective, one of the best in the country, so what were we all doing here, in a misconduct hearing? What on earth was going on? After all, Halliwell was incarcerated as a result of DNA evidence that linked him to Sian's body, which would not have been possible if he hadn't revealed to Steve Fulcher where he had left her.

Finally, it was the summing up, after which we retreated to the canteen. I saw Yvonne Fulcher there again and we sat with her. I felt sorry for the predicament they were in. I was so grateful for what DSupt Fulcher had done that day; how was it that I could be so powerless? Why was this all about how John felt? What about my and Charlie's feelings, why did we have no influence over this process?

It felt like an eternity before we were called back in. We all sat nervously; I was literally holding my breath. Once again, my heart pounded in my chest. The atmosphere in the room was tense. I looked at DSupt Fulcher. I couldn't read his expression. I guessed he was glad it was all over at last. It had taken over two long years of the IPCC investigation to reach this point. The verdict rolled off the panel members' tongues. Guilty.

They found DSupt Fulcher guilty of gross misconduct on two counts. I couldn't believe what I was hearing. Blood rushed to my face. I looked across at John and caught him smirking; I wanted to go over and wipe the look off his face. The stupid man. He had done this, the complaint was all his doing. This was the thanks he gave to the man who brought his daughter home to us. I felt slightly dizzy after they spoke. We had to rise.

While they found Steve Fulcher guilty of gross misconduct, the panel deferred their sanction to the next day. I thought this was particularly cruel of them. This would ensure that Steve and Yvonne Fulcher would have yet another very difficult and sleepless night. So, this was how senior police conducted themselves. The experience had been quite an eye-opener for me. I found the whole thing rather spiteful.

I left the room in tears. I couldn't keep them in check any longer, such was the highly charged atmosphere. If I hadn't left at that moment, my anger would have got the better of me and I would have caused a scene with John. Cathy and Yvonne were waiting, and taking one look at me they knew it was not a good outcome. I could feel my head spinning and a strange loss of control. Charlie held on to me. Once I recovered, Cathy took us over to the family room, where I could calm down.

After a while, we left via the back door to avoid the media. The police were particularly keen that we do this. But while we were driving home, Rob Murphy from ITV West Country rang me. What did I have to say? Would I speak to them? We had reached Avebury by now, on our way home.

'Stop!' I shouted. Charlie slowed to a halt.

What was I thinking? I wasn't in the police. They had no right to control me. No doubt us going out of the back door suited them. I had been totally unimpressed with every officer I'd seen in that room, with the exception of DSupt Fulcher. These were supposed to be senior officers and yet they felt like pathetic bullies to me. If that was a sample of the top brass, my confidence in chief officers was totally eroded. The panel members had sat impassive, like three dummies, their faces rigid, for days. In that room I had no choice but to sit quietly. Well, now I was going to have my say.

Charlie put the car into reverse and we drove back to Devizes. After all, someone had to stand up for Steve Fulcher and I had seen little of that. I'd written a statement for his barrister to let the hearing know how thankful we were as a family for the actions Steve Fulcher had taken, I hadn't heard it read out while were we at the hearing. Rob Murphy had a camera crew in front of Police Headquarters. He had been waiting for me to come out. Charlie pulled up and I got out and spoke to Rob. The BBC were also there. I was ready to say my piece. The cameras rolled.

The next morning the press were knocking at my door, which I was not expecting. I welcomed them in, made them tea and we all sat waiting to hear Steve's fate, as the panel would be giving their sanction. Eventually, the phone rang. It was a member of the press to tell us that Steve had received two final written warnings, but would not lose his job. I was elated. His family had been through so much for so long.

I felt disgust with the process and with the people who had sat in judgement on him, but I took some comfort from the fact that DSupt Fulcher was reinstated on Monday, 27 January 2014. At least the whole ghastly misconduct issue was finally over for him.

I now hoped that there might be some progress in relation to the enquiry. There was an information vacuum, even though I'd been passing the police what I thought were valuable leads and lines of enquiry. In my head, they were continuing to work at full pelt, at least building a picture of the man who had murdered Becky and who may well have murdered more young women. We were nearly two years down the line since Halliwell's conviction. What I desperately wanted was news, something tangible. The waiting seemed interminable.

Then, suddenly, the long information drought ended.

12

OPERATION MANILLA

It was Valentine's Day and Charlie had bought me a huge bouquet, as he always did, which sat very proudly by the fireplace. I had a call that morning from my FLO, Cathy.

'Would it be convenient for me to call over and introduce you to the new SIO, Detective Chief Inspector Sean Memory?' she asked.

'Yes, I'll put the kettle on.'

We were intrigued. We had heard nothing of any significance for so long, despite, back in 2012, DCS Kier Pritchard saying it remained a live enquiry. DCI Sean Memory was a cold-case detective and we had met him briefly between buildings at DSupt Fulcher's misconduct hearing. They arrived and we sat and listened. After only weeks since DSupt Steve Fulcher's conduct hearing had concluded, Operation Manilla was being reinvigorated and DCI Sean Memory was now in charge of the investigation. I warmed to him as I never did DI Davey. He was more approachable and, as he sat and spoke with us, I felt confident in his abilities.

'I'm not going to make you any promises,' he said before

leaving, 'but I think this may well be my last cold case before I retire and I'll do the best I can to get justice for Becky.' We thanked him and they both left. To our knowledge, this was now the third senior investigating officer to have led the case in almost as many years. We could only hope that this time things would be different. I did my usual thing and googled him anyway; I needed to be sure he was capable.

In the meantime, I continued to petition for the change to the rules of PACE. I still felt strongly about this and it was at least something *I* could do. DSupt Fulcher's misconduct hearing had a positive effect. I was finding that many police officers were now supporting and signing the petition. It was incredible. Many of them commented on how disgusted they were with the outcome of Steve Fulcher's conduct hearing and signing the petition was their way of showing support for what he had done. It was clear he was still very popular with the rank and file.

Then, just after Becky's birthday, I received a call out of the blue from a media source asking me if I knew what was happening at the field in Eastleach, which we referred to as 'Becky's field'.

'No,' I replied, 'what's going on?'

'We've received a call from a member of the public saying that police are there, searching the field.'

I called John's FLO immediately, as he was standing in for mine, who was on leave. He said he would find out what was happening. DCI Memory had told me they would be going back out to the field, but he hadn't said when this would be. He was on annual leave. When the FLO rang back he confirmed soil samples were being taken from the field. And there was more;

while taking the samples, they had discovered a human arm bone, which they would have to forensically test to see if it was Becky's.

I was shocked. I hadn't been expecting this. I had, of course, been told her head was missing. I'd assumed the rest of Becky's remains had been returned to us. Now an arm bone had been found. How many more pieces of her were there just lying around waiting to be discovered? It was then I realised I didn't know how much of Becky we had actually buried. Was this why we had been warned not to open the box containing her remains?

There was a drip, drip of information. The next day, the *Swindon Advertiser* reported that police were appealing again for witnesses into Becky's case. There was further news in the coming days that police had discovered other items in the field. DCI Sean Memory contacted us to tell us that they had recovered small foot bones, which would need to be DNA tested. Again, this was unexpected. As Charlie and I talked about this, we could only assume Becky's remains had been scattered in the field by the plough. Parts of my poor little girl were still in the field.

It was four months since the misconduct hearing, when I heard the news that DSupt Fulcher had decided to resign from the force. Obviously things had not worked out, certainly not as I'd hoped. I felt it was a tragedy for the force to lose someone of his abilities. On the same day as I heard this, there was further extraordinary news.

DCI Memory appeared on the local news channels announcing that while searching at a site in the village of Ramsbury, Wiltshire, they had discovered Sian O'Callaghan's boots in a pond. They had deployed an Avon and Somerset underwater search team, who had also discovered a number of other items, one of which was a single-barrelled shotgun. They were also deploying special cadaver dogs to search the site, as they now believed it could be the location where Halliwell had killed Sian O'Callaghan.

Of course, Halliwell had asked Steve Fulcher on the day of his arrest 'What caught me? The gamekeeper at Ramsbury?' I was dumbfounded. I found it incredible that they could find Sian's boots at this spot three years later. Over the coming days, the search continued at the pond in Ramsbury. The next startling news was that police had found 60 items of women's clothing in woods close by. The media showed a photograph of the dirty remains of a knitted cardigan that had been found there. My son Steven immediately contacted DCI Memory to say that he believed the cardigan belonged to Becky. She'd had a cream cable knit cardigan, just like the one shown by the media. Was it hers? If it was, what was it doing there?

We needed to know what was going on. We had a meeting with DCI Memory at Marlborough Police Station, where we were also introduced to new FLOs. I had a list of questions about the Ramsbury search and finds. Firstly, I asked if we could go and see the area. DCI Memory said that Sian's mother, Elaine, had already been to the site and we were welcome to go along with him. Now, if we wanted to.

I expected my request to be turned down. Even though I wasn't dressed for a visit to the Ramsbury site (I was wearing a suit and heels) I felt there wasn't a moment to lose. This might be our only chance to go so I couldn't turn it down because my clothing wasn't suitable. We agreed and followed in the car.

We drove to Hilldrop Lane in Ramsbury. The area was very rural and the lane was long and narrow. As we approached, we could see it had been sealed off with blue and white police tape. The police let us through and we pulled off to the right into a field. There was a police trailer where the officers could take a break, get warm and take a shower. The weather was cold, despite it being May. The sky was unusually dark with thick cloud and it started to rain. Charlie and I got out of the car and walked over to the trailer with DCI Memory. The officers there were so kind, giving me a police jacket to wear and an umbrella.

In anticipation of the family asking us questions when we got back, I used my phone camera to record what I saw. DCI Memory directed us towards the area of the pond. The pond itself was by the side of the single-track road and encircled by trees and vegetation. It looked like a scene from a bygone age where horses and other animals might have stopped to drink. It was being drained and they had reached the silt. The stench of it was vile. Officers were in the vicinity conducting a painstaking fingertip search.

There were police in white forensic suits searching a copse opposite the pond, when a loud shout went out. Several police officers went to a thicket along with a photographer. As we looked around, DCI Memory explained that the track opposite the pond was where he believed Halliwell had murdered Sian. He thought that Halliwell had then removed her boots and thrown them into the pond. He then said Halliwell had been disturbed, possibly by a courting couple, or a gamekeeper on a quad bike, and had panicked, placing Sian in the thicket. He said he then believed Halliwell came back later to move her to the site in Oxfordshire, where she was eventually found.

At this point, there came the rumble of thunder. It was enough for Charlie.

'I'm going back to the car,' he said. 'This place has a horrible eerie feeling, it's giving me the creeps.'

Charlie was right, the oppressiveness of the darkened sky had given the place a certain unnatural atmosphere, but I stayed with DCI Memory and we continued to talk. I looked around, taking in what he had told us. It was such a remote area. I could imagine it without the police vans and cars. As I stood there, I was haunted by what the judge had said in her remarks at Halliwell's sentencing in 2012 regarding Sian's terror. I couldn't help but remember her words again. A shiver ran down my spine. Was that cardigan Becky's? Was any of the other clothing Becky's? Was this where he'd killed her too? My poor little girl. What did she go through that night so long ago? It had been a while since I'd allowed my mind to wander back to the chamber of horrors, but standing here I couldn't help it.

The thought of Becky at that animal's hands never failed to hurt me. A lump came to my throat. I wanted to cry but fought against it. We walked back to the police trailer, where I handed back the jacket and umbrella. I thanked the officers for what they were doing and went back to the car to Charlie. We drove away. I thought about the field at Eastleach, where Becky's arm bone had been found and now this site, that might have given up an item of Becky's clothing. I thought about her missing skull – *where was that*?

Suddenly, it was as if a dark cloud had come over me. I broke down, unable to control myself, my thoughts unable to stop thinking of what Becky suffered. I hated Halliwell for what he had done. The experience at Ramsbury was awful, but I had felt compelled to go, I had to. If Becky had been there, I wanted to go there too.

Charlie took me straight to the doctor, who gave me some diazepam to calm me down. I continued to watch the news in the coming days. It was a compulsion; I wanted to know everything they found. The search of the pond area continued for three long weeks, only stopped occasionally by bad weather.

I tried to concentrate on other things. I put my focus back on the petition. I went back out to the stand at Asda. There were only a few signatures that day, but I was grateful for every single one of them. While I was there one time, I met a woman called Grace. She told me she had also got into Halliwell's taxi. He had put the locks down and started behaving peculiarly, just staring at her. She said she had been very frightened, but as she had her phone with her, she quickly called her husband and kept talking until she got out. Again, I made a note to pass on to the police.

The weeks rolled on and the news from the enquiry dried up. I continued to go out petitioning. Then I was asked if I would be a guest speaker at the North Swindon Rotary Club. By now, I was getting used to this and they made me so welcome. People were so kind and so receptive to hearing what had happened to Becky. The FLOs came round to see me, bringing with them a series of photographs, predominantly women's underwear, which had been uncovered from near the pond at Ramsbury. They wanted to see if I could identify any of it as belonging to Becky. While it was of her small proportions, I couldn't categorically say that it belonged to her.

Because of DCI Memory's progress on the case, I had started to wonder why this level of activity hadn't taken place before. My god, I was grateful for the advances he was making in the enquiry. It gave me hope. But I started to pace around at home as my mind filled with questions. I had kept in touch with Yvonne Fulcher, Steve's wife, and she told me that before Steve had left the enquiry back in June 2011, and since he had left the force a few months ago, there were a number of enquiries that he felt should have occurred before now, some of which he felt would have strengthened the case for Becky back in 2012. She was angry at the way her husband had been treated and, like him, couldn't understand why these enquiries hadn't been conducted as a matter of urgency.

Foremost of these enquiries was a spade seized from Halliwell's shed on the day of his arrest. The question was, had this been forensically examined for links to Becky's grave? The location of Ramsbury had been mentioned by Halliwell when he had spoken to Steve Fulcher on the day of his arrest in March 2011. Why had it taken over three years to discover the pond which had crucially yielded Sian's boots? In the event, hundreds of items had been recovered from or near the pond, including an old shotgun.

Yvonne told me Halliwell had also stated he'd killed two women to a doctor who had attended the police station on the day of his arrest to confirm he was fit for detention. She also said that an RAC attendant had been identified who Halliwell had called out around the time Becky had been murdered in 2003, because his car had run out of fuel near to where she'd been buried. I learnt something else too, something awful. I was told Halliwell's GP records revealed that on 3 January 2003 he had visited the doctor. He was injured, telling the doctor he had had a fight with a passenger. His finger was broken and he had scratches on his face. He had been distressed. Given the timing of his visit, police believed the injury to his finger and scratches to his face to have been done by Becky. This was absolutely dreadful to hear. It was another thing to add to the torture chamber of horrors, another thing for me to relive. Even though it caused me such pain, I needed every detail so that I could piece it all together. Once again, my thoughts went back to her at the hands of that monster. My god, I hated him.

When I heard this, it made me angry too. We'd been told the reason Becky had been dropped from the indictment had been because there was no evidence other than Halliwell's confession. This sounded like evidence to me – evidence that had been there from the start.

I shared Yvonne's anger. Having sat through Steve Fulcher's misconduct hearing and being thoroughly disappointed in the IPCC, I didn't know who to turn to. In early August 2014, I decided to send a letter to Her Majesty's Inspector of Constabulary (HMIC). I complained about the inactivity into Becky's investigation from 2011 to February 2014. I had a response back from Druscilla Sharpling of the HMIC telling us to refer the matter to the IPCC. Given the shoddy way I felt Steve Fulcher had been treated by the IPCC, I felt there was no point going there. They were the last people who were likely to take on the complaints, particularly when they hadn't wanted to listen to me with regards to my feelings over DSupt Fulcher's disciplinary investigation. Not knowing where to turn, we let the matter go.

Again, I concentrated on the petition. While I was out, I found people still willing to tell me of their suspicions and contacts with Halliwell. While at Swindon football ground, I was given information from a man who owned a guest house. He told me he had a long-term lodger, who always paid him in advance. He said that Halliwell was a friend of the lodger and called for him one evening to go out for a drink. The guest-house owner said that the lodger never returned and he never saw him again. I made a note and passed it on to the police.

This reminded me of the time not long after we had heard the news of Becky's death, when a friend of my mum suggested to her that they should go for a day out on a coach trip. Mum was in a state as everywhere she went she saw either Becky's or Halliwell's face. She couldn't get away from the press reporters at her door so she went with her friend.

They sat on the coach, and during the journey a man and woman sat in front of them. The man, a taxi driver, started to talk to another man across the aisle about the two young girls found in Swindon, meaning Sian and Becky. He then went on to talk about Linda Razzell, a woman who had gone missing in Swindon and whose body had never been found. Her husband had been subsequently convicted of her murder, despite always maintaining he was innocent of the crime. The man said that

Halliwell had stalked and killed Linda Razzell too, as he had been obsessed with her. He said Halliwell used to sit opposite the alleyway where they found her phone, sketching pictures of her. He said he was an odd man, as he used to park near him when he was a taxi driver. Mum had no choice but to sit and listen to this. It made her feel ill. When she returned and told me about it, I reported it to police.

I continued to collect signatures, but the time had come to make an application to deliver them to Downing Street. We were given a slot in January 2015. The pressure was on to collect as many more as we could. I started to look around for other venues where there was large footfall that we hadn't been before.

Not long after this, I was contacted by my FLO. Police were going to make a public appeal. They were asking the public to help them in tracing a T-registered silver Volvo S80 once owned by Halliwell. It was sold in 2004, they thought to an Irish man at an auction in Oxfordshire. The number plate was T661 LGP. The car had since disappeared. This, they said, could have been the car Becky got into. My stomach lurched at the thought of this. Had he killed her in that car? The next day, the *Swindon Advertiser* reported that police had taken several calls in relation to the appeal. It seemed the enquiry was gathering momentum again.

Officers wanted to look through Becky's belongings, letters and diaries again. I went up into the loft. We had bagged up a lot of her things and put them there from Operation Mayan; now I was sifting through it all once more. I gathered everything together and took it downstairs ready for the officers to read. It was impossible not to take a look at it all again myself.

Among all her letters, diaries and papers, I came across an A4 page of Becky's handwriting; she would have been about 15 when she wrote it for her home tutor. It was a response to *The Early Purges*, a poem by Seamus Heaney about the drowning of kittens. As an animal lover, the poem had upset Becky. As I read through it, there was an extract that leapt out at me. She had written a long sentence in a flow of indignation, saying:

Killing an animal is just as good as killing a human and should be classed as 1st degree murder and the murderer should get a life time sentence in prison for this and should not get let off of his or her sentence any earlier than what they have been given for good behaviour.

Reading this now in the context of the fight for justice for my lovely Becky, it almost felt as if she was talking to me from beyond the grave. '*The murderer should get a life time sentence in prison . . .*' It took my breath away. As I put it to one side, I found the folder she had clutched as she came out of the Diana, Princess of Wales, Treatment Centre. I had had such high hopes when we picked her up after her treatment. I remembered she'd certainly looked as if she'd turned a corner. I leafed through the folder. I realised I hadn't looked inside it before. Along with the house rules, there was a questionnaire inside, which Becky had had to fill in. I found I was now reading her answer to the question 'Describe how you get on with your parents.' Her words struck me. She had written:

'I get on really well with my mum. She has really stuck by me.'

213

I looked at the next question: 'Describe how you experienced childhood. Include a description of your family background and upbringing.' She'd written:

'My mum was always working hard to feed, clothe and house us.'

It touched me to know that, in the midst of all her troubles, she appreciated she had had a good upbringing.

Also among the papers was a bundle of letters she had sent me from when she'd been in prison. I sat and re-read them, crying at the thought of them coming from my little Becky in such a place. In one letter, she asked me to send her photos of me, Charlie and Steven and the dogs, so that she could decorate her cell with them. Another of her letters was now shockingly prophetic:

'I tried to hang myself the first day I came in but when I draped the noose around my neck I saw your face in my mind at my funeral. You were distraught. I love you . . . I couldn't do that to you.'

It was heartbreaking. And she hadn't done that to me. Halliwell had. I put the letters to one side, ready for the investigators. Strangely, as desperately sad as they were to read, Becky's words served to galvanise me further. I thought back to her school days and the battles I'd had with the school over bullying, trying to get them to listen, to help. It had been the same trying to get help with her addiction. I'd had such trouble trying to get people to listen when we were asking for help. I couldn't and wouldn't let her down in seeking justice. Halliwell would not get away with it. I was determined to get people to listen this time. I was fired up.

It was the final push for the petition. We had help coming

from everywhere, even from people I had never met before. It felt like the whole of Swindon was helping me. Charlie, Tracey, Tony and I would go round the pubs in Swindon collecting signatures. I would go in and ask the landlord for permission, which they invariably gave. One night, we went round the whole of Old Town. Each time one of us sat with someone to ask for their support it meant explaining and re-telling the story and answering questions. During the course of interactions, people would tell us where they had had contact with Halliwell, or that they knew him or their children knew his children.

It was a Friday in November and Sandy and I were covering the small Asda. We were there on our own, Sandy at one end and me at the other. We had half a dozen clipboards each, pop-up banners showing Becky's photo and the words of the petition. They were very prominent; everyone knew Becky's face by now. We had the usual laminated photographs and newspaper cuttings around the table to illustrate the case. We also displayed a large photograph of the field at Eastleach so that we could point out where Halliwell had taken Steve Fulcher and shown him where he had buried Becky. It was this day that a woman approached Sandy to sign the petition. Sandy was with her for a while before she brought her to me.

'Karen, you need to listen to this lady. She was Halliwell's former girlfriend.'

To protect her identity I'll call her Jane. Jane told me about the relationship she once had with Halliwell decades ago. As she spoke, I couldn't believe what I was hearing. The poor woman had had to live with the things she was telling me for years.

She told me that after Halliwell's arrest police had identified her as a former girlfriend and had been to see her. She said police had asked her about her sex life with Halliwell. She explained that when they visited her, she had had her child sat next to her and was embarrassed by their questioning; she therefore was unable to be more forthcoming at the time. The police left after ten minutes, without appreciating the position she was in and never made an appointment to return.

Among the things she said, she told me of Halliwell's early offending as a burglar and thief and how he would steal to order. He would steal clothes for her, bringing her the same garment in every colour. She said that he had an accomplice and that they would bury things in the garden. He had once given her an item of jewellery, a silver ring with black dots on it, that Halliwell told her belonged to his father. During one court appearance, he had even managed to escape from the courtroom.

Most disturbing of all, in hindsight, she was convinced he had killed when they were living together in the 1980s. She described him returning home one day, covered in mud, shaking and crying uncontrollably. She said he was unable to speak and she hadn't been able to console him. She never got to the bottom of his behaviour that day, as he would not tell her what had happened.

We talked for over an hour and she had disclosed a lot of information which I felt the police would be very interested in. It was incredibly brave of her. I immediately spoke to my old FLO, Cathy, and told her what I had heard and written down. She told me to email all the information across to them as she felt sure DCI Memory would want to know it. I subsequently heard that within days police did go and revisit Jane; they spent two days recording a statement from her.

The next day the phone woke me up with a start. It was my FLO to ask me if I knew where Ashbury Avenue was. She informed me that police would be searching there today and to beware of press contact. Still half asleep, I realised that Ashbury Avenue was in Nythe, where Halliwell used to live. They were searching Halliwell's former home.

It was my birthday that day and Charlie was taking me to York for a family wedding. I was pleased to be going away for a few days. However, before we went, I asked him to take me to Ashbury Avenue. We parked the car and walked down the road to where there was a police cordon. There were police cars and vans. We saw a white tent had been erected in a garden next to the front entrance of a house. There were police in white forensic suits and the place was a hive of activity.

The *Swindon Advertiser* linked the disappearance of another local Swindon woman, Sally Ann John, to the search at Ashbury Avenue. Sally Ann John had been missing for decades. The officers were reportedly taking the house apart, looking under flooring and behind wall cavities. The search also included cadaver dogs, who would be able to detect blood. There was also a renewed appeal for anyone to come forward who had seen Becky over the Christmas period in 2002. I was heartened by the activity, but I wondered what would come of it.

The time had finally arrived to deliver the petition to Downing Street. We continued to collect packs galore but each address had to be checked for a postcode, so every night I would sit and go through every list and postcode check. My sister Tracey's house looked like a post office, my house had petitions everywhere. Once checked, every thousand would be tied with a pink satin ribbon.

We then hit a problem; we were calling into places to collect petitions only to be told they had already been collected by people clearly unconnected with the campaign. Packs had gone missing from Purton, Cricklade and Cirencester. This was serious; the word was that they were being stolen. People were outraged when I reported it to the police and newspapers. People had been so very kind that I now couldn't believe at this point someone was trying to sabotage the campaign. But I wouldn't let it dampen my spirits; in total we had still managed to gather over 43,000 signatures. Considering that we'd had to explain to people the complex circumstances of Becky's case tens of thousands of times in order to persuade them to sign, it was a significant achievement.

On 13 January, Charlie and I travelled up to London the night before we went to deliver the petition. Tracey and my friends Sandy, Gladys and Dominic travelled up by train the next day and we met at the hotel we were staying at. When they arrived, we opened a bottle of champagne to celebrate our achievement. I had much to thank them all for; we had been through a lot together and they had helped me so much. I wouldn't have achieved all that we had without them; I was indebted to them.

We met Robert Buckland at Parliament, and he then escorted us to Downing Street. As we walked up to No. 10, it felt surreal; all the petitioning, all the late nights, the standing at stalls, knocking on doors, explaining to people, had led to this moment. We knocked on the door of No. 10 and the door opened. We handed over the box of petitions and took our photos on the doorstep. Then we had a surprise. Robert had organised for us to go inside and meet Max Chambers, advisor to David Cameron.

I wasn't expecting this. We left our phones in reception and were escorted upstairs. There, Max Chambers offered us coffee, poured from a beautiful silver coffee pot into a china cup and saucer. David Cameron had expressed an interest in the case years before and Max said he would update him after our meeting. Max asked me what changes I would welcome, and in addition to a change to PACE we talked about body-worn cameras. This was something I felt might have helped at the time of Halliwell's arrest, had they been available. We talked for ages, more than our allocated time, when he asked us if we'd like a tour of Downing Street; of course, we said yes.

We left Downing Street with the job done; the petition was handed in. Whether it would be enough to see a change, I didn't know, but I felt a weight lifting from my shoulders. We had done all we could.

PART THREE

13

AN ARREST

'I have something to tell you. Laura rang at two a.m. . . .'

A month later, we were on holiday with the family in Dubai, and it was the night before we were due to fly back to the UK. Someone had texted my niece, Laura, who had been dog sitting for us while we were away, telling her to look at the news. I had taken a sleeping pill that night but she FaceTimed Charlie in the early hours and relayed what she could see.

When I woke up, the TV was on with the sound turned off. It was on the BBC news channel. I could sense straight away he was edgy. Without really taking much notice, my eyes flicked on to the screen, not expecting to see anything unusual. Charlie didn't get a chance to finish what he was saying. As he spoke, I saw the breaking news running along the bottom of the TV. It said that an unnamed 51-year-old man had been arrested for Becky's murder! I rushed to get my phone from the safe and noticed that I had several missed calls, including one from the police.

I was all over the place. Was it Halliwell? It had to be, surely? What did it mean? There had been so much activity in the months up to Christmas, but then it had all gone quiet. I couldn't believe it. There had been no indication that an arrest was coming. What had happened? I tried to make contact with my new FLOs but they weren't picking up.

The long flight home from Dubai was unbearable. As soon as we landed and were inside the terminal, I called my former FLO, Cathy, as I wasn't getting an answer from my new FLOs. Charlie had gone on to collect the luggage. We had a minibus collecting us, so I needed to make this call fast. I told Cathy that Laura had called us and we'd seen the news. Who was it? She spoke to DCI Sean Memory and he asked that I call him. I was all fingers and thumbs as I pressed the phone pad. It started to ring and Sean answered. I asked him one question.

'Is it who I think it is?'

I held my breath, conscious that I was in a public place. It was all I wanted to know.

'Yes,' he said. I cried tears of relief.

'Thank you,' I mumbled. I headed off to tell Charlie and get on the minibus.

My mind was in overdrive on the journey home. It felt out of the blue. I had no idea what had suddenly prompted Halliwell's arrest. Of course, it was good news, but I was terribly apprehensive too. We had been here before and it had all gone horribly wrong. Would he wriggle off the hook again?

There was now a lot of renewed media interest and I found myself answering call after call. The police put out a statement:

We can confirm that a fifty-one-year-old man from Swindon was arrested today on suspicion of the murder of Becky

Godden, also known as Becky Godden-Edwards. He has been interviewed and enquiries continue. It is in the interests of justice for Becky that you do not speculate on the identity of the arrested man as to do so could seriously jeopardise the judicial process.

After four years of purgatory, I was in the mood to talk, but, because of the delicate nature of the case, we were still unable to discuss it for fear of it falling at the first hurdle. There was such a long way to go and we were told we needed to keep everything completely watertight. We had spent years keeping silent, so a while longer wouldn't make any difference. Through the *Swindon Advertiser*, I thanked the people of Swindon for all their support. Their kind words had helped me through some really dark times.

It is a very strange feeling at the moment. It has been a bolt from the blue. We hope and pray we will see justice and we are waiting with baited breath. Every day we live in hope . . . the day I found out that a man had been arrested, it was almost like a firework of emotions . . . I cried, but they were tears of relief. I am still feeling jittery inside and I don't think that feeling will settle until we have a conclusion. I will not believe a conviction until I see it. In the last year, Sean Memory and his team have worked incredibly hard and the smallest thing could undo it all. I would still like to thank everybody for their amazing support and wonderful messages. I have had more than

300 messages since the news broke and I would love to thank everyone individually. Becky was a Swindon girl and Swindon people have come good for her.

As Becky's birthday approached I found I couldn't settle. I was getting myself in a state, so I messaged my FLO requesting an update on the investigation. Since the news of Halliwell's arrest, I had become extremely anxious. I couldn't sleep. I just wanted all of this to go away. I was already finding the waiting a strain; I was constantly worried that the police were going to contact me with bad news. The feeling just wouldn't go away and I was running on nervous energy.

In times like this, we found ourselves out at Becky's field in Eastleach. It was now a familiar place to us, but I came here with such mixed emotions that sometimes I hated it here. It was such a desolate field and I wanted to change that. I wanted to plant a tree in Becky's memory, have something strong and permanent, something beautiful that would give blossom. We asked the farmer for his permission and he agreed.

We talked about this with the family and Tracey suggested the apple tree that she had planted in her garden all those years ago, the one that Steve and Becky had watched grow from a branch when it broken off under Tony's weight. It was a lovely gesture and seemed the perfect answer. Having made the decision we went out to plant it. It was a cold and windy day. The field was muddy but it made the soil easy to dig. The area had become a little overgrown, and as Charlie cut it back ready to dig, I suddenly had a bolt of anxiety. We were doing exactly what Halliwell had done all those years ago. He had been digging here, digging Becky's grave. I said nothing, continuing to watch as Charlie finished planting the tree. When it was planted in the ground I tied a pink ribbon around it. As he'd cleared the ground, Charlie had also found the cross left by the police among the undergrowth; the words had now worn away. We repositioned it under the tree.

We now had Becky's tree in Becky's field. We stood for a few minutes and I said a prayer for her. I hoped planting the tree would introduce life to the spot where Becky had been laid; that it might somehow make the site easier to visit. Then, much like the first time we were there, I wanted to run, get away. I couldn't explain it; I wanted to be there and yet, once there, I couldn't help but re-imagine the awful night Halliwell would have driven Becky here. We continued to visit regularly to make sure the tree thrived. We knew now that if we visited in the spring, we would see it in beautiful scented blossom.

The day of Becky's birthday arrived; she would have been 33 years old. Although I was feeling very tired, adrenalin kicked in to help me through the day. My lovely friend Shirley Bunn arrived with a birthday card. We went to visit Becky's grave and cleaned the headstone. I had made a few extra vases; jam jars put to a better use than I'd used them for before and wrapped them in some pretty paper for the extra flowers Becky would have for her birthday tribute.

After cleaning the headstone and arranging the flowers, I took some photos and we stood and had a good cry. I walked away from her grave feeling emotionally drained. I sat with

Shirley in the car for a while, just looking out of the window at her grave. I was reminded of the last time I saw Becky, when she walked away, leaving me sitting in the car. I had the same heavy, deflated feeling.

When we arrived back home another good friend, Gladys Barr, had popped over to see me. The family were coming round later for Becky's birthday celebration. She used to love celebrating her birthday. We put on Becky's R&B music and danced around the kitchen to her favourites, Usher and Daniel Bedingfield. The door knocked again and it was Sandy, my right-hand woman during the campaign. She had a bottle of champagne for us to toast Becky, which was really thoughtful. It was so lovely of them to remember Becky's birthday and share it with us.

That evening the family arrived and we sifted through photos, laughing and crying. My daughter-in-law, Kelly, made a birthday cake, complete with candles. I lit them and the grandchildren blew them all out. At 11.30 p.m. we all wrote a message to Becky on some pink and white lanterns and stood in the garden. The moon was bright and we set the lanterns off one by one. They hadn't left the garden before some disintegrated into balls of fire, falling on to the grass. It seemed Becky didn't appreciate the gesture! We laughed at the thought of her wagging her finger at us. It had been another day of mixed emotions.

Everything seemed to be catching up with me; I was lacking in energy, but my mind continued to buzz with the thoughts of bringing Halliwell to justice. Dare I hope that this time it would come good? There was now a vacuum of news from the investigation. I was left to imagine what might be happening.

I was scouring the local news as soon as I woke, checking my texts and emails for any contact from the media, who many a time found out information before I did. I had also set my phone and iPad to alert me if Halliwell's name was mentioned in the press. I didn't know what more I could do. The waiting felt interminable. There had to be more I could do.

I thought back over the last few months. The petition had gone well and unexpectedly it had also led to people giving information about Halliwell. I remembered how extraordinary it had been talking to Jane, his former girlfriend. I was pleased she felt able to approach us and be so candid. It had been chilling to hear that she thought Halliwell had killed when she had known him, back in the 1980s. But what if we hadn't been there? What if I hadn't petitioned and provided the opportunity for people to pass on their information to us? Information such as Jane had provided was crucial to murder enquiries.

There were other women still missing from Swindon: Sandra Brewin, Sally Ann John, Thi Hai Nguyen. How come there was no trace of them? There'd been no trace of Becky because he'd buried her. Had he killed these women too? If it wasn't Halliwell, were there more killers like him walking among us, just as he did, in Swindon? Were the police on top of all this? They'd let Jane's crucial evidence slip through the net until she'd approached us as we campaigned. I'd passed enough other information on to them. I thought of the people who Mum had listened to talking on the coach, linking Halliwell to Linda Razzell. I knew Linda's husband, Glyn Razzell, was in prison for her murder, although he'd always denied killing her. Her body had never been found.

Sandy remembered that Jane had mentioned the date, 19 March, as being significant, perhaps a date that a girlfriend had left him. Sandy pointed out that Sian O'Callaghan had gone missing on 19 March, as had Linda Razzell. Did this date mean something to Halliwell? Had more women gone missing on this date? I turned to the internet and put the date in, alongside 'missing women.' Immediately it returned the high-profile case of Claudia Lawrence, who lived near York. She too had gone missing on 19 March in 2009 and had not been seen since. I often recalled all the information I'd read about Halliwell, that he was a groundworker, a chauffeur, he'd travelled around the country, had once had a narrowboat, that he had 80 cars. Could his reach have stretched to York? Very possibly. I remembered reading he'd grown up in Scotland, so he certainly had travelled beyond York. I decided to research further. It gave me something to do to fill the void while I waited for an update on the investigation.

Around this time, the *Advertiser* was asking the public to help the mother of Sally Ann John so that she too could have closure. A few months earlier, Sally Ann's disappearance had been declared a murder investigation by Wiltshire Police. Sally Ann had been working as a prostitute in Swindon at the time of her disappearance in 1995. She hadn't been seen since and the only clue left behind was a postcard, allegedly sent by her from London to a friend three weeks after she was last seen. Now, nearly twenty years later, police were treating her disappearance as murder.

Of course, there were similarities with Becky, as both had

been sex workers and both had gone missing from Swindon. Whenever there were developments in the months that followed, friends would be in touch to check on me. As police made fresh searches at Sally Ann John's last known address, in Nythe, I received a Facebook message from Lisa Halliwell, Halliwell's ex-wife. I thought it was very kind of her to think of me. Her message was simple, 'Thinking of you, sending love.' My heart went out to Lisa and her children.

However, the police were not linking Sally Ann's disappearance with Halliwell, despite her father saying she would have been known to him. Some arrests were made but these people were released without charge and the case went quiet again. I felt a pang of guilt as Sally Ann's family had been waiting for answers for so long. Thanks to Steve Fulcher, Becky had been found and now we were hopefully on the road to justice. No one knew more than I what it was like to have a daughter, who you love with every fibre of your body, go missing, to not see her for years. Unless you have been in that situation, you cannot imagine the agony of not seeing your child for weeks, months and years. The not knowing, the constant wondering. I could very much relate to Sally Ann's family.

Sean Memory, who had recently been promoted to Detective Superintendent, wanted to come and see me. Out of the blue, a meeting was arranged. The FLOs arrived ahead of Sean and told me that he would be bringing others with him. They asked me how much I had been told about why we were meeting; I'd been told nothing. So when three vehicles pulled up outside and about six people got out and came into the house, I was flabber-gasted. Not only was it the police, but they had also brought the Crown Prosecution Service with them as well. We struggled to fit all of them into the living room. I was nervous; it reminded me too much of our previous meetings with the CPS. No good had come from them; in the past, meetings with CPS usually meant they had something bad to tell us. DSupt Memory did the introductions. Then the room fell quiet.

'We're here to give you an update, Karen,' Sean told me. 'We've been to the High Court.'

He could see my puzzlement so explained further.

'Because Judge Cox was not clear what should happen to restart any proceedings against Halliwell, to ensure it was transparent we opted to go to the High Court and seek their permission to recommence proceedings. As it was, they stated we didn't need to and could proceed in the normal manner, i.e. to charge and subsequent court hearings. But we wanted to be watertight with the legislation. This is what has taken a bit of time.'

A man from the CPS spoke.

'We believe we now have enough evidence that passes the threshold to proceed with the prosecution.'

This was such good news. I'd waited so long to hear something like this that I daren't believe it. They said Halliwell 'was one evil man'. I repeated it to myself; Halliwell was at last going to trial for Becky's murder.

But I was still apprehensive. I picked over their words. They said that they thought they had enough evidence to proceed. We'd lived with this for so long by now, and always at the forefront of my mind was the time we had been told that Becky was being dropped from the indictment. The system had let us down so badly that it had left an indelible feeling of mistrust. I knew I wouldn't be happy until I faced Halliwell across a courtroom again. Only when we reached that point would I believe that we might get justice. I so wanted to believe them, but I dare not. I couldn't bear the hope of conviction being snatched away again.

The situation was difficult as it seemed the wheels of justice moved so very slowly. There were months and months of more waiting. There were days when I couldn't see anything but Becky, I couldn't get her out of my mind, days when I felt as if I'd been punched in the stomach. Days when once again I asked, why did this have to happen to *her*? Why did Halliwell pick on *my* child? What could I have done differently that would have prevented all this from happening? I went back over and over the same questions, looking for answers that weren't there. The waiting was grinding and the burden of it all felt as if it was slowly killing me.

As time rolled on, we saw the back of 2015 and I could only look forward to 2016 with a sense of hope that, this year, we would finally, perhaps, get justice for Becky. I could only wait and let the police carry on with preparing the case. Endless days and weeks and months had passed with no updates. It felt like the case was in lockdown. There was, I think, a fear that if there was any leakage to the press Halliwell might again try and say he couldn't receive a fair trial.

I tried to keep busy, while wishing my life away to get to

the trial. But I was about to be dealt an unexpected blow. My lovely friend Shirley Bunn, who I had known for 32 years, died unexpectedly from a heart attack. It was hard to take in. I had only seen Shirley two days before. She told me she had been to the doctor's as she had been getting out of breath for a while. Her daughter, Sarah, and I had both nagged her to go and they thought she might have angina. Now she was dead. It was such a shock.

Over the next few weeks I spent most of my days at Shirley's with Sarah and Neil. Shirley had asked me to make sure her kids were OK if anything happened to her, as they had no one else. I promised her I would, never expecting anything to happen of course. Now we had to organise her funeral, instead of her birthday celebration.

Then, unexpectedly, things began to move forward with the enquiry again. I took a call from my FLO, Mary Parks. She wanted to come and see me today. News on progress had been non-existent, so I told her I would be back home in half an hour. I did what I needed to do and made my way back. There had been so little contact I wondered what the visit could be about. Before I could stop it, adrenalin started pumping. Charlie was already at home and Mary and her colleague arrived. As I fussed about offering them tea and talking rubbish, I tried to delay them imparting what they had come to tell us, just in case it was bad news.

They wanted to be the first to let us know. I held my breath.

'Karen, today Christopher Halliwell will be charged with Becky's murder.' She smiled.

I burst into tears and hugged them both. It was a fantastic moment and something we had waited so long to hear. It seemed Becky was going to get the justice she deserved. It wasn't quite a champagne moment, because I knew we still had such a long way to go, but we were on the road now.

14

LIMBO

As soon as the FLOs left, we went to visit Mum, Tracey and Tony, and Steven and Kelly to tell them the news. There was one other person I wished I could tell and that was Shirley. I decided that I wanted to see her, so I went to the chapel of rest where her body was being kept ahead of the funeral. I took her some flowers tied with a green satin ribbon, her favourite colour, and left them in the coffin with her. I told Shirley the news of Halliwell being charged and asked her to keep an eye on Becky for me. I left in tears, telling her I would see her next Wednesday, the day of the funeral.

It was going to be a tough day. Sarah and her brother, Neil, asked me to read a poem. They also wanted me to travel with them in the family car, which I felt honoured to do. It was a very strange feeling knowing I would never see my dear friend again. I missed Shirley dreadfully, as we'd been through so much in our lives together, both as single mums. We'd worked together and seen each other through the worst of times. She had the most caring nature and had been such a huge help to me through my troubles. Sarah and Neil gave Shirley such a lovely send-off. She would have been so proud of her 'little bunnies' as she used to call them.

I felt overwhelmed and exhausted. It had been over a year since our trip to Dubai, when we had first heard that Halliwell had been arrested. It felt like for so much of that time I had been waiting for news, then a lot had happened at once. In the midst of my dealing with Shirley's death, Halliwell appeared in front of magistrates to be charged. The case would be referred to the Crown Court for trial. It seemed at last the legal machine was slowly starting to move.

Following Shirley's funeral, and with Halliwell's trial now looming, Charlie decided we needed a break and organised a last-minute deal to Turkey.

We wanted to step off the world for a few days. It was what I needed; a chance to breathe and recover. However, with a feeling of déjà vu, some major news came in while we were away, with just a day to go until we returned. I received an email from my FLO, Mary:

'URGENT – Bristol Crown Court hearing 26 May 2016, 2 p.m. Sorry to bother you while you're away, hope you're having a lovely time.'

The hearing was going to start in just two days' time. The holiday had been good while it lasted, but now I needed to get home and be with the rest of the family.

It was an uncomfortable and long flight home, and we were both tired and apprehensive. While waiting for our flight at the airport, we had received notice that things had been moved forward to 10 a.m. It would have to be a quick turnaround. We touched down at 3.30 a.m., collected our bags, and drove home. Charlie had a couple of hours' sleep as I kept busy. I couldn't sleep so I did the washing and tidied up until Charlie's daughter picked us up at 7.45 for our journey to Bristol.

We arrived in good time to go through the security at the court. We were stood in the foyer waiting when the police team turned up. We all made our way to the second floor; there was no side room available so we all sat in the corridor. Then DSupt Memory and the prosecuting counsel, Nick Haggan, QC, approached us and said they didn't think that we would be allowed in the courtroom, so we had to sit outside. But we were not there long as it was a very short hearing. Someone managed to get the key to the family room, so when the hearing was over and everyone came out, we were able to gain some privacy.

We all bundled into the small room. At last we were told what was going on. Apparently, the day had taken an unexpected turn as Halliwell had dismissed his legal team and was not appointing another one. The big news was that he would be representing himself. No one had seen this coming. We asked a few questions about the case and how this would now work, but not even the barrister could answer the questions at this point. It seemed Halliwell had caused some commotion in the legal system by insisting on representing himself.

We were also told there would be a pre-trial hearing set for two months' time in July 2016, with the trial scheduled to start in September 2016. This was now something tangible for me to hang on to. Suddenly, after years of waiting, things seemed to be moving fast. We had a date for the trial, at last!

We spent the summer in an odd kind of limbo. There was a strange sense of anticipation, of waiting for something that we had wanted for so long to come to fruition, but was still not within grasp. I continued to grapple with my emotions; one minute I was elated by the turn of events, the next plunged into despair at the thought of something going wrong. I was torturing myself.

Just a week or so later, we attended a further court hearing at Bristol Crown Court. This time we sat in the public gallery, which was packed with people. The proceedings were directed by Justice Openshaw, who also announced that Senior Judge Sir John Griffith Williams had been called out of retirement and would be presiding at the trial in September. Halliwell again appeared via video link from Long Lartin prison to enter his plea. He pleaded not guilty to Becky's murder and confirmed he would be representing himself. Judge Openshaw addressed the court: 'If he needs access to law books, everything should be done to ensure that he can properly prepare for his defence.' The court was told that steps would be taken to ensure that Halliwell was provided with a table and papers in the dock, from where he could cross-examine witnesses. It took all of 20 minutes. I took to the internet again; I wanted to see who the judge was, I needed to see if he was competent. I discovered that he had been the judge in the trial of Mark Bridger for the abduction and murder of five-year-old April Jones.

At every turn and with every passing day, I expected to hear that something had gone wrong to prevent us reaching the trial in September. I guess I was trying to manage my expectations, trying to manage my disappointment, should this happen. This was the state of mind I had come to after so many years of this. I couldn't allow myself to believe we might nearly be there.

A further pre-trial hearing at Bristol Crown Court went head on 21 July 2016. It was reported in the news, but with no specific detail, just that it had occurred. But what happened in that hearing was extraordinary. In the run-up to it, Wiltshire Police had been busy sending out emails to witnesses to attend. These witnesses included ex-DSupt Steve Fulcher and his former PA, Debbie Peach.

I knew that Steve Fulcher was now working in Mogadishu, Somalia, as I stayed in touch with his wife, Yvonne. We spoke on the phone and Skyped one another regularly. Steve hadn't been able to find work in this country; despite being extremely capable, as soon as he applied for a job, prospective employers googled him and immediately found the IPCC misconduct report. The IPCC had insisted on it remaining on their website, despite some of the charges contained in it having been withdrawn or reworded at the misconduct hearing. The report contained no context to the charges, there was nothing in there to explain the investigation, or the fact that I was extremely happy with the actions he had taken. It was damning and it made my blood boil. So Steve had had to find work abroad, in the most dangerous of places, previously having worked in Libya.

Some time ago, Yvonne had also told me that Debbie Peach no longer worked for Wiltshire Police and had resigned a month or so before Steve had. The force had instigated disciplinary proceedings against her too. However, now it seemed they were both required for the pre-trial hearing. Steve was particularly pleased about this as Deb's evidence had never been heard at the previous *voir dire*, or his conduct hearing. But it was the reason for the hearing that was extraordinary. The prosecution were going to make a case to Judge Sir John Griffith Williams for Halliwell's original confession evidence to be heard at the trial in September.

In July 2016, the hearing took place at Bristol Crown Court. Previously, in 2012, Judge Cox had determined that the confession evidence had to be precluded, as she had been persuaded it had been obtained by oppression and Steve Fulcher had breached PACE. Now, Mr Haggan, QC, faced Judge Griffith Williams and made the case for it to be included. Steve Fulcher had travelled back from Mogadishu and was in a courtroom, waiting to be called by Haggan should he be needed.

The judge listened to Mr Haggan's argument and, in the end, was able to make his ruling without Steve Fulcher being called. We were informed the judge was going to allow the confession evidence to be heard after all! No further details were given to us about the reasons why at that time, but his comments were later reported in the *Swindon Advertiser*. Judge Griffith Williams had said that while he agreed with Judge Cox's ruling on the confession to the murder of Sian O'Callaghan, he stated the effects of oppression ended with the confession of Sian's murder:

Once the defendant had confessed and taken the police to the location where he had disposed of the body of Sian O'Callaghan, his questioning was at an end. There were no other matters to investigate, and the defendant was told he would be arrested for murder, taken to the police station and that he would be given his rights.

The defendant, who was not vulnerable, in fact knew his rights – he had earlier been cautioned and knew he would consult with a solicitor once at the police station. Importantly, the police and Detective Superintendent Fulcher knew nothing of the disappearance of Becky Godden. I am not persuaded that what the defendant then said may not have been said voluntarily. It follows that I am satisfied that the prosecution has discharged the burden of proving to the criminal standard of proof that what the defendant said by way of a confession to the murder of Becky Godden was said voluntarily.

I am satisfied also that the defendant's confession to the murder of Becky Godden and his taking police to where he had buried her was not the consequence of oppression. I am satisfied also that, notwithstanding the breaches of the Code of Practice, that the evidence is admissible in the exercise of my discretion as direct evidence of his guilt. I am satisfied that the evidence of the conviction of the defendant of the murder of Sian O'Callaghan is admissible to prove the defendant's propensity to commit murder.

He went on. He said that the fact that Halliwell had pleaded guilty 'unequivocally' to murdering Sian meant the protections of PACE and the Codes of Practice were 'no longer relevant': 'It would offend good sense to exclude the evidence . . .'

We didn't hear these comments at the time, but the fact that he was going to allow the confession evidence to be heard was significant enough. It was an extraordinary turn of events, a complete turnaround from the previous judge's ruling, who had said Halliwell's confession evidence could not be used for Becky's murder trial.

We felt huge relief, but it also left us wondering why an appeal hadn't been launched into Judge Cox's decision back in 2012. We knew that the petitioning had made a difference, by putting the pressure on police to continue with the investigation, but if it hadn't been for Judge Cox's ruling, would we have needed to spend years fighting for justice, campaigning and running around to various court appearances? We had done all this at a time when we should have been grieving for Becky. It too meant that Steve Fulcher would not have been complained about or faced a disciplinary hearing. It was a bittersweet moment, but we were so very glad of it.

As the weeks went by, I continued to struggle. I was finding the situation extremely stressful. My homicide counsellor, Audrey, came round (Rosemary had since left) and talked things through in an attempt to allay my fears. Although we'd been given the good news about the confession evidence, things were going from bad to worse. I was having an increasing amount of panic attacks and I was starting to pass out.

Even though the case seemed to be going to plan, I could not escape the feeling of dread that kept trying to overwhelm me. I couldn't seem to stop myself from contemplating the worst. What if something happened to ruin things? We *had* been here before. What if we got all the way to the trial and Halliwell was found not guilty? Where could I go then? Who would listen to me if that happened?

I was having difficulty sleeping. In the endeavour to stay busy at all times to take my mind off things, I was in overdrive most of the time. And it failed; keeping busy didn't take my mind off things. Still the thoughts crept in, worming their way down, flicking the emotional switches. I couldn't control my thoughts and this was having a physiological affect. My heart raced, beating in my ears, the panic attacks, the passing out, I couldn't eat and mostly I felt like screaming. By now I felt physically and emotionally exhausted.

Charlie made me an emergency appointment with the doctor and could only get a locum at such short notice. I spent 20 minutes outlining what was going on; she was lovely and we both ended up in tears. She made some checks, which included taking my blood pressure; it was very low, which accounted for passing out. She ordered me to rest and take care of myself. I knew she was right, I had to take care of myself to get me through the court case. If I wasn't careful, I wouldn't be fit enough to attend. After all this time, all the fighting, there was a danger I could miss the trial entirely. The doctor prescribed me some medication. It would help.

From going into overdrive, I was now tired and wanting to

sleep a lot. I would get up, make Charlie some breakfast and then go back to bed. Mum told me to listen to what my body wanted, and if it said sleep, then give in, go to sleep. So I did. There were days I spent drifting in and out of sleep all day. One day I didn't even bother to get dressed, staying in my dressing gown. We were creeping through August, getting ever closer to the trial.

Our FLO, Mary, informed us that we wouldn't be called as witnesses, which was a relief, as it meant that we could follow the whole trial from the courtroom. But as the day arrived for the start of the trial and we set off for Bristol, I was feeling terrified and suddenly I didn't want to go into court. I was a bag of nerves. I still thought the rug would be pulled from under us. I was terrified that something, somewhere, would go wrong, even at this stage. We'd been to too many court hearings and been pulled aside into too many rooms for me not to be nervous being there.

It was as if I was wired. All the time we were in the court, I was looking about me for anything, any nuance in conversations, any gesture or look between the police and barristers that would alert me to something that might be going wrong. Any time someone approached us my stomach lurched, thinking that it was to take us off to a family room to tell us something wasn't going right.

And there was something else I'd been considering. I was about to be in close proximity to Halliwell for the first time, breathing the same air as him. For days I'd be looking at the monster who had murdered Becky. I didn't know if I could do it. I already knew too much. I didn't know how seeing him and being in the same room as him was going to affect me. This was what I wanted after all, to get him back into court; this was what all the petitioning had been about.

Well, now we were here. I had got what I wanted and now I had to face him in court. My nerves were in shreds, but somehow I had to find something from somewhere inside me to get myself through this.

15

THE TRIAL

Each juror was called in turn and then had to speak to the judge. I was surprised to see it going to these lengths. Did it mean some might not be up to the job? I was totally on edge. Eventually, 12 were selected, six men and six women. As I looked at them, I couldn't help but make my own personal assumptions. Too young, too old? Were they capable of making a decision about my daughter's murderer? On top of everything else, I was fighting the grip of fierce paranoia.

The first couple of days dealt with the administrative processes and swearing in the jury, then the third day was the start of the trial proper. The whole family were with us; Steven, Kelly, Mum, Tracey and Tony, the rest of our family and friends. John and his family were there too of course. It had taken us five long years to get to this point. Again, the now familiar leaden feeling of dread had settled on me. I was sick to my stomach; as much as I wanted this to happen, I now found myself wishing my life away to the end of the trial, to get it over with. After the fight to get here, I felt I had nothing left to get me through the days ahead. My emotions were in turmoil.

I took some comfort from the heavy police presence in and around the court. The place felt as if it were in lockdown. This was due to the fact that years ago Halliwell had escaped from a court. I was pleased to see they were taking no chances. We sat in the courtroom and watched as everyone took their place. There was a respectful, low murmur in deference to the court. The public gallery filled up, the jurors came in and the usher asked the court to rise for the attendance of the judge.

Halliwell was standing behind strengthened glass with his security officers. There was now silence in the room and I held my breath. Charlie and I stole a look at one another. We'd actually made it. We were here at last. With the police presence, the judge, barristers, the jury, the court ushers, the journalists, the public gallery – the place was packed to capacity. There was no room to spare. I wasn't prepared for the confined space of the courtroom. It was oppressive. I felt an overwhelming sense of being trapped in there with Halliwell, just a few feet away. He was way too close for comfort. Furthermore, despite all the people crammed in, the room itself was unexpectedly very cold.

Judge Griffith Williams addressed the jury. He told them that Halliwell would not be represented by a barrister, but would be representing himself. He directed the jury not to speculate on the reason why.

'It has no bearing on the issue of his guilt or innocence. You will give his case the same careful consideration as if it had been advanced by counsel.'

Mr Haggan addressed the jury in the hushed courtroom and made the case for the prosecution.

What happened to Rebecca? We, the prosecution, say the short answer to that question is that she was murdered. Her naked body was buried in a clandestine grave in a field which might be described as in the middle of nowhere. You might conclude it was plain Rebecca was murdered. But secondly, this defendant, Christopher Halliwell, confessed to Police that between 2003 and 2005 – he couldn't be sure of the date – he had taken a girl from the streets of Swindon.

He told police he had sex with her and then he killed her by strangling her. He told police he stripped the girl of her clothes and concealed her naked body. Not only that but he took police to the location. Had the defendant not told police where he had buried that girl from the streets of Swindon, you might think that Rebecca's remains to this day would be in that field in the middle of nowhere.

There. It was out. At last. Halliwell's confession had been delivered to the jury. It was a dramatic moment, delivered with the air of the confident, experienced barrister that Haggan clearly was. He went on to tell the jury that the last reliable sighting of Becky had been on 3 January 2003, in Swindon town centre, when she had been seen getting into the back of a taxi.

After that, nothing more was heard from her. She made no contact with her family; she made no contact with any of the government and other agencies and financial institutions. She quite literally disappeared. She was just twenty years old.

What happened to Sian? She too was murdered. Her semi-naked body was found a few days after she disappeared. It was concealed by undergrowth, in a remote location, not a great distance from the field where Rebecca's body had been buried. What relevance is that you might think? The short answer is that this young woman was murdered by this defendant, Christopher Halliwell. How do we know that? Because he pleaded guilty to Sian's murder and is currently serving a life term of imprisonment for that offence.

Halliwell had made a short defence statement. The judge had decreed that he wear no handcuffs. Despite being behind the strengthened glass, in the confines of the court, he was just feet away from us. My stomach turned to see him.

'I Christopher John Halliwell will be pleading not guilty to the charge of murder of Rebecca Godden-Edwards. I have no knowledge of the manner of her death, nor any information regarding details of how she died.'

He was dressed in a grey suit, white shirt and blue tie and cut a very sorry-looking figure, very much like someone who no longer felt the sun, who was no longer free. It was no more than he deserved. Because he was defending himself, the judge had to ensure he had the requisite documentation he would need. It quickly became clear Halliwell was completely out of his depth as he struggled to keep up with the pace of proceedings. As a result, progress was slow. Very soon, the day was over; court was adjourned until the next day.

Each morning in the court, before proceedings began, the

judge would ask Halliwell if he had had a good night's sleep and if he had had breakfast.

'I haven't had a good breakfast,' my mum murmured, 'I feel too sick to eat. Why doesn't he ask me?'

I don't think any of us were functioning properly. All the family were attending every day, and despite the comfort of having everyone there it was a huge strain. We had been through so much to reach this point and now we were here, it was a whole new ordeal to be navigated. I felt overwhelmed by it all. I'd attended enough courts over the years to have become familiar with the environment we were in. Even so, this was different. All the pent-up frustration and emotion of having to fight to get here had reached tipping point. Just a few days in, my nerves were raw. I was a mess of tears and I was struggling to keep control of myself.

In this state, I sat and watched as a steady stream of witnesses gave their evidence. Things progressed slowly so that Halliwell was able to follow, both the judge and prosecuting counsel regularly checking to make sure Halliwell understood the implications of what he was saying and doing. But even now he was capable of cruelty. He had called as a witness his ex-partner. She was clearly terrified at being there, facing him, so much so that she requested to give her evidence behind the protection of a screen, so she could be shielded from him. We were witness to her fear as we watched a court usher erect the screen; her hand was hardly able to hold a cup of water. Then, having caused her so much distress, Halliwell refused to ask her any questions, as he said he could sense she was upset. He had put her through all that anguish for nothing.

The court listened to Miss X, whose identity was being protected. She was a friend of Becky's and a fellow sex worker. Mr Haggan took her through her evidence. In contrast, she wasn't the least bit cowed being in the presence of Halliwell.

She told the court that she knew Halliwell, as they had had sex twice. She said she often saw his car parked near the red-light district of Swindon, where she and Becky worked, and said how he used to ferry girls to their dealers. She spoke of going into Halliwell's flat and seeing a laptop open on a page showing Thai brides. She said that after that encounter with him she had mistakenly put on his trousers before leaving. She said that Halliwell knew Becky as he had had sex with her and was a regular client of hers. Furthermore, Becky was concerned he was becoming possessive of her. She said Halliwell had paid Becky not to work. In response, Halliwell denied knowing her or Becky.

'Take a good hard look at me,' he said to her, 'to confirm the person you are thinking about is me.'

'It's definitely you.'

'I've never seen this person before in my life,' he declared. 'It's a fairytale.'

'I don't know how he can sit there and say he doesn't know me. I am a hundred, million per cent sure.'

'What colour are my eyes if you know me?' he asked her. 'What colour are my eyes?'

'What colour were Becky's eyes, Chris? What colour were they?' she retorted. The court gasped and Mum squeezed my hand as I sobbed into a handkerchief.

We heard from another sex worker who knew Becky, again

only identified as Miss Y to protect her. Then Mr Haggan read out a statement from a police officer. He gave evidence to the effect that his local beat area was in the Manchester Road, Swindon. He knew Becky by sight, although he also knew her by the name of Lyndsey, one of the many aliases she used. He said he last saw her at 22.25 hours on 27 December 2002 and had made a note of it. He never saw her again.

The court was told of the other names Becky assumed in her career as a street worker; Louise Edwards, Louise Godden, Rebecca Edwards, Crystal. A list of agencies had been contacted to see if they had seen any trace of or had any contact with anyone by these names. This was for proof of life. They found none after January 2003.

Over the years, I hadn't spent much time contemplating Becky's street life. I'd chosen to ignore it for the most part. While I knew she was a sex worker, it didn't seem to sit with the lovely girl I knew her to be and I found it difficult to imagine her doing this. I'd shut it out. For some reason, I could deal with Becky the heroin user. But Becky the sex worker? She had been well brought up; I'd made sure she didn't want for anything. That had been my goal. But, ultimately, all the love in the world hadn't prevented Becky from taking drugs and selling herself.

Years later, I learnt how the seed of the idea to earn money in this way had been planted. Becky's 'friend' from Stratton Education, Holly, prostituted herself while at school and, back then, had sought to introduce Becky to doing it as a way of picking up easy money. At the time, Becky was shocked and disgusted at the suggestion. As she became dependent on drugs, however, it became a fast and endless stream of money to fund her lifestyle. It was part and parcel of that world. I just couldn't fathom how she could do it to herself. And yet there she was, my lovely, bright girl being openly described as a sex worker. It didn't make sense to me. I did though, remember how much heroin she got through and how much it cost. She must have been so desperate for drugs that it took her beyond caring what she did to herself. Charlie must have read my thoughts; he squeezed my hand as I sobbed into a handkerchief. It's alright, he was telling me, nothing can harm her now.

Each day when the trial adjourned, we shuffled back to the hotel. Each night we discussed what we thought of the day's proceedings. I could hardly believe what we were witnessing. We had waited for so long. Things seemed to be going at a fast pace but the anxiety remained.

The next day, before we went into the court, I was pulled aside by DSupt Sean Memory. My emotions continued to surface, as I could not contain my tears. I was warned that if I didn't get a grip on myself, I would no longer be allowed to sit in the court-room. Sean knew I wanted to be there, but this was no place for emotion, just cold, hard facts. It didn't matter that this had been a tortuous journey, or that it was my lovely daughter that had been murdered, or that I had to face her murderer every day. No, my wretched sobs had no place here. I had to keep a lid on it or go. I'd have to do my best. I was determined not to give Halliwell the satisfaction of seeing me excluded from the court.

Once in court, we heard evidence from another friend of Becky's, a woman called Rebecca Boast. She told the jurors that she knew Becky from Destiny and Desire nightclub in Swindon. On 3 January 2003, they were at the club and had a cigarette outside. A taxi pulled up and Becky went over to it, leaning in the window. She said Becky was speaking to the driver and then walked back to her and her boyfriend. She recalled Becky going back to the taxi and appearing to row with the driver. Becky was yelling, she said, and then went back into the nightclub, but seemed stressed and after a short while said she was leaving. Rebecca described how Becky got into the rear of the taxi and it drove away. She never saw Becky again.

Further evidence was given that Halliwell's car had run out of fuel at 05.25 on 3 January 2003 and he had been forced to call the RAC. Their records confirmed this. The location of where this had occurred made it significant. Halliwell had run out of fuel at Inglesham. It was not far from Eastleach and the field where Becky had been buried. Everything was pointing towards Halliwell having taken Becky on 3 January 2003.

The jury then heard the statement from Halliwell's GP, who had notes regarding him arriving for an appointment at 16.25 on 3 January 2003. Halliwell had attended the surgery as he said he had been attacked by a man in his taxi. The GP explained:

'He said that a man started to attack his car and then a fight ensued between them. I believe he had a fracture to his hand but I didn't do an X-ray. I simply strapped it up. I also noted that Mr Halliwell had scratches to his face; I thought they were consistent with a fight. I can remember that Mr Halliwell was emotionally distressed and upset while telling me about what happened to him.'

Of course, we already knew this information but now, here in the court, it was so upsetting to listen to. I was in absolutely no doubt that the scratches the doctor described would have been put there by Becky, who would have fought like a wildcat if she thought she was in danger. Becky had fought Halliwell so hard that she caused him injuries which had needed medical assistance. She had hurt him, broken his finger, scratched his face with her nails. I tried to stop the images coming into my mind. Now, all these years later, her fight for life was being used in evidence against him and would help to seal his fate. There was a crumb of comfort in that. I was glad she'd hurt him. God knows *I* wanted to hurt him now.

We were back in court the next morning. Each day, we took turns with John and his family in sitting at the front of a row of benches to watch proceedings unfold. It was the police's way of not favouring either of us. Today, John and his family sat at the back as we took up our positions at the front. I had mixed feelings about this as there were times when Halliwell was only a few feet away from us. It sickened me to see him unrestrained. As we listened to some of the more harrowing detail, the urge to lunge at the glass screen that he stood behind was overwhelming. I didn't think I could actually hate anybody, but what I felt towards him was pure hatred.

Today, it was the turn of Steve Fulcher to give his evidence. He had come back from Mogadishu and once again he faced Halliwell across a courtroom. It was extraordinary to think they had first faced each other at Barbury Castle five years ago. More so that at last, five long years later, the confession Halliwell gave

Steve Fulcher near the Uffington White Horse could now be heard. The atmosphere was electric. Steve Fulcher told the court of his encounter with Halliwell, when he had confessed to the murder of Sian O'Callaghan, with him taking officers to where he had left her. Then the question from Halliwell, 'Do you want another one?', which led to another confession of murder and the discovery of Becky.

Halliwell tried to take issue with various points of his evidence, one of these being the depth of Becky's grave. Steve Fulcher maintained Halliwell had told him Becky was buried in a five-foot grave, whereas the grave Becky was found in was actually quite shallow. Moreover, said Halliwell, the ground was difficult to dig.

'It wasn't five foot deep was it?' Halliwell put to Steve Fulcher.

'No, it wasn't, but that's what you told me at the time.'

'You know from your enquiries that I spent most of my time as a groundworker or building. So in that capacity I knew the difference between a five-foot hole and a six-inch hole. Shouldn't it stand out?'

'It does. What this indicates to me,' Steve Fulcher said as Halliwell tried to imply he was lying about their exchange, 'is that you were confused about the nature of this deposition. You couldn't recall whether you had murdered Becky in 2003, 2004 or 2005. That tells me that you didn't recall it correctly and somewhere there is another grave, five foot in depth, that contains another victim.'

Halliwell didn't like that. It caught him off guard. To end their exchange, Halliwell started to talk in riddles, saying that when it was his turn to speak, everyone would find out what the truth was. The reference to a further victim knocked him back. As a parting shot, Halliwell told Steve Fulcher that it had been a pleasure ruining his career. Everyone took a sharp intake of breath.

The court adjourned for lunch. In the afternoon, the court heard evidence from a man who had seen Halliwell and Becky together at a pub in Eastleach. He said he had had to intervene when he witnessed Halliwell become aggressive towards her and throw a drink over her.

Then there was a statement from Dr Ali, a police surgeon. Dr Ali had been called in to examine Halliwell and assess whether he was fit for detention at the police station when he was initially arrested for the murders of Sian O'Callaghan and Becky back in March 2011. During the time he was being examined, Dr Ali and Halliwell had a conversation. The doctor had asked him what he was there for and Halliwell told him he had killed two people. This, of course, followed Halliwell's confession to DSupt Fulcher, so Halliwell had continued to want to unburden himself. After Halliwell made his protestations regarding Dr Ali's statement, it was time to adjourn for another day.

Before we could go back to the hotel, we were pulled aside into a family room by our FLO. She had a brown envelope in her hand.

'Have you ever seen a picture of Becky's grave?' she asked.

'No.' I hadn't even thought to ask if such a thing existed.

'I have a photograph of it here. The jury will be shown this in the morning. Do you want to see it now? I'll understand if you don't want to, but I'd rather you see it than catch a glimpse of it for the first time tomorrow in the courtroom.'

I took a breath. I wasn't expecting this. I looked at Charlie. 'It's up to you,' he said, knowing already what effect it would have on me. I didn't know what to do. I was struggling to keep my emotions in check as it was.

'Give me this evening to think about it, I'll let you know in the morning.' I had to give myself time to prepare for what I would see. We left for the hotel. Charlie and I spoke about it all evening. I was undecided, but then I had to know, didn't I? I couldn't sleep as I turned this over all through the night. In the morning, we met the FLO again. We went into the family room and she took the brown envelope out of her briefcase. She slid the photograph out upside down.

'Are you absolutely sure you want to see it?'

'Yes.' I was sure this time.

She turned the photograph over. It was then I saw Becky's remains as they had been found in the shallow grave at Eastleach. There was her skeleton lying straight in her grave, minus her head. It was shocking to see this, even though I already knew her head was missing. Her arms including her hands were also missing, as were her feet. At the same time, I was given an A4 sheet of paper which had a skeleton printed on it. It was coloured in, mainly in green, but there were different colours too. The colours, it was explained, denoted what parts of Becky's skeleton had been found and when.

'This is the first time I've seen this,' was all I could say as I looked at the photograph. My mind was spinning as I looked at the image of an incomplete skeleton. This was my Becky. Why hadn't I been shown this at the time I asked how Becky had been found, back in 2011? Why hadn't I been given this at the time of her burial? Why hadn't I been shown this for the inquest? Here we were at court; I now had to go in and come into close proximity with the monster who had dug and put Becky in this grave. Furthermore, it appeared to be confirmation of what I'd feared a while ago; there were still parts of Becky's remains in the field and with the police. As we went into the courtroom, I carried the images of Becky's grave in my mind. I watched proceedings through the blur of unshed tears, trying to keep myself under control.

Once things were under way, the jury were directed to a pack in front of them, containing the photo I had just been shown. We then heard from a forensic archaeologist, Professor John Hunter. He described how Becky's remains had been found in a grave that had been dug some 35–40 centimetres from the surface and confirmed that, when found, Becky's skull, arms and feet were missing. There could, he said, be four possible reasons for this. They could have been removed prior to burial; however, he confirmed there was no evidence to suggest this had happened. Secondly, it may have been caused by animal scavenging, but in his opinion, it would be unusual for animal scavenging to be so selective and take just the head and arms. The third possibility was that the body had been disturbed by plough damage, but he would have expected to find missing components within the immediate vicinity given the way the field had been ploughed and there was no evidence of that.

Lastly, that the body had been revisited and these body parts had been removed at a later date.

I recalled being told years ago they didn't know why Becky's remains weren't intact. They'd speculated then as to the possible reasons. They told me that Halliwell said he had revisited the field in 2008; was this when he took her head and arms? Or had he revisited earlier? There was more. In a statement read to the court, a consultant pathologist said that between 50 and 75 per cent of Becky's skeleton had been recovered. Four of her teeth had also been recovered from her chest cavity, suggesting that her head had been intact at some point, then removed. The detail was absolutely harrowing to listen to.

As I spoke about all this detail with Charlie back at the hotel later, something occurred to me as I recalled the photograph of her remains. Her arms were missing when she'd been found, including her hands. Yesterday, we had heard about the scratches to Halliwell's face. I remembered reading that Halliwell was forensically aware; he had removed and burnt his seat covers when he had murdered Sian. If Becky had indeed scratched his face, then his skin, his DNA, would have been under her fingernails. Was this why her arms and hands were missing? I couldn't wait for it all to be over. I hadn't factored in having to hear such grim detail. It was too much. But I felt determined to see it through now we had come through the worst.

The next day, forensic evidence was heard in relation to the spade seized as an exhibit from Halliwell's shed. The spade was brought into the court. I knew of its existence of course, it had been talked about for so long, but it was quite another thing to see it for myself. To think that it had been used to dig Becky's grave was absolutely chilling. The large spade was wrapped in a thick clear plastic bag with a tag attached to it. It was brought into court by a woman who was showing it to the jury and the court.

'Oh my god!' My mum was taken unawares. 'Is that the spade that he used to dig Becky's grave?' She put her head in her hands to shield her eyes from it. 'Oh my god.'

'It's alright, Mum.' I put my arm around her but I knew exactly how she was feeling.

Professor Lorna Dawson was called to give evidence on the forensic analysis that had taken place on the spade. They had conducted analysis on the soil in the field through a complicated and lengthy process which she explained in great detail. She informed the court that soil found on the blade of the spade matched that found in the field where Becky had been found.

'The chance of finding such similarities of soils from other samples from elsewhere is negligible,' Professor Dawson said. She described the soil as 'sticky' and said it would 'adhere to something that it came into contact with'. The court heard the texture, colour, alkanes, alcohol content, organic matter and mineralogy had been compared with over 500 other soil samples, linking it to Becky's grave quite categorically. The farmer had been able to confirm the field hadn't been ploughed since 2003. This is what had helped give the soil its unique nature.

Professor Dawson went on to explain further evidence relating to soil found on black tape on the handle of the spade. It matched that of the field. It was a stunning denouement; Halliwell's spade, found in his shed, was linked directly with the field at Eastleach through the soil left on it. The spade had indeed proved to be an incendiary piece of evidence. A piece of silver gaffer tape had also been found in Becky's grave which she was also able to prove, through soil analysis, had not come from anywhere else.

Halliwell's response was limp. He asked Professor Dawson whether the spade found in his shed would be able to dig a grave in the field. The professor replied:

'I didn't measure the penetration resistance of the soil in that field so I cannot comment on the particular strength of the tools.'

'I can assure you that they are not,' Halliwell replied. 'I have worked on over 200 properties in that area. Those shovels aren't capable of going anywhere close to getting through that field. I've seen thirty-six-tonne excavators break their teeth trying to get through the limestone.'

All he had served to demonstrate was why Becky's grave was so shallow. I recalled the evidence of the forensic archaeologist yesterday. It was looking highly likely that Halliwell had revisited her grave. Like taking her hands, had Halliwell taken Becky's head in an attempt to prevent her being identified through dental records in the future? Or was there another reason? These thoughts floated around my mind, as the vile, evil beast who knew all the answers to these questions stood feet away from me.

Police officers gave evidence from an interview they had undertaken with Halliwell when he had been arrested for Becky's murder in 2015. They informed the jury how Halliwell had told them that in 1998, while he was still a groundworker, in order to earn extra money he became a taxi driver at weekends. He explained that he had worked as both a hackney and private hire driver. The first taxi firm he worked for had offices in Manchester Road.

He'd described having one-night stands with women, as well as using sex workers, at the time of his marriage and while in his other relationships, admitting he didn't remember the names of any of them. He denied knowing Becky. When asked if he knew the area of Eastleach, Halliwell explained that he did as he went there on 'probably hundreds or dozens' of occasions when he'd worked on a house refurb there for about six months. He couldn't be exactly sure but it may have been 1996. He also said he'd visited Eastleach as a taxi driver. It was clear from this that he knew the area well. A statement was read out from Halliwell's sister. She said her brother had a dark side and displayed a 'disturbing aura'. She said after he was born in Swindon, his parents had split up and he had been brought up in Scotland by his mother and stepfather. He had been subject to beatings with a leather strap, showing no emotion when this occurred. She also said that he was 'not a normal child'. He 'used to enjoy trapping spiders and butterflies and taking his time to pull off their legs and wings one by one. It was like a hobby to him. He lived in a strange world of his own.' She described him as 'a very cold, detached person who could never handle normal relationships'.

She'd said, 'If you ever had a go at him he would just stare you out with those vile eyes and say nothing.' His mother placed him into foster care when he was 15 as she could no longer cope with him. She said he had showed virtually no emotion when he was handed over, simply telling his mother how much he hated her and how he would get her back for what she had done.

The court also heard that during the search for Sian O'Callaghan in Savernake Forest Halliwell had commented to his taxi colleagues, 'Who knows what or who you might find buried out there. There could be loads of people over the years.' I thought of all the other women missing from Swindon, further afield. Was this Halliwell giving a cryptic clue as to how prolific his crimes were?

The evidence against him was mounting. Listening to it all was exhausting. We were, after all, just sitting there, but the sheer effort of hearing what each witness said, then the input of the prosecuting counsel and watching Halliwell conduct a cross-examination, was draining. Every now and then I would take a peep at the jury; what were they thinking? With every passing day, Halliwell looked more dishevelled and agitated. The suit had been discarded, along with his tie. His short-sleeved shirt was now hanging outside his trousers.

Eventually, Halliwell took the stand himself. He had had years to prepare a response, to tell everyone why he was not guilty of Becky's murder. What he came up with was almost laughable. Mr Haggan let him ramble on, but it was shambolic. I felt nothing but pure hatred for him as I watched him. He was pathetic.

'I want to start by saying I am telling the truth. I have no reason to lie. Getting life anyway and I have no real prospect of getting out. I deserve every day that I got . . . my actions were brutal. What I put Sian's family through was inhumane.'

Halliwell started to talk of the night he picked Sian up near the nightclub she had left to walk home. He described a version of events of what happened when she realised Halliwell was driving her away from the direction she wanted to go. Halliwell made out that Sian attacked him and he'd retaliated, injuring her in self-defence. I thought of Elaine O'Callaghan. Halliwell continued:

'Whether I get out or not is irrelevant. Whether you, the jury, find me guilty or not guilty it doesn't matter.'

Halliwell then went on to outline his working life. He told the jury that he was a construction worker, working mainly in London, when he bought a house in Ashbury Avenue, Swindon. Prior to this, he said, from around 1989 to 1998, he had lived in the red-light area in Swindon. He then started working as a part-time taxi driver. He gave up construction work for full-time taxi driving and chauffeuring. However, in 2009 he went bankrupt. After this, he worked for taxi firms, rather than himself.

He then gave a bizarre speech about how he didn't care that DSupt Fulcher hadn't cautioned him, or not taken him to the police station after their meeting at Barbury Castle. He said he deliberately told him about the site of Becky's body, not knowing it was her, but wanting to use the occasion to delay going into custody. This, he said, was because he knew he would cause DSupt Fulcher difficulties if he did so. He acted as he did, he said, as a form of revenge on DSupt Fulcher for threatening his family. He offered no further explanation than this.

The crux of his defence was that he had been paid by two drug dealers from Swindon to take them in his taxi out into the countryside. They had a large sports bag with them, which was put in the boot of the taxi. He drove them out to Eastleach. Once there, they took the bag and told him to return an hour later, paying him £700 to keep quiet about it. They went into the field and he returned to pick them up.

He thought they had drugs or guns in the bag. Then one of them later told him they had buried a prostitute from Swindon. So, according to Halliwell, it was the two men who buried Becky in the field. When he took DSupt Fulcher there, it was because he thought there might be a body there. He didn't *know* she was there. He acknowledged he had told police he had had sex with a prostitute, strangled her, stripped off her clothes, left her body in a field and dug a grave. This, he said, was merely 'an account'. But when Haggan asked him if he'd murdered Becky, he replied, 'No, I didn't.' It was utterly ridiculous.

When Haggan questioned him as to what the names of the drug dealers were, he said he couldn't divulge them for fear of reprisals against him and his family. Quite rightly, Haggan dismissed this as fantasy. It was a pretty lame defence considering that Halliwell had had so much time to come up with something.

Mr Haggan took him piece by tiny piece through all the witness evidence. Why, he asked, hadn't Halliwell reported to the police the assault on him that necessitated treatment for his broken finger on 3 January 2003? After all, he had done so on nineteen previous occasions when he had been assaulted by customers. Halliwell had no answer.

Miss X, Miss Y and Becky's friend were absolutely sure in their identification of Halliwell, despite him denying knowledge of them or Becky. But there were also times when Haggan had

Halliwell totally confused as to what he was saying. Halliwell didn't know whether he was coming or going.

It was Thursday and the judge deemed that summing up would now occur on Friday. We met everyone in the family room and exchanged a few encouraging words. We had at least reached the end of the trial. There were times when I thought we would never get here and yet tomorrow we would be in the hands of the jury.

We went back to the hotel for the evening. We were like zombies. The trial had felt like months and yet it had been only days. I could not eat. I lay awake that night, only drifting off for two hours, waking with a start. This was the day I'd waited years for. Lying in the darkness, I tried to envisage what the day would bring. Dare I hope that Halliwell would at last be convicted for Becky's murder? It was out of our hands now. But then, it always had been.

16

THE VERDICT

As we sat in the courtroom the next morning I felt as if I was in a daze. The lights were on but there was no one at home as far as my head was concerned. All our family were there that day. No one wanted to miss anything. Haggan did his summing up to the jury, as did Halliwell, rubbishing all of what had been heard and presented in court. They retired to consider their verdict.

We had been listening for nine days now and it was over. There was nothing more to be done except wait for the twelve jurors to return. The atmosphere was again electric with anticipation. We didn't know how long we would have to wait. We adjourned to the family room. All Charlie and I could do was look at each other. This had been such a long and complicated journey and now it was almost over. There was no knowing how long we might have to spend waiting; some juries stayed out for days, deliberating.

My head was banging with a fierce pulse. I didn't know if it was my heart I could hear through my ears or something else. My stomach churned. I took a diazepam to calm myself. The last thing I wanted was to miss this if I fainted. After just three hours, we were told the jury had a verdict. So soon! What could we read into this? Was this a good sign? Bad? What was the form on how long or short a time they stayed out?

My hands started to sweat and I wondered if I could put one foot in front of the other. Everything now rested on the next few minutes. We all went back into the courtroom and sat down. Again, the room was packed with people. The foreman of the jury stood up. I looked at his impassive face. The judge spoke.

'Members of the jury, have you reached a decision on which you are all agreed?'

It seemed to take an age for him to speak.

'We have.'

'How do you find the defendant?'

My eyes locked on him and I held my breath.

'Guilty of the murder of Rebecca Godden-Edwards.'

A large cheer suddenly punched through the tension in the room. After all these years, we had it, justice for Becky. Momentarily, there was triumph. The relief was incredible. My mum, who is normally as quiet as a church mouse, leapt up from her seat and threw her arms in the air.

'I hope you rot in hell,' she shouted.

My sister quickly pulled Mum back in her seat. It was completely out of character for her, but I guess she felt the need to vent her anger as much as we did. I fell into Charlie's arms. I was shaking and crying. Sitting up in the public gallery Yvonne Fulcher texted the good news to her husband, Steve, who had stayed away from court.

The judge briefly addressed Halliwell, telling him that the sentencing would be on Monday. Court was dismissed and we filed out. Around us people were huddled into groups talking; it was a strange feeling. I was elated and yet it was as if the last five years caught up with me right there and then. I'd suddenly slammed into a brick wall. Everything seemed to be moving in slow motion, all the adrenalin and tension seemed to leave my body, only to be replaced by a tiredness the like of which I hadn't felt before.

I remember walking away at that point into the arms of our family. We went a few yards down the road to the pub on the corner. Someone ordered a bottle of champagne, and before I knew it I was holding it to my lips and having a photo taken. We did it. At last we had justice for Becky. It wasn't so much a triumphant moment, more one of satisfaction. It had been a long time coming. But, despite all the fighting and now Halliwell's conviction, it didn't bring our Becky back to us.

We returned on Monday for sentencing. It had been absolutely harrowing having to sit and face my daughter's killer, to watch him walking past us, talking freely, to see him looking at me. Now back in court, Halliwell was again behind glass with prison guards beside him. He was back in handcuffs. The jury had taken their places, not wishing to miss the judge's sentencing remarks. Judge Griffith Williams addressed Halliwell:

You have been convicted by a jury of the murder of Rebecca Godden. Sadly, her young life was troubled and blighted by her drug abuse which forced her into prostitution to fund her addiction. While she had returned to the company of friends and to her life of drug taking, it remained her hope that she would one day free herself of her addiction and belatedly return to her family to live the decent life her early years had promised and of which her addiction had deprived her. When you murdered her, you deprived her of a potentially fulfilling life.

Your account of the circumstances in which she met her death bears all the hallmarks of a contrived explanation designed to avoid conviction in the hope that the minimum term you are presently serving will not be increased. But the account which you advanced so glibly with little or no regard to the truth made no sense at all.

You told Superintendent Fulcher that you had sex with an unnamed prostitute, strangled her before undressing her, you then left her body in bushes by the wall of Oxo Bottom field and returned the following night to dig the grave and bury her. I am firmly of the view that that was only partially truthful.

I have had the opportunity of observing you throughout the trial and listening to your evidence. I have no doubt that you are a self-centred and domineering individual who wants his own way. You are both calculating and devious.

Having heard the evidence, I am satisfied so as to be sure to the required criminal standard of proof of the following;

1) You knew Rebecca Godden and had known her for some time. It was not a conventional relationship. I consider it unlikely that you were besotted with her. In my

judgement your behaviour towards her was controlling. You used her for sex whenever you wanted to, taking advantage of her vulnerability as a drug addict and prostitute. She had little or no time for you.

2) In the early hours of 3rd January 2003 when she was standing outside the Destiny and Desire club with Rebecca Boast, you drove up in your taxi and summoned her. That could only have been because you wanted her to go with you for sex but she was clearly not interested. She returned to join her friend but you remained and so she went to speak to you a second time. A row developed during which she yelled at you, clear evidence that she did not want to go with you. She returned again to her friend but you did not drive off and so it was that she went to your taxi and got in to a rear seat. Rebecca Boast described her as 'huffed', that is to say annoyed and I conclude she joined you unwillingly.

3) You then drove to somewhere private, most probably to the south of Swindon and to Savernake Forest where eight years later you took Sian O'Callaghan. What then happened must be a matter of inference. I take as my starting point the evidence of your injuries when you were examined later that day by your general practitioner – a broken little finger and scratches to your face. I reject your evidence that you had been involved in a fight with a would-be passenger. I conclude you must have attacked Rebecca Godden; that attack must have been prompted by her refusing you sex. When she put up a struggle, you

273

killed her. You clearly intended to kill her. I add that I am certain she struggled desperately in an attempt to save her life but she was physically no match for you.

4) You then drove to Oxo Bottom field which you knew to be very isolated. There you had the presence of mind to remove her clothing to ensure, if her body was found, that there would be no forensic links to your taxi and to you. You returned the next night to bury her and returned again and again over the following years to make sure that her body was not visible in that shallow grave.

5) When on 24th March 2011 you realised you had no chance of avoiding detection for the murder of Sian O'Callaghan, you very briefly allowed the little conscience you have to prompt your confession to the murder of Rebecca Godden. I consider that but for that confession, there is every prospect that Rebecca Godden's remains would not have been found but such mitigation that provides is overweighed by your subsequent behaviour. Following your arrest you answered 'no comment' to all questions and you have since sought to manipulate, first the police investigation and then the court process in a futile attempt to avoid the punishment you so richly deserve.

I am satisfied that your conduct amounted to abduction. Rebecca Godden did not want to go with you and would certainly not have gone with you had she known you were prepared to rape her and to use violence if she did not do as you told her. There was clearly sexual conduct and your offending was aggravated by your concealment of the body.

Mrs Justice Cox said Sian O'Callaghan would have been terrified and panic stricken right from the moment she realised you were not going to drive her home. She was satisfied that you made extensive efforts to conceal her body and would have made more but for the police activity searching the area for her. She ignored, as I shall ignore, your previous convictions, all for offences of dishonesty and committed many years ago. She allowed a discount of five years for your guilty plea and determined the minimum term as 25 years.

I observe that you lied to the jury about the circumstances of the murder of Sian O'Callaghan just as you lied to the jury about the circumstances of the murder of Rebecca Godden. A feature of your evidence which I would have not been alone in considering disgracefully unfeeling was the contradiction in your claims that you wanted to spare the family of Sian O'Callaghan further grief and yet you did not take the police straight to her body and despite your confessions to Superintendent Fulcher, you made 'no comment' answers when you were interviewed about her murder; you then pleaded not guilty and so compounded and added to the grief of her family.

You have put the family of Rebecca Godden through similar anguish, first confessing to her murder and then answering no comment to all questions in interview. After what must have been hours of trawling through the prosecution papers, you devised a cock and bull story about two drug dealers. I cannot add to your sentence for such cynical indifference to the concerns of the families but it is clear to me that there is nothing which can mitigate your sentence.

I have considered the heartfelt evidence of Rebecca Godden's mother and father.

I am satisfied that there are real similarities between the two murders. The fact that some nine years elapsed between them probably reflects the absence of opportunities.

With the Transitional Provisions in mind, I have considered paragraph 18 of the Practice Statement under the heading 'Very Serious Cases' – 'A substantial upward adjustment may be appropriate in the most serious cases, for example, those involving a substantial number of murders or if there are several factors identified as attracting the higher starting point present. In suitable cases, the result might even be a minimum term of 30 years . . . which would offer little or no hope of the offender's eventual release. In cases of exceptional gravity, the judge, rather than setting a whole life minimum term, can state that there is no minimum period which could properly be set in that particular case'.

Applying Schedule 21 of the Criminal Justice Act 2003, I have concluded both murders involved the abduction of the victim and sexual conduct and both were aggravated by the concealment of the bodies. I am satisfied your offending is exceptionally high and satisfies the criteria for a whole life term and that the Transitional Provisions do not require me to impose a minimum term. Were I to impose a minimum term it would be of such length that you would in all probability never be released.

I sentence you to Life Imprisonment and direct there will be a whole life order.

I want to take the opportunity of saying a few words to Mrs Edwards and Mr Godden. You have had to live with every parent's nightmare of a missing child and then the discovery that she had been dead for some years, buried naked in a field. You have been deprived of the opportunity we all want, to say farewell to our closest and dearest. And then you have had to live through the criminal processes as Christopher Halliwell was brought eventually to justice. There must have been moments when you wondered whether the case would ever be completed. If I may say so, you have behaved throughout with quiet dignity and courtesy. I hope you will feel that justice has been done and that while that cannot bring Becky back, that it may at least bring you some solace.

I will include Mr and Mrs O'Callaghan because this trial must have been an ordeal for them as they had to relive the evidence of how Sian died. They too have behaved with dignity and courtesy. I pay tribute to you all.

At last. It was over, it was truly over. With a Whole Life Order Halliwell would indeed spend the rest of his miserable life in jail, which meant he would die there. But Halliwell had not quite finished. In response to the judge's remarks, he replied, 'Thank you', and as he was led from the dock, he smirked back at us, a callous act that the press were quick to pick up on.

We finally left court for the last time. We walked towards

the door and to the waiting media. I had to be ready now to face them. With Charlie standing next to me, I tearfully read the statement I had prepared over the weekend:

Today Christopher Halliwell has been found guilty of Becky's murder. We have waited over five years for this momentous day. It has been an extremely painful journey but today we have received the justice that has felt like an eternity coming for our beautiful little girl Becky.

We have all sat and listened to heartbreaking evidence day after day to enable the jury to come to their decision. We have all sat and listened hard. Firstly I would like to thank from the bottom of my heart Steve Fulcher for bringing my little girl home.

I had to pay tribute to Steve Fulcher; without his actions neither we nor the O'Callaghans would have had our precious girls back, much less justice. I continued:

I will also respect him and will be indebted to him for making that moral decision as a police officer, but he should have never have suffered the terrible consequences, loss of reputation and career for doing such a thing.

My message to any family out there who have waited so long for justice as we have is, never give up hope.

We caught up with Steve and Yvonne Fulcher, who had also attended court to see Halliwell sentenced. As Halliwell was driven back along the motorway to his prison cell, we went for lunch. It had been a long time since we'd last met Steve and we all sat around and chatted about Becky and about the long road to justice we had all been on. Looking back, it had been an extraordinary series of events.

We were exhausted. It had indeed been a long journey to reach this point, and the judge was right: there were times when I never thought we would get there, but there were never times when I thought of giving up. I would have gone on fighting for justice for Becky until my dying breath. It had been important to secure Halliwell's conviction. It took away his hold over us as a family. The need for him to confess again to Becky's murder as the only way for him to face justice was gone. He no longer held the key to justice for Becky. He had no power over us now he'd been processed by the law. And, most importantly, he could never come out.

17

REVELATIONS

In the weeks that followed the trial, my feelings of exhaustion slowly turned into a strange kind of energy. I'd been unable to relax for so long that now I didn't know how to. I thought the conviction meant it was over, but I was wrong. What followed was like being caught in the middle of a storm.

The trial had fuelled media interest in Halliwell and they were now focused on the same question that had often been at the back of my mind: how many more might he have killed? If he believed that he needed to kill three or more people to be classified as a 'serial killer', had he achieved this?

Speculation in the media grew as to how many possible victims there were. Once again, I pored over the stories behind the headlines. Halliwell's sister was convinced he would have committed more than the two murders he had been convicted for. His former partner Heather said he had once told her he had done 'horrendous' things in the past. Likewise, Steve Fulcher was informing the media that Halliwell had once indicated that there were eight victims. The newspapers reported that police had conducted searches of Halliwell's computer back in 2011 which had revealed his interest in murder, violent sex and rape. It was such a contrasting picture to his outward persona; neighbours described him as a 'normal bloke' and even 'smashing'. It was clear Halliwell was a split personality, able to put on a convincing front at home and work, while masking the fact he was a depraved killer.

Now Becky's fight for justice was over, I too had questions. What were the police doing about discovering Halliwell's previous offending history? How could the gap between Becky and Sian's murders be accounted for? Listening to the police in the press briefings that followed, they said there was nothing else to link Halliwell to further offences. They were keeping an open mind, they said, but there was no evidence. But I wasn't so sure about that. Back in 2012, the police had declared in the press that they were looking over the last thirty years of Halliwell's life to determine his offending. What had happened regarding that? I had passed on further information myself, gathered during our petitioning days, and didn't know whether this had all been followed up.

I wanted to learn all I could about the monster I'd sat listening to for days in court. There was a rash of reports from people who had known Halliwell over the years. There were further accounts of his various jobs as a window cleaner, groundworker, chauffeur. There were details about his love of fishing and his 'encyclopaedic' knowledge of waterways and ponds from his time living on a narrowboat. What struck me about Halliwell was how he had managed to normalise himself over the years. He had lived in various locations around the country, been married, had children, held down many jobs. All that time he had functioned just as anyone else might and yet we knew for certain that from 2003 he was a killer. He would have been in his late thirties by the time he murdered Becky. He had been, by then, a husband, partner, father and colleague, when all the while he was a murderer. I wondered what caused someone like him to kill women and yet be able to still live harmoniously at home?

All through his relationships there had been evidence of him using sex workers. If he killed others, is that how he'd got away with what he'd done for so long? Had he chosen women who were not readily missed, who were under the radar? In Sian, he'd picked on the wrong woman. Sian was immediately missed because she had a regular, normal life, unlike the chaotic lives of sex workers. This meant the police were on to him from the get-go; he had randomly taken Sian off the streets and had met his match in Steve Fulcher. But what about the cases of missing women in Swindon whose bodies had never been found? The enquiry into Sally Ann John, a sex worker, remained unresolved. Then there were the other missing women from the area; Sandra Brewin, aged 21, who went missing from Peatmoor, Swindon, in 1994 and Thi Hai Nguyen, aged 20, who went missing in Swindon in 2005. Another woman, Tina Pryor, had not been seen since getting into a taxi in Trowbridge in 2001.

After the trial, Wiltshire police released a recording of an interview with Halliwell in 2015 in which he was shown trying to bargain with officers when they questioned him regarding Becky's murder. He appeared to be saying that he would tell officers what they wanted to know about Becky if, in return, they would guarantee to him that they would not keep returning and asking him about any other crimes he may have committed. Not only did it demonstrate that, far from his stance in court, he *did* know Becky, but it also suggested that there were other crimes. They must have been serious crimes for them to be a concern to him, so was it a veiled acknowledgement that there were indeed other victims? I found it sickening.

Following Halliwell's conviction, it seemed I, along with Steve Fulcher, was much in demand. I had spent so long unable to voice my frustrations, constrained by police and legal protocols, and now they were no longer in place. TV and radio stations wanted to know my thoughts and feelings following such a lengthy road to justice, and after all this time I was only too happy to speak. After all this time, I had a lot to say. I found myself on *Good Morning Britain* on the sofa with Piers Morgan and Susanna Reid, on *BBC Breakfast* with Charlie Stayt and Naga Munchetty, *Channel Four News*, Radio 4 with Jenni Murray. It was a blur of activity. It seemed to me that there were so many unresolved questions still, and the idea that there could be more victims out there, undiscovered, troubled me. I couldn't bear the thought that other families might have to go through what we did: the agony of not knowing.

One of my FLOs made contact with me. She told me that Chief Constable Mike Veale wanted me to go and see him. It was strange: I hadn't seen a chief officer in Wiltshire Police during the whole five years of two murder investigations. Now I was free to speak, suddenly they wanted to meet? I could only guess that this would be an attempt to keep me quiet, stop me talking about other victims; an attempt to put a stop to all the headlines in relation to him being a serial killer that had occurred since Halliwell's conviction. I had no intention of meeting with him. It was too little, too late.

Shortly afterwards, I saw a long piece in the *Swindon Advertiser* by Chief Constable Veale in response to criticisms in which he lauded the police investigation led by DSupt Memory, saying that 'officers had worked relentlessly' and spoke in terms of thousands of statements taken and exhibits catalogued. He pointed out that the case had been the subject of an independent review by an outside force in 2015, at which time 'no concerns were raised'. There followed a long diatribe about PACE and a further reminder that Steve Fulcher had been found guilty on two counts of gross misconduct. Chief Constable Veale also said that 'there has been some suggestion in the media that there are people out there with a dossier of evidence linking Halliwell to other murders. If anyone has any information they wish to share with us to assist with the ongoing enquiry, I would encourage them to make contact with us.'

As I read it, my blood started to boil. I took the comments to be aimed at me, but I *had* passed on to the police all the information people had told me while campaigning. There was plenty that I shared with them, but never heard what they'd done with it. The police seemed to want to move on now, happy that Halliwell was locked up for good. They were saying that while they may suspect he had committed further crimes in between the times of Becky's and Sian's deaths, they had no further evidence of his offending history. But even if there wasn't clear-cut proof, why did that mean the matter shouldn't be investigated?

It had always been clear to me that Halliwell must have committed more murders than those of Becky and Sian. I had heard enough to know that he was a very dangerous individual. His use of prostitutes and internet searches revealed a disturbing attitude to women. There were numerous accounts of close calls from passengers in his taxi when he had locked the doors and gone off route. Those that knew him well – his sister and his former partners – were all convinced he had committed more murders. Steve Fulcher, whose instincts I so trusted, strongly believed there were more victims. We'd heard Halliwell allude to them himself, when he'd hinted at additional crimes and asked how many he'd need to kill to become a serial killer.

No, there was no doubt in my mind. But the police seemed to be saying that now I had justice for Becky I should go home, put the kettle on and be quiet. After all this time, how little did they know me.

The FLOs made contact a couple of weeks after the trial. We were to be 'signed off'. During the course of the two enquiries we had had five FLOs. We were very grateful for their input over the years, as there were certainly times when they went above and beyond for us. To show my appreciation I bought them both bouquets of flowers, but, even so, that didn't seem to adequately reflect how indebted we were to them. During this process, I also had returned to me a number of Becky's belongings, such as her hairbrush, lock of hair and letters that had been taken to help with the enquiry.

With the FLOs signing us off, it was natural around this time to reflect on everything. It was different now; we had the conviction, we had justice for Becky. But the more I thought about the enquiry and the length of time it had taken, the more uneasy I became. I thought back to the letter of complaint I had sent to the HMIC back in 2014, in which I had flagged evidential issues that I had then listened to in court two years down the line. A large feature of the trial had been the soil on the spade; Steve Fulcher had seen that the spade was seized on the day of Halliwell's arrest back in March 2011. The soil on the spade matching the soil at Becky's grave *was* new evidence, that much was true, as was the soil found on the tape on the handle of the spade. But why hadn't all this been established much earlier, given that the spade had been seized in March 2011?

In spring 2017, the Sally Ann John case appeared on *Crimewatch*, with officers appealing for help in the enquiry and police offering a £25,000 reward for information. There was a development; the postcard that had allegedly been sent by Sally Ann to a male friend all those years ago, saying that she was living in London, had been examined and was declared a fake. Following the appeal for help, a former housemate of Sally Ann's appeared in the national news. She said they shared a house together and she herself had come into contact with Halliwell when she was a sex worker. He had, she said, put his hands around her throat and she escaped. She said that she had left Swindon for London in 1995 and had asked Sally Ann to go with her. She stayed in Swindon. She was convinced her friend Sally Ann had been murdered by Halliwell and said he used to pay Sally Ann to stay in. This was similar to what Becky's friend had said about Halliwell, that he had paid her to stay off the streets.

Suddenly, the police started excavating gardens and garages of premises in Broad Street, another former home of Halliwell. The local and national news was buzzing, but this activity went on for ten days without any result. Once again, it fizzled into nothing. The question of what happened to Sally Ann John was still left unanswered.

Although the trial was over and Halliwell had been convicted, the Justice for Becky Facebook page continued to attract more posts. I had been inundated with messages of support, but among all those was one with quite a different message. There was a lady whose male friend had told her he had seen Halliwell talking to Claudia Lawrence. The lady said that her friend had been to the police but they weren't interested. He was saying that he saw Claudia speaking to Halliwell through an open taxi window, as she asked him if he had any change so that she could ring her dad. When Claudia Lawrence had disappeared, her phone and rucksack were also missing; her rucksack contained her chef's whites for her 6 a.m. shift as a chef in the kitchens of the local University of York, in walking distance of her home. It had therefore been assumed that she had left her home on the morning of 19 March 2009 to go on shift and never arrived.

The message shocked me. Here was a man saying he'd seen Halliwell talking to Claudia Lawrence. Furthermore, he said he'd been to police with his information and they weren't interested.

I realised that because both I and Steve Fulcher had speculated whether Halliwell was responsible for Claudia's disappearance, further witnesses might come forward. With the man having said the police weren't interested in what he had to say, I didn't know what to do with this message; nevertheless, I did pass it on to Wiltshire police and told Steve Fulcher.

On 18 June 2017, Steve Fulcher published a book, *Catching a Serial Killer*, detailing the Halliwell case and outlining the issues around PACE. I was excited for Steve and couldn't wait to read it, although it was strange seeing the story laid bare in black and white for the first time, particularly as it was written with his insight into events. I had continued to keep in touch with his wife, Yvonne, who had let me know about the book and kept me updated as to its progress to publication. It was a great achievement, being well received by the public. A documentary based on the book was also filmed for ITV in the summer of 2017. Both Charlie and I had agreed to appear in it. The writer and director came out to see us and invited us to London, where they explained what would happen. We found it an interesting process and were shown a reconstruction they had previously filmed of Steve Fulcher questioning Halliwell.

It was with some astonishment when I received an email message from Wiltshire Police a few days after Steve's book was published. It had been a while since I had had any contact with the force, particularly since going public and stating there were other potential victims of Halliwell. I could well imagine I was being dismissed as some kind of nutcase by the hierarchy there. What they wrote took me by surprise. They were asking if I had given Steve Fulcher the information I had been given while campaigning and if he had withheld it from Wiltshire Police! I actually couldn't believe what I was reading. What they were suggesting was wholly bizarre. Not least because Steve Fulcher had been suspended all the time I was campaigning and I had no contact with him then. I had only told Steve information subsequently, because he seemed to want to listen, but this was after he'd left the force.

I replied to them, telling them that I had given all the information to Wiltshire Police in the first instance, years ago. Steve had mentioned the information regarding the man seeing Halliwell talking to Claudia Lawrence in his book, but I'd certainly passed that on to police immediately. They replied, asking me if I could attend the police station and give them the information again. Of course I would, I would be only too happy to. But why had it taken the publication of Steve's book for them to be interested? Why couldn't they have acted on the information I gave them at the time?

I arranged to go to the police station. I also decided to make some phone calls to the people who had given me the information over the years. I asked them if they had ever been contacted by police and asked about the information they had given me. With the exception of Jane (who, once I told them about her, provided a very lengthy statement to police), not one of them had had any contact from them.

I went along to Marlborough police station with Charlie to meet with Detective Chief Inspector Jeremy Carter of the Major Crime Unit. When we arrived, a microphone was set up on the table. It was explained this was in readiness for a call to be made to Detective Superintendent Dai Malyn, from North Yorkshire police, who was in charge of the Claudia Lawrence case. It was a surprise, but I welcomed the chance to hear what he had to say.

DSupt Malyn was adamant that Halliwell was not in any way connected with the Claudia Lawrence case. Furthermore, he told me that Halliwell had never been to York. I asked how could they know this with such certainty; I'd been told that Halliwell worked in the north as a groundworker and that Halliwell's father had lived in Huddersfield, less than 50 miles away from York. Halliwell had demonstrated he was capable of driving across counties to deposit his victims. What about the man who said he'd seen Halliwell speaking to Claudia through his car window? Dai Malyn was dismissive; he said it wasn't Halliwell.

Once we had finished our conversation I continued to give Jeremy Carter all the information I had gathered while campaigning. This was information I had given before to others over the years. I was glad I'd done my duty and passed on what I had been told, but it felt very much as though Wiltshire Police wanted me to go away and shut up. They wanted the whole matter of Halliwell closed.

Out of the blue one day, I took a call from a journalist, Rob Murphy. He had been contacted by another ITV journalist contact of his, Christine Talbot, a crime reporter in Yorkshire. She had been following the Claudia Lawrence case and had a good relationship with Claudia's mother, Joan. Obviously, Christine was very interested in the information contained in Steve Fulcher's book and what I had told him about a man seeing Halliwell speaking to Claudia. After we spoke, Christine informed Joan Lawrence of the information that had been passed to me. On hearing this, Joan asked to meet. We arranged for her to come to Swindon. Joan had a good reason for wanting to meet me and hear what I had to say in person: North Yorkshire Police were scaling down the investigation into Claudia's disappearance. After nine years, they were no nearer to discovering what had happened to her.

When we met, she was accompanied by Christine Talbot. I warmed to Joan straight away and we had a good conversation in which I informed her of the information I had been given regarding the man seeing Claudia speaking to Halliwell. Christine was going to film us the next day for a programme for both ITV Yorkshire and Wiltshire News. I had every sympathy with Joan Lawrence. Similarly to my fight for Becky, Joan needed to keep Claudia's disappearance in the public consciousness. As in Becky's case, over the years the enquiry into Claudia's disappearance had passed through the hands of different senior investigating officers. But as time went by and Claudia remained missing, the investigation into her disappearance stalled. Joan Lawrence was continuing her fight to know what had happened to Claudia, despite years of police investigation. I felt so desperately sorry for her and her predicament as I knew only too well what she was going through.

Our meeting was publicised in the *York Press* newspaper on 6 October 2017. The next day, I was contacted by a lady in the north of England via Facebook who had seen it. She told me about a believed sighting of Halliwell in York about two weeks prior to Claudia going missing, as her daughter was walking home from the Nestlé factory after her night shift. It had been very early in the morning when her daughter saw a vehicle parked with its engine off and no lights on. She described it as an old-type Rover and not parked outside the Nestlé factory gate, but further away, as if to keep out of sight of anyone picking up a relative after their night shift. The car was parked near a bus stop. Whoever was in the car, however, was near enough to see if anyone started to walk home. She said that as her daughter left work and walked over the Nestlé bridge approaching the car, she could see a man sat inside.

As her daughter walked by the car, the man inside leant across towards the passenger side and stared at her. His movement in the car frightened her, as she believed he was either about to try and get her in the car or draw a knife, so she immediately drew out her mobile phone and pretended to speak into it. On quickly passing his car, she heard the engine start up and the car drive off. She initially thought it might turn around and come back for her. She thought it very odd that he didn't pick anyone up from the factory and that he was just parked up, watching. Fortunately, she lived very near and once she arrived home she phoned her mother, as the incident had frightened her. She described him as having the most evil stare.

Her daughter reported the incident to the police when she heard of Claudia Lawrence's disappearance. It took them a while for them to visit, but they took a statement from her back in 2009. Then, when Halliwell's face appeared in the local *York Press* following his trial for Becky's murder in 2016, her daughter rang her and said, 'I swear that's him, that's the man in the car that morning near Nestlé, he had the same face, the same piercing eyes.' She contacted the police again in December 2016 and was told by them that Halliwell wasn't in York at the time and didn't drive that make of car.

I wasn't sure what to do with this information. The lady seemed clear it was Halliwell, but would the police even look at it if I passed it on? How would I know? Having been told by Dai Malyn that Halliwell hadn't been to York, I could imagine they wouldn't take any notice of me. I felt it wasn't my place to raise this, and instead gave it to Christine Talbot, so that Joan Lawrence could discuss it with the police herself if she wished to. Subsequently, I had a letter of thanks from Joan, who was going to meet the lady and her daughter to hear the information herself. I was later told that North Yorkshire Police made contact with the daughter and took a further statement from her, but they were dismissive of her claims to have seen Halliwell where she stated. As far as I was concerned, again, I'd done all I could to bring information to the attention of the police.

But there was more. While on a train to London shortly after the trial, I received an email from another lady making contact regarding Halliwell. She told me that she believed she had been stalked by Halliwell between 1996 and 1998 in Bath, Somerset. She reported it to the police at the time and made a statement to this effect in 1999, when she said they questioned her about him in relation to the disappearance of Melanie Hall (who had last been seen in a Bath nightclub in 1996). She said when his face appeared on her mobile following the news report of conviction, she recognised him instantly. Yet again, I had been given information from a woman who had seen Halliwell's face and was convinced she had had contact with him. It was extraordinary. A common denominator was the description of Halliwell's evil stare, or piercing eyes. Again and again, his eyes were commented upon.

At the same time, I received an email from Wiltshire Police to tell me they would be making contact with my mum to ask her about the conversation she had heard on the coach all those years ago. Perhaps they were starting to listen?

But there was more to come that made me feel angry. Within months of Steve Fulcher's book being published, it was suddenly reported on the local news that the Wiltshire Police and Crime Commissioner was referring a complaint to the IPCC. The Gold Policy book that Steve Fulcher's barrister had requested at his misconduct hearing and which no one could find had suddenly 'appeared' three years on.

No explanation for this was given in the news report, only that a referral to the IPCC had been made for an investigation. I remembered that day at the misconduct hearing when Chief Constable Geenty had been asked about it; it had been lost and this was accepted. He had retired from the force in 2015, to be replaced by Mike Veale. I found it very strange that it could not be found for the purposes of a misconduct hearing, but then three years later could suddenly reappear. I thought it was all over when Halliwell had been convicted. It seems this was not the case.

I followed with interest news about the IPCC. It seems my misgivings about the organisation weren't without foundation. I had no truck with them after their investigation of Steve

Fulcher, which led to his misconduct hearing. In 2018, they were overhauled and rebranded as the Independent Office for Police Conduct (IOPC). This, they said, was to ensure a faster, more transparent response to complaints against the police. God knows, they needed to do this, if my experience of them was anything to go by. But after all this time and all that had happened, I was dubious.

One day, along with Steve Fulcher, I received a letter from the IOPC following the investigation into the Gold Policy book that had mysteriously appeared. There was nothing by way of explanation as to what had occurred, just that there was nothing untoward and therefore no action to be taken. They were basically saying, 'Nothing to see here.'

But in September 2018 something extraordinary burst into the press. Chief Constable Mike Veale, who had since jumped forces from Wiltshire to Cleveland, had been under investigation by the IOPC. This was for causing damage to a mobile phone. While the IOPC found he had not deliberately caused damage to the phone, they did however, take issue with his version of events. In a press release, the IOPC stated:

> Chief constables are expected to promote ethical values, lead by personal example and act as ambassadors for the standards of professional behaviour. That Mr Veale chose to give a different account to the truth, both verbally and in writing, on several occasions and for some time, in our view amounted to a case to answer for misconduct relating to honesty and integrity.

It was reported widely in the press that he had lied to colleagues. This was, after all, the man who had been in charge of discipline at the time of Steve Fulcher's misconduct hearing. Once again, my confidence in senior police officers was eroded.

I clashed with Wiltshire Police repeatedly in the media – me asking what they were doing in relation to investigating further victims of Halliwell and the information I had been giving over the years, with them stating there were no links between Halliwell and other murders. It was frustrating. All during Operations Mayan and Manilla they had asked us for information about Becky and we had supplied it to them. They had been more than happy to engage with us. We couldn't give them enough information as they returned to us again and again with their questions. Now I was contacting them regarding other women saying they had seen Halliwell in connection with different incidents, it seemed to me I was being treated as a nuisance.

I don't feel I should apologise for asking questions about Halliwell having other victims in the aftermath of the trial. I knew from past experience that evidence could be overlooked for years. Despite Halliwell's conviction, I kept going back to the evidence that had proved so crucial at court. It still rankled with me about the spade. It directly linked Halliwell to Becky's grave, so why hadn't that been used in 2012 to prevent Becky being dropped from the indictment?

Our family had been in the grip of two murder investigations – *their* murder investigations – for five long years, by the time of Halliwell's conviction. I felt the police had asked a lot of us as a family and we had more than played our part in bringing

Halliwell to justice. There were so many times when we were asked not to say anything about the enquiry and we had done as asked. And it had taken its toll.

I would have appreciated some sort of debrief on the Op Mayan and Op Manilla investigations: an opportunity to air things like the information I'd given to them and ask what was being done. We were never offered the chance to do this, which, on reflection, does seem extraordinary after such a long enquiry. As soon as Halliwell was convicted, it very much felt like 'job done' as far as the police were concerned. They were moving on. And we as a family were obviously expected to do the same, but it wasn't that easy when there were questions outstanding.

Don't get me wrong; I was so very grateful for what Steve Fulcher had done in returning Becky to us and to Sean Memory for bringing Halliwell to trial. But I really didn't take kindly to being shut down about the information I was being given, information that might ultimately bring resolution for another mother with a missing daughter. Because if I could do anything to end that pain and misery for another person, I would.

18

THE END IN SIGHT

One day we heard from Steve Fulcher with some exciting news. His book, *Catching a Serial Killer*, had been picked up by an award-winning writer and producer at ITV, Jeff Pope, for a TV drama series. He had previously won BAFTAs for his work and the early signs were encouraging.

He wanted to meet the people involved in the story, including Charlie and myself. Jeff and his son, George, visited us and listened as I outlined Becky's story: all her troubles, the events she had gone through and the searches we had made for her when she was missing. Although he'd obviously read the account of the investigation in Steve's book, Jeff seemed quite taken aback by Becky's story. He said he had been searching for an angle from which to tell the story and now knew what he was going to do.

When I next spoke to Yvonne Fulcher, she said that originally the drama was going to be in three parts; after Jeff Pope had spoken to me and Charlie, the idea now was to make it into six parts. I was flabbergasted. It would involve all of us, Elaine O'Callaghan and her family too, who were also agreeable to the story being dramatised. I had been involved in making the documentary about the case the year before, but what was being suggested now was something altogether different.

Our story – Becky's story – would be writ large on national TV for all to see, on the basis of Steve's book and an intensive period of research interviews with Steve, me, Elaine and others. I talked it over with Charlie. We were told the director, Paul Andrew Williams, had directed *Broadchurch* and the producer, Tom Dunbar, had worked on *Poldark* and *Downton Abbey*. It wasn't a decision we took lightly, but we were reassured by the quality of people involved in the production. We decided that we would participate and furnish Jeff Pope with all the detail he needed. I hoped the drama would provide the oxygen to keep police looking for more victims. For all we knew, it could even touch Halliwell's conscience. In any event, it was an extraordinary story that it seemed was not quite over.

Then my whole world went dark.

Charlie died suddenly.

Only two weeks before, he had been for his private medical check-up and was told all was fine. There was no reason for us to suspect otherwise. Charlie had no underlying issues and the yearly check-up was his way of ensuring he kept healthy. On this particular day, we were getting ready to go out.

'I know,' he said. 'We'll go out for afternoon tea.'

'That's a nice idea,' I said, 'Let's just go and get ready.'

There was no warning before Charlie suddenly fell into a chair. I called paramedics and we got him to hospital. After three days in intensive care, there was no more they could do. The family gathered and we had to say our goodbyes. The man I loved with all my heart, who had stood by me for twenty-two years through all my troubles and who had been such a tremendous support was suddenly gone. I was devastated.

He had been such a fantastic husband and father, to his own girls and especially to Steven and Becky. In their late teens, both Steven and Becky acknowledged this by wanting Charlie to adopt them. He wanted this too, but they were too old for this to happen. Instead, Becky was in the process of changing her name from Godden to Edwards when she last disappeared, so I always asked the press to refer to her as Becky Godden-Edwards.

Steven was bereft. Charlie had taught him so much in the twenty-two years he'd known him. He had been Steven's father as much as if Steven had been his own son. So much so that Steven completed the process to change his surname. It had been a fitting tribute, as Charlie always had their best interests at heart and had made such a positive difference to their lives. Charlie had made a huge impact on them both.

The days passed in utter turmoil while I fell into a deep pit of misery. This wasn't how it was supposed to be. We should have had years stretching out before us. Many more years with the children and grandchildren. Many more birthdays and Christmases. We'd had enough misery to last a lifetime, so we had lots of good times to look forward to. But it wasn't to be.

I felt cheated. After everything we'd been through, life should have been kind to us now. Didn't we deserve to see our retirements filled with long, sunny, happy days in which there was lots of laughter, surrounded by children? I thought so. The shock of Charlie's death so unexpectedly had an enormous impact on all our family and friends. He was such a big-hearted man, funny and easy company.

Somehow we managed to get through the weeks to the funeral. It was a very strange time and, of course, the way I felt took me right back to Becky's funeral. I couldn't believe it was happening. The suddenness of finding myself standing behind Charlie's coffin was such a dreadful blow. Steven, Kelly and the family helped me through it. Life was going to be very different without my adorable, funny rock of a husband. I was back on my own and I didn't think I'd be able to properly function again. I missed him terribly. It changed my world in so many unimaginable ways. Just like I had with Becky, I had to say goodbye to Charlie prematurely, too suddenly, unexpectedly. It had all come as an enormous shock. I now had both Charlie's and Becky's graves to tend to.

One thing that had continued to cause us pain as a family was the fact that the police still held some of Becky's remains. I had long wanted these to be returned to Hillier's, the undertakers. Recalling the photograph of her remains, I had to try and bring as much of Becky as I could into one place. In the midst of arranging Charlie's funeral, issues around Becky's remains had come up. An arm bone and some foot bones that had been discovered when the scientists had taken soil samples from Becky's field were at last returned to Hillier's. The remains had been put into plastic capsules and labelled. The thing was, when these had been delivered to Hillier's, there had been some empty capsules, so I wasn't entirely sure whether I had all that they intended me to have. Charlie and I had always said that whichever one of us 'went first', we would have the rest of Becky's remains buried with us, but with Charlie's death being so sudden, this remained outstanding and we couldn't do as we'd wished. It would have been a great comfort to me to have at last laid Becky to rest with Charlie, rather than have parts of her still at Hillier's and possibly still with the police.

Slowly, I emerged from the fog of grief. Life does go on, as much as you don't want it to, or think it will at times. The children and grandchildren were such a godsend, as were my ever wonderful friends. Everyone rallied round, they were absolutely superb. I had grandchildren staying the weekends with me, friends staying during the week, everyone wanting to make sure I wasn't left on my own. But it was a tremendous shock not to have Charlie with me.

In the weeks and months following Charlie's death, I certainly wondered what on earth life was all about. I just couldn't come to terms with him not being there. It was all so sudden. It seemed as though we were all in shock, none of us able to believe what had happened. It was a beautifully warm summer but it did nothing to lift us; we were struggling to come to terms with it all.

Since Charlie's death, Jeff Pope had kindly been in touch to offer his condolences. He and his son had met Charlie several times, or exchanged emails and phone calls to discuss details. I found the TV drama a welcome distraction during this time. It was something different to think about, something to take us out of our gloom following Charlie's death.

Jeff let me know there would be a meeting soon, for everyone to meet the cast. They would be re-creating our family on screen and, of course, that gave us something else to think about. For something light-hearted to do, this had been a topic of discussion with the family whenever we needed cheering up. We speculated about who might play us; the suggestions went from the sublime to the ridiculous and we always ended up having a laugh about it. Of course, my curiosity got the better of me. I wanted to know who would be playing Becky. I needed to be sure that Jeff had understood her and that might be reflected in the actress who would play her. We had had a conversation about it, but he was still undecided as to who to cast. Understandably, it made me anxious.

Then, one afternoon, I took a call from Jeff to tell us who would be playing various family members. It was teatime when he rang me.

'The person who we've cast for Becky is an actress called Stephanie Hyam.'

'Oh?' I couldn't place her immediately.

'She's played parts in BBC's *Peaky Blinders*,' he explained, 'and more recently, as Chanel Dyson in the BBC drama *The Bodyguard*. She's petite like Becky. She'll be perfect for Becky's part in the drama.'

After some googling, I agreed. She would be perfect. I knew it would be very strange seeing her. In fact, the whole thing was starting to feel a little peculiar. In another call, he told me who would be playing me.

'I don't want you to think in terms of someone who looks like you,' said Jeff cautiously. 'That's not how it works.'

'OK,' I said tentatively.

'It's all to do with performance, who we think would be best to portray you, what you've been through.'

By now I was intrigued. I had already learnt from Yvonne Fulcher who would be cast as Steve. I couldn't believe it; it was to be Martin Freeman of *The Hobbit*, *Fargo*, *Sherlock* and *Black Panther* fame. We were really impressed by this, as it signalled that the series was going to be very watchable.

'So the actress who'll be playing you is Imelda Staunton.'

'Wow!' was about all I managed to say. She wasn't a choice I had considered, but, my goodness, what a great actress.

'You will, of course, have to meet her,' he said. 'We've got a date, how are you fixed?'

The drama was certainly a welcome distraction for us all. I had to make arrangements to meet Imelda Staunton and asked Tracey if she would come with me. Of course she would. We met with Imelda Staunton, and the hair, make-up and wardrobe team, in London at Soho House for lunch. The director and Jeff's son were also with us.

Imelda was a lovely lady. My nerves set in and Tracey told me that, apparently, I didn't stop talking. To be fair, that's what they wanted, but Tracey said I didn't draw breath! Imelda sat and asked me lots of questions. She was very sensitive and when I told her all about Becky's troubles and losing Charlie so recently, she held my hand and sat and cried with me. She was obviously looking to capture some of my mannerisms and to see how I reacted to things. It was all very clever and I trusted her to do what she is obviously very good at.

Tracey and I returned home and told the rest of the family all about our day. We couldn't mention anything to anyone wider than close family at that time, as ITV wanted to give the programme a big launch on their website. We had to wait until then before we could share the news with friends. Eventually the news broke; the crime drama was to be called *A Confession* and was scheduled to be aired in the autumn of 2019.

A few weeks later, Jeff ran through the script with me and outlined the six parts from beginning to end. It sounded extremely good; I just couldn't imagine it on screen, how all these years could be condensed into six hours of television. He had written it from the perspective of Steve Fulcher, Elaine O'Callaghan and myself, and the story would unfold through us, as the three main characters. He would need to employ a degree of artistic licence, and whilst not able to fit everything in, it would by and large, remain true to events. It was a strange and extraordinary thing to happen. But like many a time during the last eight years, we used to say, 'You couldn't make it up.'

We had a further meeting with Imelda Staunton and the actors who would be playing our family members. Tracey came with me; she was introduced to the actress Morwenna Banks, who would be playing her. We were also introduced to the actors and actresses who would play Charlie, my son, Steven, and daughter-in-law, Kelly, and of course Stephanie Hyam, who would play

Becky. We were confronted with our new look 'family'. There had been a few surreal moments over the last few years and this was another of them.

During the gloomy winter months, the drama continued to provide the distraction we all needed. The actor Peter Wight, who would be playing Charlie, wanted to come and see me at home, so that he could get a sense of who Charlie was. I was only too pleased to do this and we sat and talked, as I leafed through photos of us together. Peter was such a sweet man and wanted to find out all he could about Charlie, where he worked, where he went to school. He had brought a large map of Swindon with him and I pointed out where the various locations were so he could mark them on the map. I relished the opportunity to talk about Charlie like this.

Meanwhile, the documentary that we had taken part in during the previous year was finally aired on ITV. It now formed part of a Trevor McDonald crime series and he was the narrator. I had almost forgotten about it. Charlie had also taken part, so it was bittersweet to watch. We were told we could also attend a small party to celebrate its airing, but none of us went in the circumstances.

The purpose of making the documentary had been to support Steve Fulcher's book. He had recently shared with us that the book had sold over 28,000 copies, which was an enormous achievement. Steve had felt compelled to write the book in order to provide the context to all the headlines and the wretched IPCC report that sat on the internet for all to see. Since the trial in

2016, the IOPC had taken the report off their website. I was glad this had happened at last. In any case, I felt that Judge Griffith Williams ruling on Halliwell's confession to Becky's murder had rather undermined the IPCC investigation into John's complaint. Steve was still working in Mogadishu, in extremely dangerous conditions.

I managed to get through the Christmas season of 2018 largely by ignoring it. It was too soon after Charlie's death to celebrate in any meaningful way. Christmas had always been a special time for us both, and without him I wanted it over as quickly as possible. Life had become a series of hurdles to get round now Charlie was no longer with me. At times, life threatened to overwhelm me. My doctor had referred me to trauma counselling because of everything that had happened with Becky and Charlie dying. I was keen to see if counselling would help.

Charlie's death had knocked the stuffing out me and had inevitably led to my revisiting a lot of emotions that I'd felt around Becky's death, emotions that I hadn't dealt with because we'd been fighting for justice. I had to deal with both of their deaths because otherwise I would end up doing myself untold damage from a mental health point of view. I couldn't put it off any longer.

In the New Year, we had a visit to the set of the drama, and I took my friend Gladys Barr. It was to watch Imelda Staunton and Peter Wight enacting a scene where Charlie and I visit Robert Buckland, MP.

The actress Stephanie Hyam, who was playing Becky, met us

on set. She was uncannily petite and pretty like Becky. I put my arm around her for a photograph. The unexpectedness of the familiar feeling made me immediately tearful. She fitted into my arm just as Becky had. I was holding her again.

EPILOGUE

As I face a new year without Charlie by my side, I look forward to a time when peace can settle on us as a family; when the drama has been aired and when we can at last enjoy our memories of Becky with the benefit that hindsight brings, knowing we'd succeeded in doing all we could to bring to justice the man who'd cut her life short.

Looking back, a moment that I wish could change is that Judge Griffith Williams had been the one to hear the *voir dire* in 2012. From my understanding, what he'd said in his ruling in 2016 meant that, had he been there, Halliwell's confession for Becky's murder would have been deemed admissible at the *voir dire* in 2012. If that had been the case, so much misery would have been saved, so much time and public money would not have been spent. Charlie and I wouldn't have spent so much precious time worrying, driving around the country to different courtrooms from Preston to Bristol, or going round TV and radio studios, me leaving him while I campaigned or did speeches.

I will always be indebted to the people who helped in our fight for justice for Becky: my family and friends, Robert Buckland, the reporters of the *Swindon Advertiser*, and the good people of Swindon and beyond who signed the petition. The people who with endless patience listened to our story and supported us have my heartfelt thanks and gratitude. In the aftermath of the trial, as a family, we have many times gone over the case, if nothing more than to try and make sense of it all. We still do this, because even now the need to do this will catch us unawares.

I still try to find the point in all the years where I could have done just one thing that might have made a difference to how things turned out for my beautiful Becky. I could have insisted she came home with me the last time I saw her. I know from experience she would have gone again. But maybe, just maybe, if I had dragged her out of her boyfriend's flat that day, that would have been enough to change her fate. To put a dent in the series of events that ultimately led her into Halliwell's path on the night she got into his taxi. Or perhaps, as he knew Becky, there was a terrible inevitability to the final outcome.

I know I'll never stop analysing my actions in relation to Becky's murder, but likewise have always questioned those of Wiltshire Police during the course of their investigation. I wondered why an appeal to Judge Cox's ruling had not been made back in 2012, or at the point when Halliwell pleaded guilty to Sian O'Callaghan's murder. I wondered why Becky had been dropped from the indictment when a spade that held such incriminating evidence had sat for years in an exhibit room? Who was ultimately responsible for that?

I wanted answers of senior officers, those whose job it was to oversee and drive the original Operation Mayan and Manilla investigations, who should have been giving direction and ensuring timely reviews had been conducted. This would have highlighted outstanding actions, such as the forensic examination of the spade. The complaints I'd written to the HMIC in 2014 still nagged at me. As ever, I had to have answers, I wanted to know. So I submitted 12 complaints to Wiltshire Police, who passed them to the IOPC, who passed them back to Wiltshire Police. They in turn found an outside force, Hertfordshire, Bedfordshire and Cambridgeshire Professional Standards Unit, to investigate them. As my complaints involved two chief constables, it was referred back to the IOPC, who determined they would 'manage' the investigation while Herts., Beds. and Cambs. continued to investigate. Two years on, I await their findings.

It takes enormous strength to come out of this situation intact. But, of course, you don't. It's not possible. You lose so much along the way that even if you survive, when it's over you're a much different person. Having been caught in the 'justice system', I think it is, at times, utterly heartless and devoid of understanding from a family perspective. We found ourselves very much in the hands of others, having no control over what was happening, waiting for people to do their jobs, waiting for them to decide when to tell us what they were doing. The interminable waiting for information is the worst. Hanging on for any tiny piece of information that might bring with it a shred of hope among the searing pain.

Now I have to pick up the pieces of my life and move on. I'm able to do this because we did finally get justice for my beautiful, spirited Becky. And one day I'll have answers to questions that would have kept me awake for more years, if I had not finally pursued my complaints. Because in years to come, when I recount this story and people question me about it, as will invariably happen, I want to be able to answer them. I want to have as complete a picture as possible, so that I can make sense of it all. I wish I didn't need to have recourse to a complaint investigation; the time and effort this takes could have been saved by some kind of formal debriefing with us as a family.

Apparently, the police too continue to seek answers to Halliwell's offending. Perhaps it was the pressure of the media attention and asking questions that prompted them to continue their enquiries under a new name, Operation Major. It's the third operation into Halliwell, since 2011. I hope this will bring some resolution to other families. Whether Halliwell is linked to other missing person enquiries or not, if asking questions finds answers and ultimately ends the pain and misery for another mother with a missing daughter and others are convicted, then it would have served a good purpose. I maintain contact with Joan Lawrence and we continue to exchange letters of support. We've both become members of a terrible 'club' of sorts, one that no parent would ever want to join.

If anything comes out of my whole experience, I would like to think someone, somewhere, might agree that the service to the families of murder victims needs to be improved. It would be good to formalise engagement with victims' families through established best practice, along with a well thought-through 'exit' strategy for victims' families once an investigation and trial are over. This needs to include an honest 'question and answer' session to discuss things that went right and things that did not go so well. Only then can understanding, learning and improvements in service take place. It would be good to see the judicial system included in this, providing families with a clear understanding of the intricacies of the law and the motivations of barristers.

All these years on, I often wonder about Mr Richard Latham, QC, Halliwell's barrister. I want to believe that he didn't really want a self-confessed murderer to go free, and that he instead chose to defend Halliwell in order to ensure the case was properly tested by the court, so that it closed down any avenue of future appeal for his client. Perhaps that day at the High Court, when he held the door open for me, he was going to explain exactly that. I'll never know for sure, but I'd like to think this was the case.

When the drama airs, my hope is that in raising the PACE issue again it might cause a conversation to be had around it. I can't bear the thought of another family (or another police officer for that matter) going through the same thing as we have. Steve Fulcher had decided he must breach the rules of PACE to ask Halliwell to immediately reveal where he had left Sian. As he faced Halliwell in that single moment, as they stood eye to eye, he somehow managed to penetrate the evil of the man who stood before him. Using all his skill as a detective, Steve Fulcher sought and found the tiniest chink of humanity Halliwell, an accomplished and manipulative murderer, had left in him. And, having found it, he appealed to it. As far as I'm concerned, it was good old-fashioned coppering. But Steve Fulcher paid a professional and personal price for a morally justified and audacious piece of policing.

In facing Steve Fulcher, I am convinced Halliwell knew he had finally met his match. At last, someone had stopped him in his tracks. And it took someone to push through the rules in order to stop a man on a killing spree. In giving up his victims, Halliwell had acknowledged the skill of the man who caught him. From what I could understand, what was being said by the upper echelons of the legal profession was that proper application of PACE would have prevented Halliwell from confessing and revealing the bodies. This it seems was what barristers and chief police officers would have preferred, over Halliwell being identified as a killer. Is this how they wanted *justice* to work?

As far as I'm concerned, if your son or daughter is abducted, as Sian and Becky were, and the suspect is arrested and is the only person who knows where they are, what parent would not want police to immediately ask the suspect where their loved ones had been left? That was what Steve Fulcher did. That was *all* he did. And Halliwell answered his plea.

During this process, there must have been times when Halliwell could hardly have believed his good fortune – no wonder he looked so smug at court. Ignoring the two horrific murders he had carried out, the legal profession instead were advocates in his favour regarding the niceties of the circumstances under which he'd been detained and revealed his victims' bodies.

It is utterly devastating when loved ones are abducted and murdered. To never be reunited with them, while their whereabouts are never revealed by the perpetrator, is a superior act of cruelty. It is the ultimate act of power a suspect has over the families of their victims. It is controlling behaviour that they relish while being incarcerated. And that cruelty is further exacerbated when the law appears to collude with the perpetrator. I will be eternally grateful to Steve Fulcher for returning Becky to me. To be able to spend the time I did with her when we brought her home for the last time, and to be able to lay her to rest with the dignity she deserved, was such an enormous comfort to us as a family. I cannot imagine the alternative. Despite everything, in that respect I had to consider myself lucky.

But I know others live with this iniquity on a daily basis. Since December 2015, I have followed another mother's campaign, that of Marie McCourt. There were similarities with us as mothers looking for our daughters and having to campaign for a change to the law. Marie's daughter, Helen, was murdered on her way home from work in 1988. While a man was convicted of her murder in 1989, he has never revealed where her body is. Because of this, Marie spent years conducting her own searches for Helen. In 1992, she wrote to the killer asking him to reveal where Helen was, only for him to threaten and abuse her. Having spent a lot of her time supporting other families of victims of murder, she realised how her situation was replicated in other cases. She decided to do something about it and launched a campaign calling for a 'no body, no parole' law: 'Helen's Law'.

I followed Marie because, like me, Marie campaigned and petitioned. She delivered 320,000 signatures to Downing Street. Marie managed to have a private members' bill presented to Parliament which passed through its first reading unanimously. Delays in the parliamentary process meant that she had to continue to fight, her campaign eventually achieving over 600,000

signatures. This finally paid off in May 2019 when the government agreed to adopt Helen's Law. As a result it will be
harder for convicted criminals who cruelly hide their victims'
bodies to be granted parole. I have the utmost admiration
for Marie McCourt and her inspiring fight against injustice.
She has stood up and fought for all of those in this disgusting
situation, where mothers and fathers go to their graves not
knowing what happened to their sons and daughters. It is a
truly hideous thing.

I consider I was lucky Steve Fulcher was on call the day he
was contacted to respond to Sian O'Callaghan's disappearance.
I was lucky it was Steve Fulcher who faced Halliwell and who
brought my daughter back to me; no doubt, in hindsight, Marie
McCourt would have appreciated a 'Steve Fulcher' at the time her
daughter's killer had been arrested. What haunts me is the fact
that but for Steve Fulcher's actions I would be totally oblivious
of Becky being buried in that field. What if it happens again
with another incarnation of Halliwell? Who would be there to
find the victim of abduction for another family? How many
more mothers are there who are oblivious of their daughters
having stepped into the path of a Halliwell and who are buried
in a field somewhere? God forbid, if you are ever in the dreadful
situation of being denied justice, as I have been, you must never,
ever give up fighting.

My friends and I talk about setting up a foundation in Becky's
memory. She'd said if she could have got herself free of drugs,
she wanted to go into schools and tell them of her experiences,
to prevent them from repeating her mistakes. We are thinking

about starting something along these lines, so that, in some respect, Becky would have achieved her aim.

I have now started trauma and bereavement counselling which will help me on the road to recovering from what has happened. I have been so fortunate in having such wonderful support from family and friends. We talk of happier times and remember Becky and Charlie in our conversations every day.

A Poem by Rebecca Godden aged nine

I should like to walk on the sun and go to Mars as a holiday
I should like to go to Jupiter and
I should like to fly in space and smell the moon
I should like to go to the edge of the earth
I should like to be a shooting star.

ACKNOWLEDGEMENTS

I would like to thank all my family and friends for their unending patience and whose support I am so very grateful for – the list is long. They have all been with me during this time. I would like to pay tribute to my wonderful husband, Charlie, whose support never wavered throughout Becky's troubles and of course, to my lovely friend, Shirley Bunn. To my Mum, Steven and Kelly, Tracey, Tony, Sam and Laura and all my wonderful grandchildren, with whom I now look forward to spending better times as we remember Becky.

I need to also especially thank my dear friend Gladys, who provided such support to both Becky and I and to Jenny who has been with me since the early days. My fellow campaigners need a special mention – my 'wingwomen' Sandy, Shan, Josie and all the other supporters have my heartfelt thanks. Robert Buckland, my MP, who has helped enormously and the One25 charity in Bristol, to whom I am so grateful for helping Becky.

I would particularly like to thank the journalists and media outlets for listening to my story and helping with my campaign. Notably amongst these are Rob Murphy, Steve Brodie,

Scott D'Arcy, Claire Hayhurst, the *Swindon Advertiser*, the Press Association, *Western Daily Press*, *Daily Mail* and the *Mirror*. I also have to thank Sean Memory and Mr Nicholas Haggan for bringing Halliwell to trial. My grateful thanks also to Sir John Griffith Williams.

Thanks also need to go to my agent, Robert Smith; my ghost-writer, Deborah Lucy, for articulating my story; and to my editor, Fiona Crosby, and the publishing team at Headline. And to Andy, for all the culinary delights while this book was being written.

And, of course, I will be for ever grateful to Steve Fulcher, the man who returned my beautiful Becky, and to his wife Yvonne, for her support and friendship.